PARTNERSHIP INCOME TAXATION

FIFTH EDITION

By

WILLIAM H. LYONS
Richard H. Larson Professor of Tax Law
University of Nebraska College of Law

JAMES R. REPETTI
William J. Kenealy, S.J. Professor of Law
Boston College Law School

CONCEPTS AND INSIGHTS SERIES®

FOUNDATION PRESS
2011

This publication was created to provide you with accurate and authoritative information concerning the subject matter covered; however, this publication was not necessarily prepared by persons licensed to practice law in a particular jurisdiction. The publisher is not engaged in rendering legal or other professional advice and this publication is not a substitute for the advice of an attorney. If you require legal or other expert advice, you should seek the services of a competent attorney or other professional.

Nothing contained herein is intended or written to be used for the purposes of 1) avoiding penalties imposed under the federal Internal Revenue Code, or 2) promoting, marketing or recommending to another party any transaction or matter addressed herein.

© 1991, 1995, 1999 FOUNDATION PRESS
© 2005 THOMSON REUTERS/FOUNDATION PRESS
© 2011 By THOMSON REUTERS/FOUNDATION PRESS

    1 New York Plaza, 34th Floor
    New York, NY 10004
    Phone Toll Free 1–877–888–1330
    Fax 646–424–5201
    foundation–press.com

Printed in the United States of America

ISBN 978–1–59941–382–2

Mat #40638385

To Karen, Ginger, Kevin, Andy, Rachel, Jeanette and Bill
W.H.L.

To Susan, Jane, Tom, Caroline, Cleo and Memore
J.R.R.

PREFACE

This book attempts the simplest possible introduction to an intricate body of law. Any "simplified" description of the rules of partnership taxation would be so misleading as to be useless. We have therefore tried to make the subject accessible not by paraphrasing the rules, but by including numerous illustrations that are as straightforward as possible. The text focuses on simple partnerships holding few assets and engaging in routine transactions. It places the rules in context by pointing out the purposes of the statute and regulations and presenting background information about practical matters such as how partnerships maintain capital accounts and how nonrecourse financing works. Using many examples, it then shows the operation of the rules in everyday cases encountered by practitioners.

This is not a reference book: many interesting and difficult issues have been ignored. Some matters, such as the application of § 736 to noncash distributions and tiered partnerships, are not discussed at all, and some problems, like mandatory basis adjustments under § 732(d), receive only passing mention. Most of the points that are dealt with are, however, discussed at considerable length. Our goal has been to give students background material and illustrations so that they can begin to understand and work with a statute that was drafted for (and by) experienced practitioners.

Most chapters end with a section comparing the tax treatment of partners with that of the shareholders of S corporations. Many students encountering partnership taxation for the first time have already studied subchapter S. We expect that an examination of some of the basic differences between subchapters S and K should help those students understand both subjects.

We thank our previous coauthor, Alan Gunn, for all of his contributions to this book. We greatly benefitted from Alan's invaluable insights about partnership taxation and his good humor. He is a masterful teacher to whom we owe much. We also thank James E. Tierney and Larry D. Ward for helpful comments on previous editions.

Lastly, William Lyons gratefully acknowledges the generous support for a portion of this project provided by the McCollum Fund at the University of Nebraska College of Law and James

PREFACE

Repetti gratefully acknowledges support provided by the Paulus Endowment for Tax.

The cover picture is John Tenniel's drawing of the mad tea party. It seems a perfect match for a subject that has grown so intricate as to have become, in practice, almost a legal fiction.

William H. Lyons
Lincoln, Nebraska

James R. Repetti
Newton, Massachusetts

January 2011

TABLE OF CONTENTS

Preface	v
Chapter One: Choice of Entity: Taxation of Partnerships, C Corporations and S Corporations	1
A. INTRODUCTION	1
B. THE FLOW–THROUGH FEATURE OF PARTNERSHIPS AND S CORPORATIONS	2
Chapter Two: The Pass–Through Principle of Partnership Taxation	6
A. INTRODUCTION	6
B. ILLUSTRATION	7
C. THE TIMING OF PARTNERSHIP INCOME	9
D. THE DURATION OF A PARTNERSHIP	10
E. PARTNERS AS SELF–EMPLOYED TAXPAYERS	10
F. PARTNERS AND SOCIAL SECURITY AND MEDICARE TAXES	12
G. THE "ANTI–ABUSE" REGULATIONS	12
H. COMPARISON WITH SUBCHAPTER S	14
Chapter Three: An Introduction to Partnership Basis and Limits on Losses	16
A. THE TAX BASIS OF PARTNERSHIP INTERESTS AND PARTNERSHIP PROPERTY	16
B. THE EFFECTS OF PARTNERSHIP DEBT TRANSACTIONS UPON BASIS	18
C. LIMITS ON THE DEDUCTIBILITY OF PARTNERSHIP LOSSES	19
1. Section 704(d)	20
2. The At–Risk Rules of Section 465	20
3. The Passive–Loss Rules of Section 469	22
D. COMPARISON WITH SUBCHAPTER S	23
Chapter Four: Contributions to Partnerships	24
A. CONTRIBUTIONS OF PROPERTY	24
1. The Statutory Pattern	24
2. Holding Periods	25
3. Contributions of Encumbered Property	26
4. Depreciation Recapture	27
5. Character Issues: Section 724	28

TABLE OF CONTENTS

B. CONTRIBUTIONS OF SERVICES — 28
 1. Receipt of an Interest in Partnership Capital — 29
 2. Receipt of an Interest in Partnership Profits — 31
C. CONTRIBUTIONS DISTINGUISHED FROM OTHER TRANSACTIONS — 38
 1. Contribution vs. Sale to Partnership — 38
 2. Contribution vs. Sale or Exchange Between Partners — 41
D. COMPARISON WITH SUBCHAPTER S — 42

Chapter Five: Allocations of Partnership Income, Deductions, and Credits: An Introduction — 44
A. AN OVERVIEW OF THE CODE AND REGULATIONS — 44
B. THE "SUBSTANTIAL ECONOMIC EFFECT" TEST — 45
 1. Introduction — 45
 2. Capital Accounts — 46
 3. The "Simple" Capital Account Test for Substantial Economic Effect: Orrisch v. Commissioner — 49
 4. The "Substantial Economic Effect" Regulations — 53
  a. Determining "Economic Effect" When Capital Account Deficits Need Not Be Repaid — 54
  b. The "Substantiality" Rules — 56
  c. Some Special Problems — 60
   i. Depreciation — 60
   ii. Deductions Attributable to Nonrecourse Debt — 63
   iii. Interaction of Nonrecourse Deductions With the Alternate Test for Economic Effect Test — 68
   iv. Allocating Credits — 69
C. COMPARISON WITH SUBCHAPTER S — 70

Chapter Six: Allocations Attributable to Contributed Property: Section 704(c) — 71
A. ALLOCATIONS OF GAIN OR LOSS — 71
B. ALLOCATIONS OF DEPRECIATION — 74
 1. The Traditional Method — 75
 2. The Traditional Method With Curative Allocations — 77
 3. The Remedial Allocation Method — 79
C. "REVERSE SECTION 704(c) ALLOCATIONS" UNDER SECTION 704(B) — 82
D. DISTRIBUTIONS OF SECTION 704(c) PROPERTY — 83
E. DISTRIBUTIONS OF PROPERTY TO A PARTNER WHO HAS CONTRIBUTED SECTION 704(c) ASSETS — 85
F. COMPARISON WITH SUBCHAPTER S — 86

Chapter Seven: Partnership Allocations: Assignment-of-Income Problems — 87
A. FAMILY PARTNERSHIPS — 87
B. LAST-MINUTE PARTNERS: SECTION 706(d) — 90

TABLE OF CONTENTS

C. ASSIGNMENTS OF INCOME NOT DEALT WITH BY SPECIFIC CODE PROVISIONS: THE ANTI–ABUSE REGULATIONS	91
D. COMPARISON WITH SUBCHAPTER S	95

Chapter Eight: Allocation of Partnership Debt — 96
A. INTRODUCTION	96
B. WHAT IS A PARTNERSHIP LIABILITY UNDER SECTION 752?	96
C. THE DEFINITION OF RECOURSE AND NONRECOURSE DEBT	97
1. Introduction	97
2. Economic Risk of Loss and Constructive Liquidation	98
D. ALLOCATION OF RECOURSE LIABILITY	100
1. In General	100
2. Effect of Guarantees and Indemnifications of Recourse Debt	102
3. Contributions of Property Encumbered by Recourse Debt	103
E. ALLOCATION OF NONRECOURSE LIABILITY	104
1. The First Tier of Nonrecourse Debt Allocation	104
a. Sufficient Basis for Nonrecourse Deductions	104
b. Refinancing	105
2. The Second Tier of Nonrecourse Debt Allocation	106
a. No Gain Recognized When Contributing Property Encumbered by Nonrecourse Debt	106
3. The Third Tier of Nonrecourse Debt Allocation	106
4. Effects of Guarantees of Nonrecourse Debt	108
F. OBLIGATIONS THAT ARE NOT "LIABILITIES" UNDER § 752	109
G. COMPARISON WITH SUBCHAPTER S	112

Chapter Nine: Transactions Between Partnerships and Their Partners — 113
A. INCOME–RELATED PAYMENTS: DISTRIBUTIVE SHARES AND SECTION 707(a) PAYMENTS	115
B. FIXED PAYMENTS: GUARANTEED PAYMENTS AND SECTION 707(a) PAYMENTS	117
C. DETERMINING WHETHER A "PARTNER CAPACITY" PAYMENT IS A DISTRIBUTIVE SHARE OR A GUARANTEED PAYMENT	118
1. Minimum Payments	118
2. Payments Measured by a Partnership's Gross Income	121
D. SOME OTHER ASPECTS OF TRANSACTIONS BETWEEN PARTNERS AND PARTNERSHIPS	121
E. COMPARISON WITH SUBCHAPTER S	122

TABLE OF CONTENTS

Chapter Ten: Sales of Partnership Interests — 123
A. TAXATION OF THE SELLER — 123
   1. The Seller's Amount Realized — 123
   2. Section 751(a) — 124
   3. Taxation of Look-through Gains Under Section 1(h) — 128
B. THE BUYER'S OUTSIDE AND INSIDE BASES — 129
   1. The Buyer's Outside Basis — 129
   2. Inside Basis Adjustments Under Section 743(b) — 130
      a. Determining the Transferee's Share of Inside Basis — 131
      b. Allocating Section 743(b) Adjustments to Particular Assets — 133
      c. Using the Section 743(b) Adjustment — 137
      d. The Section 754 Election and Adjustments Required Without a 754 Election for Substantial Built-in Loss — 138
   3. Basis Adjustments Under Section 732(d) — 139
C. COLLATERAL EFFECTS OF A SALE OF A PARTNERSHIP INTEREST — 140
D. COMPARISON WITH SUBCHAPTER S — 141
   1. Calculating Gain on the Sale of Stock — 141
   2. Character of Gain and Inside Basis Adjustments Upon Transfers of Interests — 141
   3. Termination by Sale — 143

Chapter Eleven: Partnership Distributions: An Introduction — 144
A. THE GENERAL PRINCIPLE OF NONRECOGNITION — 145
B. CASES IN WHICH GAIN OR LOSS IS RECOGNIZED — 151
   1. Gain Recognition — 151
   2. Liquidating Distributions on Which Loss Is Recognized — 152
   3. "De Minimis" Distributions of Property — 154
   4. Distributions of Section 704(c) Property — 155
   5. Distributions Taxed Under Section 737 — 155
C. TAX TREATMENT OF THE PARTNERSHIP — 156
D. COMPARISON WITH SUBCHAPTER S — 157

Chapter Twelve: Distributions Subject to Section 751(b) — 158
A. LIQUIDATING DISTRIBUTIONS OF ASSETS OTHER THAN SECTION 751 ASSETS — 161
B. LIQUIDATING DISTRIBUTIONS OF SECTION 751 PROPERTY — 164
C. SECTION 751(b) AND CURRENT DISTRIBUTIONS — 167
D. THE SCOPE OF SECTION 751(b): AN EXAMPLE — 168
E. COMPARISON WITH SUBCHAPTER S — 170

Chapter Thirteen: Payments to Retiring Partners: Section 736 and Related Problems — 171
A. INTRODUCTION — 171
   1. Interpreting Section 736—In General — 172
   2. Payments by Service Partnerships to Retiring General Partners — 173

TABLE OF CONTENTS

B.	HOW SECTION 736 PAYMENTS ARE TAXED	176
C.	EXAMPLES	178
D.	SOME COMPLICATIONS	181
	1. The Relationship Between Section 736 and Section 751(b)	181
	2. A Refinement in the Definition of Section 736(a) Payments	182
	3. Liquidation of an Entire Partnership	183
E.	SALES AND RETIREMENT PAYMENTS DISTINGUISHED	183
F.	PROBLEMS OF "FORM" AND "SUBSTANCE"	186
G.	COMPARISON WITH SUBCHAPTER S	187

Chapter Fourteen: Basis Adjustments Under Section 734 — 188

A.	ADJUSTMENTS UNDER SECTION 734	189
	1. Distributions That Change the Basis of the Distributed Property	189
	2. Distributions on Which Gain or Loss Is Recognized	190
	3. Allocating the Adjustment to Particular Assets	192
	4. Adjustments Required Without a Section 754 Election: Substantial Basis Reductions	194
B.	SECTION 734 AND THE ANTI–ABUSE REGULATIONS	195
C.	COMPARISON WITH SUBCHAPTER S	196

Chapter Fifteen: The Death of a Partner — 198

A.	INCOME IN RESPECT OF A DECEASED PARTNER	198
	1. Introduction	198
	2. The Basis of an Inherited Partnership Interest	199
B.	CLOSING THE PARTNERSHIP'S TAXABLE YEAR UPON THE DEATH OF A PARTNER	203
C.	SALE OR LIQUIDATION OF A DECEASED PARTNER'S INTEREST	204
D.	COMPARISON WITH SUBCHAPTER S	204

Chapter Sixteen: What Is a Partnership? — 206

A.	CO–OWNERSHIP OF PROPERTY	207
B.	COST–SHARING AND EMPLOYMENT ARRANGEMENTS	208
C.	PARTNERSHIP VS. CORPORATION	210
D.	ELECTION OUT OF SUBCHAPTER K	212
E.	PUBLICLY TRADED PARTNERSHIPS	213
F.	ELECTING LARGE PARTNERSHIPS	215

TABLE OF CASES	217
TABLE OF INTERNAL REVENUE CODE SECTIONS	219
TABLE OF TREASURY REGULATIONS AND RULINGS	223
INDEX	225

PARTNERSHIP INCOME TAXATION

FIFTH EDITION

Chapter One

CHOICE OF ENTITY: TAXATION OF PARTNERSHIPS, C CORPORATIONS AND S CORPORATIONS

A. INTRODUCTION

The central principle underlying the federal income taxation[1] of partners is that the existence of the partnership should matter as little as possible. As an American Law Institute study put it, "the ideal mode for taxing partnership earnings is to tax each partner as though he were directly conducting his proportionate share of the partnership business."[2] This mode of taxation is usually referred to as the "aggregate" approach because it treats the partnership as an aggregate of individuals, each conducting her share of the partnership's business. The ALI emphasized, however, that this principle controls only in the absence of countervailing factors.[3] A "countervailing factor" that often makes it undesirable to try to tax partners as if they were conducting their shares of the business as sole proprietors is administrative convenience. Administrative convenience normally suggests that the partnership be treated as an entity separate from the partners, i.e. that the "entity" approach be used.[4]

To illustrate the considerations raised above, think about a laundry business conducted by Alice and Bill as equal partners. Each of them contributed equal amounts of cash, each does identical work, and each takes the same amount of money out of the business. In this very simple case, it is easy to apply the aggregate approach and tax Alice and Bill as if each were conducting half of the business: Each of them can include in income half of the income of the laundry.

Treating the partnership as an "aggregate," as in the example above, is not always practical; sometimes an "entity" approach must be used. Suppose that the laundry building burns down, and that Alice wants to reinvest the insurance proceeds in a new building, electing nonrecognition of gain under § 1033. Bill (who has a large, deductible

---

1. This discussion focuses on federal income taxation of partnerships and partners. State taxation of partnerships and partners may differ from the federal income tax rules.
2. American Law Institute, Federal Income Tax Project, Subchapter K, 5 (1984).
3. Id. (emphasis omitted).
4. Indeed, concerns about administrative convenience prompted the drafters of the Revised Uniform Partnership Act (1997) to recommend that states use the entity approach in formulating laws that govern the conduct of partnerships so that partnerships can own property as an entity, contract as an entity and be sued as an entity.

loss from another activity) would prefer that the gain be recognized. Can both partners get the tax treatment they want? No: Section 703(b) adopts the entity approach and allows nonrecognition only if the partnership itself makes the election and replaces the building. Section 703(b), with three exceptions, provides that elections affecting the computation of partnership income must be made by the partnership, and § 1033(a)(2)(A) allows nonrecognition only if "the taxpayer" which realized the gain (in this case, the partnership) purchases qualifying replacement property.

As a rule, the amount and character of a partnership's income are calculated using an "entity" approach. The income, however, is taxed to the partners, not to the entity, using the "aggregate" approach. For example, if a partnership realizes gain of $10,000 from the sale of an asset, the entity approach causes the character of that gain to be determined at the partnership level. The gain will be capital gain if the partnership does not hold the property for sale to customers in the ordinary course of business and the other exceptions for capital asset treatment in § 1221 are inapplicable. The aggregate approach will then cause that gain to be taxable to the partners regardless of whether the gain is actually distributed to them.

B. THE FLOW–THROUGH FEATURE OF PARTNERSHIPS AND S CORPORATIONS

Application of the aggregate method to partnership income is one of the most attractive features of partnerships because it results in a single tax being applied to partnership income. When a partnership recognizes taxable income, such income is taxed directly to the partners. The partnership, itself, does not pay a tax on its income.[5] In addition, the subsequent distribution of that income to the partners does not usually trigger an additional tax liability because the aggregate method treats each partner as though she had directly conducted her share of the rental business and had already received her share of the income.

This single-tax approach stands in stark contrast to the double taxation of income of a corporation subject to the tax regime contained in Subchapter C of the Internal Revenue Code.[6] (Corporations subject to the double-tax regime of Subchapter C are often referred to as "C corporations.") Income realized by a C corporation is taxable to the corporation because the corporation is treated for all purposes as an entity separate from its stockholders. When the corporation distributes

---

5. Although a partnership will not pay federal income tax on its income, a partnership that has employees will be subject to various federal and state employment taxes.

6. Subchapter C consists of §§ 301 through 385.

that income to its stockholders, the stockholders also recognize taxable income.

Example 1–1: Andrew and Rachel are considering whether they should organize a real estate investment business as either a limited liability company (LLC), which is taxable as a partnership, or as a corporation, which is subject to the double-tax regime of Subchapter C. They anticipate that their real estate investments in land will generate rental income of approximately $500,000 per year. Andrew and Rachel have significant income from other sources and are subject to tax at the maximum marginal rates. They have asked their attorney which entity they should use.

Their attorney has advised them of the following tax consequences. If they place their land into an LLC, the $500,000 rental income will be recognized by Andrew and Rachel and they will pay a federal tax of $175,000 (35% of $500,000). No further tax liability will be incurred when the LLC distributes the rental income to Andrew and Rachel since the aggregate principle treats them as having directly conducted the rental business. In contrast, if they place their land into a C corporation, the income will be taxable to the corporation and will be taxed again when distributed to them. This will result in a total tax of $223,750, since a tax of $175,000 is incurred at the corporate level (35% of $500,000) and an additional tax of $48,750 is incurred when the income remaining after payment of the corporate tax is distributed to Andrew and Rachel (15%[7] of $325,000).

Clearly, application of the aggregate method causes an entity taxable as a partnership to be an attractive alternative for conducting a profitable business. In addition, the aggregate method often causes a partnership to be the preferred choice where the business will hold assets that are likely to appreciate in value. The aggregate method means that when a partnership distributes appreciated assets to its partners, neither the partnership nor the partners recognize taxable income. The logic is that since the aggregate method treats each partner as though he holds his share of partnership assets, nothing changes as the result of an actual distribution of those assets. In contrast, when a C corporation distributes appreciated assets to its stockholders, both the distributing corporation and its stockholders recognize taxable income since the corporation is treated as an entity separate from its stockholders. The distribution of an appreciated asset is a realization event for the corporation, triggering

---

7. Section 1(h)(11) provides that "qualified dividend income" received by an individual will be taxed at a rate of not more than 15 percent.

the corporation's recognition of income. Similarly, receipt of the property also results in income recognition by the stockholders.

Example 1–2: The land that Andrew and Rachel's entity purchased in Example 1–1 for $500,000 has appreciated in value to $1,500,000. If Andrew and Rachel formed the real estate entity as an LLC, the LLC may distribute the land to Andrew and Rachel and neither Andrew and Rachel nor the LLC will recognize taxable income. In contrast, if Andrew and Rachel formed the entity as a C corporation, the corporation will recognize the $1,000,000 difference between the land's tax basis and its fair market value as gain, and the stockholders will also recognize income upon their receipt of the land.

This favorable treatment of the distribution of appreciated assets from a partnership usually leads tax advisors to recommend that assets likely to appreciate in value not be placed into a C corporation. For example, a person considering purchasing a farm or marina should consider placing the farm's or marina's real property into a limited liability company that would be taxed as partnership, not a corporation.

If all the stockholders of a corporation elect to have the corporation subject to the provisions of Subchapter S of the Internal Revenue Code,[8] instead of Subchapter C, a different approach applies. A corporation subject to taxation under Subchapter S, (an "S corporation") has some, but not all of the advantages of an entity taxable as a partnership. Like a partnership, income of an S corporation is taxable to its owners, i.e. to its stockholders, not to the corporation. However, unlike a partnership, taxable income is recognized when an S corporation distributes property that has appreciated in value. Thus, the S corporation provides less flexibility than a partnership.

Example 1–3: The facts are the same as in Examples 1–1 and Example 1–2 except that Andrew and Rachel are conducting their real estate investment business in the form of an S corporation. The $500,000 rental income collected by their S corporation is not taxable to the S corporation. Instead, Andrew and Rachel are each taxed on their share of the corporation's income.

If the S corporation distributes the land that has appreciated in value to $1,500,000, it recognizes $1,000,000 of gain (the difference between the $1,500,000 value and $500,000 tax basis). This gain flows out to and is recognized by the S corporation stockholders on their individual tax returns. The stockholders normally do not also recognize additional taxable income as a result of receiving the distribution. Thus, only one level of tax

---

8. Subchapter S consists of §§ 1361 through 1379.

is usually assessed as a result of an S corporation's distribution of appreciated property. This means that the S corporation is preferable to C corporation, which is subject to a double tax, but not to a partnership, which would generate no tax.

Similar to income, expenses of a partnership and an S corporation also flow out to partners and stockholders. The ability of partners and S corporation stockholders to obtain immediate tax benefits from such expenses, however, may be significantly affected by limitations discussed in Section C of Chapter 3.

Chapter Two

THE PASS–THROUGH PRINCIPLE OF PARTNERSHIP TAXATION

A. INTRODUCTION

As discussed in Chapter 1, the amount and character of a partnership's income are calculated using an "entity" approach, but the income is taxed to the partners, not to the entity. The basic Code provisions which implement the taxation of partnership income to the partners are:

Section 701, which provides that partners, and not the partnership itself, shall be subject to the income tax. (Note, though, that Code provisions referring to "the taxpayer" can refer to partnerships. Section 7701(a)(14) defines "taxpayer" as "any person subject to any internal revenue tax." Although a partnership cannot be subject to the income tax it can be subject to some Federal taxes, such as payroll taxes and excise taxes.)

Section 702(a), which provides that each partner shall take into account that partner's share of various kinds of partnership income, deductions, and credits. Items of income and deductions which, because of their character, could affect each partner's tax liability differently are "separately stated." For example, capital gains must be separately stated so that each partner's share of partnership capital gains can be treated as though the partner had realized those gains. Sections 702(a)(1) through 702(a)(6) list some items which must be separately stated, but these sections are so obvious as to be almost meaningless. The most important information appears in the regulations under § 702(a)(7), which require separate statement of any item of income or deduction (even if not listed in §§ 702(a)(1) through 702(a)(6)) if separate accounting makes a difference.[1] Income and deduction items that do not require separate statement pass through to the partners under § 702(a)(8). In the trade, the partnership's net income or loss not counting separately stated items is called "bottom line" income or loss.

Section 702(b), which says that the character of any item of income, deduction, or credit is determined at the partnership level. Thus, if a

---

1. Treas. Reg. § 1.702–1(a)(8)(ii). Section 1366(a), the subchapter S equivalent to § 702(a), simply requires shareholders of S corporations to take into account their shares of separately stated items and other items. Separately stated items are defined as items "the separate treatment of which could affect the liability for tax of any shareholder." In practical terms, § 702 and § 1366 are identical.

partnership recognizes a $10,000 gain from the sale of property, the question whether that gain is capital gain, ordinary income, or § 1231 gain is answered at the partnership level.

Section 703(a), which provides, with exceptions to be discussed later, that a partnership's taxable income is computed in the same way as the taxable income of an individual.

Many "partnerships" today are limited liability companies, which are taxed as partnerships unless they elect to be taxed as corporations.[2] All of the rules discussed in this book apply as much to LLCs that are taxed as partnerships as to conventional state-law partnerships. The use of the LLC form does present some special problems. For instance, it sometimes matters whether a partner is a general partner or a limited partner. LLC members resemble general partners in being able to participate in management, but they are like limited partners in not being personally liable for partnership debts. The application of partnership-tax rules distinguishing between general and limited partners may therefore be uncertain at times. Cases in which it may matter whether a partnership (in the tax sense) is an LLC will be noted in discussing particular issues.

B. ILLUSTRATION

An example may help to clarify and extend the discussion of the previous section.

Example 2–1: Clarissa and David are equal members of the CD partnership. During the current year, the partnership recognizes the following income and deduction items:

$50,000 of gross income from the performance of services.

$35,000 of ordinary and necessary business expenses incurred in earning income from the performance of services.

$4,000 long-term capital gain from the sale of investment securities held by the partnership.

$2,000 in expenses for the management of investment property. This cost would be deductible under § 212 if incurred by an individual taxpayer.

$1,000 charitable contribution.

Clarissa and David will each report the following on their individual income-tax returns:

$7,500 income from the partnership's business operations. The partnership's "bottom-line income"(that is, income that

---

2. See Chapter 16.

does not have to be separately stated under §§ 702(a)(1) through 702(a)(7)) is $15,000. This consists of $50,000 of gross income from the partnership's business less $35,000 in business expenses. Each equal partner reports half of this amount.

$2,000 in long-term capital gain, which must be separately stated because of §§ 702(a)(2) and 703(a)(1).

$1,000 of expenses deductible under § 212. These expenses are not deductible in calculating the *partnership's* taxable income under § 703(a) because of § 703(a)(2)(E). Nevertheless, the partners can deduct them on their individual returns (subject to the two-percent floor for "miscellaneous itemized deductions"[3]). The expenses pass through to the partners under § 702(a)(7).

$500 share of the partnership's charitable contribution (a separately stated item under § 702(a)(4)). Like the partnership's investment expenses, this contribution is not deductible in computing the partnership's taxable income under § 703(a).

Note that § 703(a) creates a two step process. It requires that the deductions and income in Example 2–1 that are described in § 702 be separately stated and taken into account by each partner. In addition, partners take into account their shares of the other partnership items that do not have to be separately stated and, therefore, are combined into a single number.

The Code's requirement that many kinds of partnership income and deductions be separately stated stems from the pass-through principle discussed at the beginning of this Chapter. Separate statement of capital gains is needed because different partners are likely to have different amounts of capital gains and losses from their non-partnership activities and so their shares of partnership capital gains will be treated just like capital gains they had recognized individually. Similarly, the deductibility of investment expenses and charitable contributions will vary among partners; some, for example, will take the standard deduction and will therefore not deduct these outlays at all. The controlling principle is "to tax each partner as though he were directly conducting his proportionate share of the partnership business."[4]

Partners must report their shares of partnership income even if the partnership does not distribute any money or property during the year

---

3. § 67.

4. American Law Institute, Federal Income Tax Project, Subchapter K at 5 (1984).

in question. Partners are taxable on their "distributive shares" and not (usually) on distributions.

C. THE TIMING OF PARTNERSHIP INCOME

Subchapter K adopts an "entity" rather than an "aggregate" approach in dealing with accounting methods. Suppose that Karen uses an accrual method of accounting and that her partner, Ludwig, uses the cash method. Keeping two sets of partnership books would be a mess, and so the partnership must use one accounting method. Section 706(a) requires Karen and Ludwig to include in their incomes their shares of partnership items for partnership years that end "within or with" their personal taxable years. In the everyday case in which Karen, Ludwig, and the partnership all use a calendar year, Karen and Ludwig will report their shares of items for the partnership's calendar year 2011 on their 2011 tax returns, because the partnership's 2011 year is the taxable year that ends "within or with" (in this case, "with") the partners' 2011 calendar years. Note that the partnership's accounting method controls. If the partnership, using an accrual method, accrues but does not receive a $10,000 income item in calendar year 2011, both Karen (an accrual-method partner) and Ludwig (a cash-method partner) must report the item on their 2011 returns.

> **Example 2–2:** The MN partnership reports income on a fiscal year ending on January 31; MN's partners, Michelle and Norman, are calendar-year taxpayers. Income and deduction items received or accrued during the partnership's fiscal year ending January 31, 2011, are reported by Michelle and Norman on their returns for calendar year 2011. This is the taxable year "within" which the partnership's taxable year in question ended.

Without special rules, partnerships could elect any fiscal year. Under the timing rules discussed above, this would permit income deferral for up to 11 months. In Example 2–2, for instance, partnership income earned mostly during calendar year 2010 was not taxable to anyone until 2011. Section 706(b) prevents most partnerships that consist of calendar-year individual partners from doing this by requiring that they use a calendar year. There are two exceptions. First, partnerships that convince the Service that they have a "business purpose" for using a fiscal year different from that of their principal partners can use that fiscal year (a partnership operating a professional basketball team would be an example); see § 706(b)(1)(C). Second, § 444 lets some partnerships use a fiscal year that § 706 would not allow. Partnerships that elect otherwise-impermissible fiscal years under § 444 must make "required payments" under § 7519. These payments are intended to take away the tax advantage of the income deferral that results when a partnership uses a taxable year other than that of its partners.

D. THE DURATION OF A PARTNERSHIP

Under some state partnership statutes, a partnership is dissolved whenever a partner withdraws from the partnership or dies. Although the partnership agreement can, and often does, provide for the remaining partners to continue as a partnership, the new partnership is technically just that—a new partnership. For income-tax purposes, however, dissolution of a partnership is almost always irrelevant. Section 708(a) provides that an existing partnership continues until it terminates under § 708(b). Section 708(b), in turn, says that a partnership terminates only if none of its activities are carried on by any of its partners in a partnership or if fifty percent or more of the total interest in partnership capital and profits is *sold* within a twelve-month period.

A partner's withdrawal from a partnership is not a "sale" under § 708(b). If 98 of the 100 partners of a large partnership retire, leaving two of the old partners to carry on a tiny fraction of the original partnership's business, the partnership will not terminate. (If there had been only one person left, the partnership would have terminated under § 708(b)(1)(A) because the remaining partner would not be carrying on any of the partnership's business "in a partnership.") Section 708(b)(2) and the regulations under that section provide some rules for determining whether a partnership created by combining or splitting up older partnerships is a "continuation" of one of those older partnerships.

E. PARTNERS AS SELF–EMPLOYED TAXPAYERS

Partners performing services for their partnership are considered self-employed taxpayers; they are not employees of their partnerships for federal income tax purposes.[5] In some cases, classification as a self-employed taxpayer is preferable to being treated as an employee. For instance, deductions for business expenses of self-employed workers are above-the-line deductions under § 62(a)(1) that are not subject to some limitations that apply to itemized deductions. Most employee business expenses are itemized deductions, and are also "miscellaneous itemized deductions" as defined in § 67. Taxpayers can deduct miscellaneous

---

5. This is so even if part of a partner's compensation for services performed as a partner is a fixed payment (called a "guaranteed payment" in partnership-tax jargon). Treas. Reg. § 1.707–1(c). One Fifth Circuit decision, which should not be relied on in planning, holds that a partner who received payment for work done for the partnership but not in his "capacity as a partner" was an employee for purposes of § 119; Armstrong v. Phinney, 394 F.2d 661 (1968). Even if this decision is correct, it has nothing to do with compensation for a partner's services as a partner to the partnership.

itemized deductions only to the extent that the total amount of those deductions exceeds two percent of adjusted gross income.[6] For many taxpayers, this means that miscellaneous itemized deductions cannot be deducted at all. Furthermore, above-the-line deductions reduce the taxpayer's adjusted gross income. For many high-income individuals, a reduction in adjusted gross income lowers the taxes imposed by § 151(d) ("phasing out" personal exemptions) and the many other sections that phase out tax benefits.

One of the major benefits of being considered self-employed arises when a taxpayer has to pay for premiums for health insurance. Self-employed taxpayers, such as partners performing services for their partnerships, can fully deduct the cost of their health insurance.[7] In contrast, employees can only deduct the cost of premiums that they pay to the extent the premiums exceed ten percent of their adjusted gross income.[8]

With respect to tax-favored fringe benefits allowed by the Code, a partner's status as self-employed is sometimes a drawback. Some fringe benefits receive favorable tax treatment only if the recipient is an "employee."

Example 2–3: Mary and Norm are forming a small business. Each will spend $150 a month for parking while at work. If they form a C corporation and work for it as employees, the corporation can pay for their parking and deduct the cost as a business expense; Mary and Norm will not be taxed on the value of their parking.[9] If Mary and Norm form a partnership, the $150 that each of them spends each month for parking will be a nondeductible commuting expense.[10]

Other fringe benefits available tax-free only to employees include qualified transportation fringes other than parking[11] and premiums on group term life insurance.[12]

Until 1984, many doctors and other professionals incorporated their practices so that they could be employees. Under pre–1984 law, tax-favored pension and profit-sharing plans for employees received much more favorable income tax treatment than the "Keogh plans" available to self-employed taxpayers. The Deficit Reduction Act of 1984 eliminated

---

6. § 67(a).
7. § 162(*l*). The deduction is an above-the-line deduction.
8. § 213(a).
9. § 132(a)(5).
10. Treas. Reg. § 1.132–9(b) Q & A 24.
11. Treas. Reg. § 1.132–9(b) Q & A 1.
12. § 79.

most of the important differences between employee plans and Keogh plans, considerably reducing the incentive of professionals to incorporate.

F. PARTNERS AND SOCIAL SECURITY AND MEDICARE TAXES

Taxpayers are subject to Social Security and Medicare taxes on wages they earn as employees and on income they earn from conducting a trade or business while self employed. Section 1402 imposes Social Security and Medicare taxes on a general partner's share of partnership income arising from the partnership's conduct of a trade or business.[13] In effect, a general partner is treated as though she directly conducted her share of the partnership's trade or business. In contrast, a limited partner's share of income arising from the limited partnership's conduct of a trade or business is generally not subject to Social Security and Medicare taxes.[14]

Amazingly, despite the popularity of LLCs, current law is unclear whether members of the LLC should be treated like general partners or limited partners for purposes of Social Security and Medicare taxes.[15] In contrast, current law is clear that S corporation stockholders pay Social Security and Medicare taxes only on the salaries they receive from the S corporation. Trade or business income of the S corporation that flows out and is taxable to stockholders for income tax purposes is currently not subject to Social Security and Medicare taxes. There have been recent proposals, however, to also subject such income to Social Security and Medicare taxes.

G. THE "ANTI-ABUSE" REGULATIONS

The regulations under § 701 provide two "anti-abuse" rules. The first of these allows the Commissioner to recast transactions "to achieve tax results that are consistent with the intent of subchapter K."[16] The other allows the Commissioner to "treat a partnership as an aggregate of its partners ... to carry out the purpose of any provision of the Internal Revenue Code."[17] Several other sections of the regulations contain their own anti-abuse rules for particular matters.

---

13. § 1402(a); Treas. Reg. § 1.1402(a)–1(a)(2).

14. Social Security and Medicare taxes do apply, however, to a limited partner's share of income that constitutes a guaranteed payment to the partner, as described in § 707(c) and Chapter 16.

15. See Prop. Treas. Reg. § 1.1402(a)–(2); P.L. 105–34, § 935.

16. Treas. Reg. § 1.701–2(b).

17. Treas. Reg. § 1.701–2(e).

The regulations describe the "intent of subchapter K" as being to allow taxpayers to conduct activities without incurring an entity-level tax, provided the tax results "accurately reflect the partners' economic agreement" and "clearly reflect" the partners' incomes.[18] Of special concern are transactions that produce tax results more favorable than those that could have been achieved if the partners, rather than the partnership, had owned the partnership's assets and conducted its activities.[19] There are, however, cases in which rules adopted for administrative convenience or other policy purposes allow tax results that do not clearly measure incomes.[20] Applications of the "intent of subchapter K" anti-abuse rule will be discussed in connection with particular issues.

The other general anti-abuse rule, allowing the Commissioner to treat a partnership as an aggregate of its partners, seems to have been designed mainly to coordinate provisions applicable only to corporations with the partnership provisions. For example, § 163(e)(5) defers or disallows some interest deductions on high-yield discount obligations issued by corporations. What if a partnership, all the members of which are corporations, issues a high-yield discount obligation? Although the obligation was not issued by a corporation, and so is not literally subject to § 163(e)(5), an example in the regulations provides that each corporate partner will be treated as if it had issued its share of the partnership's obligation in determining whether the partner can deduct its share of the interest.[21] Without this rule, § 163(e)(5)'s attempt to limit the deductibility of interest would be undermined. Another example, however, concludes that a partnership's corporate partners will not be treated as the owners of stock of a foreign corporation owned by their partnership. In this example, if the corporate partners had owned the foreign corporation's stock, the foreign corporation would not have been a controlled foreign corporation ("CFC") under § 957. If the partnership, itself, is treated as owning the foreign corporation's stock, the foreign corporation would be a CFC. The example concludes in a cursory manner that "Congress clearly contemplated that taxpayers could use a bona fide ... partnership" to obtain CFC status for a corporation that would not have been a CFC if owned directly by the partners. This conclusion appears to be based on the statement in § 957 that the persons listed in § 7701(a)(30) shall be treated as the owners of a CFC.[22] Because § 7701(a)(30) lists several types of entities, including partnerships, the example's drafters apparently felt that Congress intended the

---

18. Treas. Reg. § 1.701–2(a)(3).

19. Treas. Reg. § 1.701–2(c)(1), listing this as the first of seven factors to be considered in deciding whether a particular use of a partnership is abusive.

20. Treas. Reg. § 1.701–2(a)(3).

21. Treas. Reg. § 1.701–2(f) (Example 1).

22. Treas. Reg. § 1.701–2(f) (Example 3).

partnership to be treated as an entity separate from its partners in determining who owns a CFC. The example's failure to provide a full explanation, however, leaves an impression that the drafters believed that treating the interest on high-yield obligations as fully deductible would be a bad thing, while treatment of foreign corporations as CFCs is a good thing.

Many have criticized the anti-abuse rules for being too general and vague. In response to the criticism, the IRS announced in 1994 that its agents cannot apply the regulations without the approval of the National Office.[23] The rules remain controversial today. One prominent commentator has concluded that "[t]he antiabuse regulations seem destined to play no part in the affairs of most partnerships."[24] Another article has concluded that the regulations should be applied to combat tax shelters and has said that "Treasury needs to focus the attention of the bar once again on these regulations and declare its intention to apply them."[25]

H. COMPARISON WITH SUBCHAPTER S

Most of the rules discussed in this Chapter correspond closely to those that apply to the taxation of S corporations and their shareholders. Section 1366(a), the pass-through provision for S corporations, is identical in substance to § 702, and the timing rules discussed above have close parallels under subchapter S. Shareholders of S corporations who receive salaries for the work they do are generally treated as employees of the corporations. However, § 1372 says that S corporation stockholders who are employees of the corporation and own more than two percent of the corporation's stock shall be treated as partners for purposes of determining the income tax treatment of employee fringe benefits provided to them.

Unlike a partnership, the distribution of appreciated property by an S corporation to its stockholders triggers a tax liability. Also, unlike the uncertainty surrounding LLCs, it is clear that, under current law, distributions of profits from an S corporation that are attributable to a trade or business are not subject to the Social Security and Medicare taxes.

The subchapter S regulations contain no anti-abuse rules. In many ways, subchapter S is less well suited to than subchapter K to aggressive

---

23. Ann. 94–87, 1994–27 I.R.B. 124 (1994).

24. Alan Gunn, The Use and Misuse of Antiabuse Rules: Lessons From the Partnership Antiabuse Rules, 54 S.M.U. L. Rev. 159, 173 (2004).

25. Noel Cunningham and James Repetti, *Textualism and Tax Shelters*, 24 Va. Tax Rev. 1, 62 (2004).

tax schemes, and it may have been thought that abuse of subchapter S was not a serious problem. Furthermore, the rules of subchapter S tend to be very rigid. Imposing anti-abuse rules, which tend to emphasize substance over form and to rely on judgments based on "all facts and circumstances," to a system based on mechanical formalities would be awkward.

Chapter Three

AN INTRODUCTION TO PARTNERSHIP BASIS AND LIMITS ON LOSSES

A. THE TAX BASIS OF PARTNERSHIP INTERESTS AND PARTNERSHIP PROPERTY

Consistent with the pass-through model of taxation, a partner's contribution of property to a partnership is not ordinarily a taxable event. (The rules for nonrecognition are discussed in Chapter 4). A partner's basis for a partnership interest acquired by contributing property is the same as the basis of the contributed property. The partnership takes the contributed property with the partner's basis. See §§ 721, 722, and 723. These rules preserve whatever gain or loss is "built in" to contributed property so that it will be recognized later: either when the partnership disposes of the property or when the partner disposes of the partnership interest. Similar rules preserve pre-contribution holding periods for capital and § 1231 assets (see §§ 1223(1) and 1223(2)).

Example 3–1: Ellen becomes a partner in the CDE partnership by contributing a capital asset with a basis of $40,000 and a value of $50,000. Ellen's basis for her partnership interest is $40,000 under § 722. If she sells her partnership interest for $50,000 she will recognize a $10,000 gain, just as if she had sold the property. The partnership's basis for the asset is also $40,000: if the partnership sells the asset for $50,000 after Ellen contributes it, its gain on the sale will be $10,000.

The basis of a partner's interest in a partnership is often called the partner's "outside basis." A partnership's basis for property it holds is often called "inside basis."

To prevent a partner from being taxed more than once on the same economic gain, a partner's outside basis must increase to reflect that partner's distributive share of partnership income. Similar considerations require that a partner's outside basis be reduced to reflect losses and other items.

Example 3–2: The CDE partnership (Example 3–1) earns $150,000; Ellen's distributive share of this income is $50,000. Under § 705(a)(1)(A), Ellen's outside basis increases by $50,000 to $90,000. Were it not for this increase, a sale by Ellen of her partnership interest for $100,000 (its value taking into account the partnership's receipt of $150,000, of which Ellen's share is

$50,000) would cause her to recognize a gain of $60,000. In substance, she would be taxed twice on her $50,000 increase in wealth: once when she reports her distributive share of the partnership's income and again when she sells her partnership interest.

Considerations similar to those discussed above underlie basis adjustments required by § 705 for tax-exempt income and for losses and non-deductible outlays (other than capital expenditures).

Example 3–3: Frank and Gail form the FG equal partnership by contributing $50,000 each. Under § 722, each has an outside basis of $50,000. The partnership invests its $100,000 in tax-exempt bonds and earns $6,000 in tax-exempt interest during its first year. At this point, the partnership's assets consist of the bonds (which have a cost basis of $100,000) and $6,000 in cash. Each partner's outside basis increases by $3,000 under § 705(a)(1)(B). Therefore, a partner's sale of a 50 percent interest in the partnership for $53,000 will produce no gain.

Example 3–4: Harvey and Iris form the HI equal partnership by contributing $20,000 each. In a desperate attempt to make money, HI uses $30,000 of its $40,000 cash to bribe a public official in an attempt to get a liquor license; this is HI's only activity during its first taxable year. The bribe is non-deductible. Section 705(a)(2)(B) requires that each partner's outside basis be reduced by that partner's $15,000 share of the non-deductible bribe. Without this adjustment, the decline in the partnership's value attributable to its no longer having the $30,000 on hand could be reflected in a deductible capital loss for a partner who sold a partnership interest. For instance, if Harvey were to sell his interest for $5,000, he would have a loss of $15,000 without the downward basis adjustment required by § 705.

Likewise, a partner's basis is reduced, but not below zero, to reflect distributions from the partnership to the partner. See §§ 705(a)(2) and 733. In general, a distribution is not taxable to the partner to the extent that the distribution does not exceed the partner's outside basis. Distributions in excess of a partner's outside basis result in gain recognition. § 731(a)(1). (Distributions will be explored in much more depth in Chapter 9.)

Example 3–5: James acquires a one-third interest in the HIJ partnership by contributing $100,000. During the partnership's first taxable year, James's distributive share of ordinary income net of deductions (bottom-line income) is $4,000; his share of tax-exempt interest is $1,000; and he receives a distribution of $3000. James's basis, as adjusted to reflect these transactions, is

$102,000, computed as follows: Original basis of $100,000 (§ 722), plus $5,000 for his share of taxable and tax-exempt income, less $3,000 for the distribution. The distribution is not taxable because it does not exceed James's outside basis. § 731(a).

B. THE EFFECTS OF PARTNERSHIP DEBT TRANSACTIONS UPON BASIS

Changes in the partnership's debt affect the outside basis of partners. If a partnership increases its debt, partners are treated as though they contributed cash to the partnership to the extent of their share of the increase in partnership debt. § 752(a). Since contributions of cash increase a partner's outside basis (§ 722), the increase in the partner's share of partnership debt also increases that partner's outside basis.

Example 3–6: Ellen, Francesco, and Georgia are equal partners in the EFG. EFG borrows $12,000 from the Acme Small–Loan Company. If each partner shares equally in the $12,000 borrowing, each partner is treated as having contributed $4,000 to EFG under § 752(a). As a result, each partner's outside basis in EFG will increase by $4,000. § 722.

Decreases in a partner's share of partnership debt are treated as cash distributions to that partner. § 752(b). Since cash distributions decrease a partner's outside basis (§ 733), the partner's outside basis is decreased (but not below zero) by the decline in that partner's share of partnership debt.

Example 3–7: The EFG partnership (example 3–1) repays $9,000 of its loan from Acme. Section 752(b) treats each partner as having received a distribution of $3,000. As a result, each partner's outside basis is decreased by $3,000. § 733.

Complex rules, which are discussed in Chapter 8, determine each partner's share of debt. In general, partners share recourse debt in proportion to how they share partnership losses. Nonrecourse debt is generally shared among partners in proportion to how they share partnership profits.

Why does § 752 treat partnership debt in this manner? Section 752 applies an aggregate approach to partnership debt. It treats each partner as having borrowed a share of the partnership debt and having contributed that share to the partnership. When the partnership debt is reduced, the reduction is treated in effect as a cash distribution to each partner, with the partner then using the cash to reduce the debt.

Ch. 3   *LIMITS ON THE DEDUCTIBILITY*

Sometimes a partner will have both a decrease and an increase in debt as part of the same transaction. Suppose, for example, that Keith, who owes $90,000 to the Third Bank, becomes a one-third partner in KLM. The partnership assumes Keith's debt, so that it, rather than Keith, is the debtor after Keith joins the partnership. The partnership has no other debt. Assume that Keith's share of the partnership's debt is $30,000. Under § 752(a), Keith's share of the partnership's liabilities has increased from zero to $30,000, so Keith is deemed to have contributed $30,000 to the partnership. But, under § 752(b), Keith's "individual liabilities" have decreased by $90,000, so the partnership is considered as having distributed $90,000 to Keith. To simplify things, Keith's $30,000 constructive cash contribution to the partnership and the partnership's $90,000 constructive cash distribution to Keith are netted and treated as one transaction: a $60,000 constructive cash distribution by the partnership to Keith.[1]

C. LIMITS ON THE DEDUCTIBILITY OF PARTNERSHIP LOSSES

This Section examines three Code provisions that limit the extent to which partners can deduct their shares of partnership losses: (1) § 704(d), which limits a partner's deduction for losses to the partner's outside basis; (2) § 465, which limits deductions based upon nonrecourse debt; and (3) § 469, which allows individual taxpayers to deduct losses from "passive" activities only against income from passive activities.

The connections among these three sections are practical and historical, not theoretical. Partnerships were for many years the preferred way of organizing tax shelters, many of which depended on deductions based on debt for their success. Section 704(d), which limits loss deductions to outside basis, does not seriously impede tax sheltering, because partners' outside bases reflect those partners' shares of their partnerships' debts. In the 1970s, Congress attacked tax shelters by adopting § 465, which lets many taxpayers take deductions only to the extent that the taxpayers are "at risk" with respect to the activity in question. When the tax-shelter industry continued to flourish, Congress adopted the passive-loss rules in 1986.

A word about the term "loss" is in order here. For purposes of §§ 704(d), 465, and 469, a "loss" is the excess of a partnership's (or an activity's) deductions over its gross income. For instance, if a partnership earns $30,000 and incurs $50,000 in business expenses, the partnership's "loss" is $20,000. Therefore, a partnership which has recognized a

---

1. Treas. Reg. § 1.752–1(f).

1. Section 704(d)

Suppose that the FG equal partnership has $40,000 in income and $100,000 in deductions this year. Partner Fred's basis for his interest in the partnership is $100,000; partner Georgia's basis is only $10,000. Although each partner's equal share of the partnership's $60,000 loss is $30,000, only Fred can deduct the full $30,000. Section 704(d) lets a partner deduct a partnership loss "only to the extent of the adjusted basis of such partner's interest in the partnership at the end of the partnership year in which such loss occurred." Therefore, Georgia can deduct only $10,000 of her share of the loss. The other $20,000 becomes a carryover to future years,[2] so she will deduct the loss whenever her outside basis increases. (For example, if she contributes $20,000 to the partnership, or if the partnership borrows $40,000, or if her share of partnership income in some later year is $20,000, her outside basis will go up and the previously disallowed $20,000 deduction will be allowed.)

Section 704(d) seems to embody a familiar principle of income taxation. An individual taxpayer's deductions cannot normally exceed the amount of the taxpayer's cash plus the basis of the taxpayer's property. (There are exceptions: Deductions for charitable contributions can exceed the basis of property contributed to a charity, and deductions for percentage depletion can exceed the basis of the mineral property in question.) Suppose that Georgia, as an individual, owns one asset with a basis of $10,000. Ordinarily, that asset can generate only $10,000 in tax deductions. Georgia should not be allowed larger deductions by contributing the asset to a partnership and claiming a share of the partnership's deductions than she could have gotten by holding the asset as a sole proprietor.

2. The At–Risk Rules of Section 465

The ability of partners to include their shares of partnership debt in basis creates opportunities for abuse. Consider a much-simplified version of the kind of tax shelter which flourished during the 1960s. A promoter produces a motion picture at a cost of $20 million and then sells the picture to a partnership for a nominal purchase price of $200 million. (The purchase price consists of $30 million in cash and $170 million of nonrecourse purchase-money debt.) The partners, as a group, will deduct depreciation calculated by using a basis of $200 million, even though they have paid only $30 million in cash, and even though they will pay little if anything more if the picture flops. (Remember, they are not

---

2. § 704(d) (second sentence); Treas. Reg. § 1.704–1(d)(1).

personally liable on the debt.) Section 704(d) will not limit their deductions, as the debt portion of the purchase price will be reflected in the partners' outside bases under § 752.

One reason for doubt about the legitimacy of the partners' deductions is that the $200 million purchase price may not represent the true value of the film. Neither the seller nor the partners have any incentive to limit the amount of nonrecourse debt in the example to the film's real value: the higher the "debt," the greater the partners' deductions. If the partners are subject to a fifty percent income tax, and if the first year's depreciation deductions for the film are $60 million, the tax savings from the deductions in the first year of the venture will equal the entire cash portion of the purchase price.

Section 465 limits an individual taxpayer's deductions for losses from an activity to the amount the taxpayer has "at-risk" in the activity. One gets an at-risk amount by contributing cash or property to an activity or by borrowing on a recourse basis; nonrecourse financing doesn't count. The at-risk rules apply to partners, not to the partnership.

> **Example 3–8:** The HIJ limited partnership consists of Helen, the general partner, who has a ten percent interest in the partnership, and Isaac and Joan, the limited partners, each of whom has a forty-five percent interest. Isaac and Joan got their partnership interests by contributing $40,000 in cash each to the partnership. The partnership owns a very short motion picture, which it purchased for $50,000 cash plus a $500,000 nonrecourse purchase-money debt. During the partnership's first year of operations, the film earns $35,000 in revenues. Current expenses are $35,000 in deductible cash outlays plus $100,000 in depreciation.
>
> Isaac and Joan have outside bases of $265,000 each (forty-five percent of the $500,000 debt plus $40,000). Section 704(d) would therefore not prevent their deducting all of the $45,000 loss allocated to each of them. But because they are at risk only to the extent of $40,000 each, § 465 limits their deductions for losses to that amount. As with deductions disallowed by § 704(d), deductions disallowed by § 465 carry over to future years and become deductible when the taxpayer's at-risk amount increases.

The at-risk rules did not stop promoters from marketing some very shady tax shelters. For one thing, § 465 did not apply to real-estate ventures until 1986. (Even today, certain nonrecourse loans for real-estate activities ("qualified nonrecourse financing") are exempt from the at-risk rules.[3]) Furthermore, tax-shelter promoters devised schemes purporting to make investors personally liable, but in fact imposing little or no real risk. (One tax shelter involved beavers. The investors were, in form, personally liable to pay the full purchase price, but they could satisfy this liability by paying in beaver pelts, rather than in cash.) Many of these schemes stood little chance of holding up in litigation, but the promoters could provide at least a colorable claim to tax deductions, and for many investors that was enough. In 1986, Congress put an end to most tax shelters by enacting the passive-loss rules.

3. The Passive-Loss Rules of Section 469

Section 469 allows individuals to deduct losses from "passive activities" only against income from passive activities. Income from the active conduct of a business, or from portfolio investments, cannot be reduced by passive losses.[4] (Similarly, credits from passive activities can be used only against the tax attributable to those activities.)

Example 3-9: Ken has $100,000 gross income from salary ("active" income), and $20,000 in interest and dividend income ("portfolio" income). He has $40,000 gross income and $60,000 in business expenses from a passive activity. Ken can deduct only $40,000 of the business expenses from the passive activity. The other $20,000 becomes a carryover to future years; he can deduct it against future years' passive income or when he disposes of his entire interest in the passive activity that generated the expenses.

A partner's losses can be classified as passive in two ways. First, if the partner does not materially participate in whatever business the partnership carries on, that business activity is a "passive activity" with respect to that partner. Second, a limited partner's interest in a partnership normally produces passive losses because, by statute, limited partners are usually not material participants.[5] If a partnership is publicly traded, additional restrictions apply. Passive losses from a publicly traded partnership can be deducted only against passive income from the *same* partnership. Thus, a partner who has a $40,000 passive loss from a publicly traded partnership and $10,000 in passive income from some other source cannot deduct any of the loss.[6]

---

3. § 465(a)(6).

4. §§ 469(a)(1); 469(d)(1).

5. § 469(h)(2). Treas. Reg. § 1.469–5T(e) carves out several exceptions for very active limited partners.

6. § 469(k). Some publicly traded partnerships are taxed as C corporations; see Chapter 16. Losses from these partnerships cannot be deducted by the partners because losses of C corporations do not pass through to the shareholders.

Real estate is usually "passive," even if the taxpayer does participate actively. But two important exceptions apply. First, low-and middle-income taxpayers can deduct up to $25,000 a year in real-estate losses against active and portfolio income.[7] Second, taxpayers who are real estate professionals such as brokers may deduct rental real estate losses from their active and portfolio income.[8] Therefore, a real-estate broker who owns and operates rental property on the side can deduct losses from the activity; a doctor who has an identical rental operation cannot.

The passive-activity rules (particularly for limited partners) have made most tax shelters of the traditional kind obsolete for investors who are individuals. Few investors in tax shelters want to get involved in the day-to-day activities of a business, or to become general partners. Tax-shelter investors typically tried to buy deductions, not real opportunities to make money. The passive activity rules do not apply, however, to corporations in which more than five individuals own more than fifty percent of the stock.[9]

D. COMPARISON WITH SUBCHAPTER S

Shareholders of S corporations do not increase their outside bases (that is, their bases for either their stock or for loans by them to their corporations) when their corporations incur debt from third party lenders. For this reason, the outside-basis limit is a more serious problem for the shareholders of S corporations than for partners when the entity has debt-financed losses. If the shareholders of an S corporation are to deduct losses generated by the corporation spending borrowed funds, they must often borrow the funds themselves, and then either lend the funds or make capital contributions of the funds to the corporation, in order to have enough outside basis to cover the losses.

Although the basis rules for S corporations made those entities unsuitable for tax sheltering, the passive-loss rules apply to the shareholders of S corporations as well as to partners.

---

7. § 469(i).
8. § 469(c)(7).
9. §§ 469(a)(2)(B), 469(j)(1).

Chapter Four

CONTRIBUTIONS TO PARTNERSHIPS

A. CONTRIBUTIONS OF PROPERTY

1. The Statutory Pattern

Section 721 provides that neither the partners nor the partnership recognize gain or loss when the partners exchange "property"[1] for partnership interests.[2] (The one exception is that transfers to investment-company partnerships are taxable.[3] This exception deters investors from exchanging securities without tax by contributing them to partnerships.) The transferred property keeps its basis. That basis also becomes the transferor's basis for the partnership interest acquired in the exchange.[4]

The provisions governing transfers to partnerships do not deal directly with the effect of the transferor's receiving cash (or other) "boot" in addition to a partnership interest. Instead, the distribution of cash or property is governed by the Code provisions dealing with distributions. Under § 733, a cash distribution reduces the partner's outside basis. The distribution is tax-free unless it exceeds the partner's outside basis immediately before the distribution. § 731. (This exception prevents the distributee from having a negative basis.) If a cash distribution does exceed the transferor's pre-distribution outside basis, the excess is taxed as gain from the sale of the transferee's partnership interest.[5] (This rule differs from that governing the recognition of gain upon transfers to controlled corporations—that kind of gain is treated as gain from the sale of the transferred property.)

Gain recognized under § 731 does not increase the transferor's outside basis.[6] Nor does it increase the basis of partnership assets unless

---

1. Although in most instances there will be no doubt about whether a partner has transferred "property," questions will occasionally arise. Because, as discussed in Section B, *below*, services are not "property," the borderline between property and services can be uncertain. For example, a patent, which is the result of a person's efforts, is "property," but a person's "know-how" in most instances would not be "property" for purposes of § 721(a).

2. Unlike § 351(a), § 721(a) does not require that the transferors be in "control" of the partnership immediately after the exchange of property for partnership interests.

3. § 721(b).

4. §§ 722; 723.

5. § 731(a).

6. Gain recognized under § 721(b) when property is transferred to an investment company partnership does increase the transferor's outside basis. See § 722.

Ch. 4   CONTRIBUTIONS OF PROPERTY

a basis-adjustment election under § 754 (described in Chapter 14) is in effect.[7]

Example 4–1: Gwen contributes a capital asset with a value of $102,000, a basis of $10,000, and a holding period of one month to the GHI partnership. In exchange, she receives $12,000 in cash and a one-third interest in the partnership. Gwen's initial outside basis is $10,000 under § 722 (the basis of the property she contributed) [*Transferred Basis*]. She recognizes a $2,000 short-term gain, because the amount of cash distributed to her ($12,000) exceeds her initial outside basis immediately before the distribution ($10,000). After the distribution, Gwen's outside basis is zero ($10,000 initial basis under § 722, reduced to zero by § 733). The partnership's basis for the asset is $10,000 under § 723 unless an election under § 754 is in effect.

2. Holding Periods

When a partner contributes property that is a capital asset or property described in § 1231(b) to a partnership, § 1223(1) permits the partner to tack the holding period for the capital or § 1231(b) asset to the partner's interest in the partnership. In addition, the partnership's holding period in the contributed property is the same as the contributing partner's, regardless of whether the property contributed by a partner is a capital or § 1231(b) asset.[8]

Example 4–2: Ryan and Sarah each own parcels of land that they have held for more than one year and that qualify as capital assets. Each has a tax basis of $10,000 in the parcels.

Ryan and Sarah contribute the parcels to a newly formed partnership in exchange for a partnership interest. Each has a tax basis of $10,000 and a holding period of more than one year in their respective partnership interest. (§ 722, § 1223(1).) In addition, the partnership takes each parcel with a tax basis of $10,000 (§ 723) and a holding period of more than one year (§ 1223(2)).

Since § 1223(1) only allows a contributing partner to tack the holding period of contributed property to the contributor's partnership interest if the contributed property qualifies as a capital or § 1231(b) asset, a partner can have a bifurcated holding period. That is, if the partner contributes a capital or § 1231(b) asset and other types of property, the partner will have two holding periods for the partnership interest—a tacked holding period for the portion of the partnership

---

7. § 743(a). As with outside basis, inside basis does increase when gain is recognized under § 721(b). See § 723.

8. § 1223(2).

interest attributable to the capital or § 1231(b) asset and a new holding period for the remaining portion of the partnership interest. The portion of the partnership interest that qualifies for the tacked holding period is based upon the relative values of the capital or § 1231(b) asset and the other property.

Example 4–3: Quint and Ricki form the QR partnership. Quint contributes $50,000 cash and vacant land that has a fair market value of $50,000. Quint has held the land for more than one year and the land qualifies as a capital asset. His basis in the land is $25,000. Ricki contributes depreciable property that she has held for three months. The value of the depreciable property is $100,000 and Ricki's tax basis in it is $98,000. The depreciable asset is not described in § 1231(b) because Ricki has held it for less than one year.

Quint has a holding period of more than one year in one-half of his partnership interest since one-half of his contribution (measured by value) was a capital asset that he had held for more than one year. Treas. Reg. § 1.1223–3(a). His holding period for the other one-half of the partnership interest (the portion he received for cash) is zero. His tax basis in his partnership interest is $75,000 ($50,000 cash plus $25,000 tax basis in contributed land). § 722. The partnership's holding period in the land is more than one year (§ 1223(2)) and its basis in the land is $25,000 (§ 723).

Ricki's holding period in her new partnership interest is zero, since she did not contribute a capital or § 1231(b) asset. Ricki's tax basis in her partnership interest is $98,000. § 722. The partnership's holding period in the depreciable property is three months, the same holding period that Ricki had. § 1223(2).

3. Contributions of Encumbered Property

A partner contributing property encumbered by recourse debt may recognize gain on the contribution. If some of the recourse debt is shifted to other partners, the contributing partner is treated as receiving a cash distribution under § 752(b) to the extent the debt was shifted. The contributing partner will recognize gain to the extent the deemed cash distribution exceeds the partner's outside basis. This gain is characterized under § 731 as arising from the sale of a partnership interest.

Example 4–4: Dawn and Edward form the DE partnership. Dawn contributes property encumbered by $1,000 of recourse debt. Her tax basis in the property is $100.

Suppose that $500 of the recourse debt is shifted to Edward. (Chapter 8 discusses how debt is allocated among partners.) As a result, Dawn is treated under § 752(b) as receiving a constructive cash distribution of $500. Dawn's initial basis in her partnership interest is $100 (the tax basis of the property she contributed). As a result of the $500 distribution, Dawn recognizes $400 of gain ($500 distribution less $100 basis) under § 731(a)(1). This gain is treated as though it arose from the sale of Dawn's partnership interest, not the property she contributed.

Additional complexities of contributing property encumbered by debt are explored in Chapter 8.

4. Depreciation Recapture

Suppose a partner transfers a machine having a zero basis, a $10,000 recomputed basis (§ 1245(a)(2)), and a $10,000 value to a partnership in a § 721 exchange. A sale of the property would have given the partner $10,000 of ordinary income because of depreciation recapture under § 1245. At first glance it appears that § 721 does not prevent the partner from recognizing this ordinary income when the asset is transferred to a partnership, because § 1245(a)(1) says that recapture income "shall be recognized notwithstanding any other provision of this subtitle."[9] However, § 1245(b)(3) rescues the transferring partner by saying that depreciation recapture on a § 721 transfer cannot exceed the transferor's recognized gain on the transfer.

If someone who transfers § 1245 property to a partnership recognizes gain because cash is received, depreciation may be recaptured. Suppose a partner who would have had $10,000 of depreciation recapture upon selling an asset transfers the asset, subject to a liability, to a partnership. Suppose further that the partner recognizes a $1,000 gain under § 731 because some of the debt that encumbered the property is shifted to other partners and results in a constructive cash distribution to the partner under § 752(b) in excess of the partner's outside basis.[10] Section 1245(b)(3) recharacterizes the $1,000 gain as depreciation recapture.[11]

---

9. § 1245(a)(1). See also § 1245(d) ("This section shall apply notwithstanding any other provision of this subtitle").

10. See pages 26–27, above, for a discussion of § 752(b).

11. Treas. Reg. § 1.1245–4(c)(4) (Example(3)). If both § 1245 property and other assets are transferred in an exchange on which gain is recognized, the gain is allocated between the two kinds of assets. Only the portion of the gain allocated to the § 1245 property counts in calculating recapture. See Treas. Reg. § 1.1245–4(c)(1).

5. Character Issues: Section 724

Suppose a partner who owns an appreciated ordinary-income asset, such as an item of inventory, contributes that asset to a partnership. If the asset is a capital or § 1231 asset in the partnership's hands, § 702(b) would make gain on the sale of the asset by the partnership a capital or § 1231 gain even though the gain would have been ordinary if the partner had sold the property. However, § 724 limits § 702(b) by "tainting" some kinds of contributed property having undesirable tax attributes. Partnership gain or loss on tainted property contributed by a partner has the same character it would have had if the partner had sold the property.

Sections 724(a) and 724(b) limit the ability of partners to convert ordinary income into capital gain by contributing "unrealized receivables" and "inventory items" to partnerships in whose hands the property would be capital or § 1231 assets. "Unrealized receivable" and "inventory item" are terms of art, defined in §§ 751(c) and 751(d). The definition of these terms will be discussed in detail in Chapter 10. The definitions are so broad that almost any item of ordinary-income property is either an "unrealized receivable" or an "inventory item" (or both). Gain or loss recognized by a partnership that disposes of unrealized receivables contributed by a partner is ordinary. § 724(a). Gain or loss on a partnership's disposition of inventory items contributed by a partner is ordinary if the disposition takes place within five years of the contribution. § 724(b). (Of course, the disposition of inventory items more than five years after a contribution will also generate ordinary income if the property is "inventory" in the partnership's hands. Section 724 has practical effect only when the character of an asset in the partnership's hands differs from its character in the partner's hands.)

Under § 724(c), partnership losses on disposing of contributed property within five years of the contribution may be treated as capital losses if the property was a capital asset in the partner's hands. Unlike the ordinary-income taint of §§ 724(a) and 724(b), the capital-loss taint applies only to capital losses "built in" to the property at the time of the contribution. Suppose, for instance, that a partner contributes a capital asset with a basis of $10,000 and a value of $9,000, and that the asset is ordinary-income property in the partnership's hands. If the partnership recognizes a $4,000 loss upon selling the asset within five years of the contribution, $1,000 of that loss will be capital because of § 724(c).

B. CONTRIBUTIONS OF SERVICES

Nothing in the Code provides for nonrecognition when a partner acquires a partnership interest in exchange for performing services (or promising to perform services in the future). The taxation of these transactions may turn upon whether the partner receives an interest in the partnership's capital or only an interest in the partnership's future profits; for this reason, these kinds of cases will be discussed separately.

1. Receipt of an Interest in Partnership Capital

The regulations provide that a partner who receives an interest in partnership capital as compensation for services recognizes income.[12] Under current law, the amount and timing of the service partner's income depend upon the application of § 83. The service partner will ordinarily have income when the right to a share of partnership capital becomes substantially vested.[13] As is always the case when property is received in a taxable transaction, the service partner's basis for the partnership interest will be the amount includable in the partner's income.[14]

Example 4–5: Karen performs services for the HIJ partnership. As compensation, she receives a one-fourth interest in the partnership, including a one-fourth interest in the partnership's capital. If this interest is worth $25,000, Karen has $25,000 income from the performance of services and her basis for the partnership interest is $25,000.

Just as the partner who receives an interest in the partnership is treated as receiving compensation for services, the partnership is treated as paying compensation for those services. The partnership will usually get a deduction or be treated as having made a capital expenditure.[15]

Example 4–6: If Karen's services in Example 4–5 were non-capital (that is, if a cash payment by the partnership would have been deductible as an expense), the partnership will deduct $25,000. The deduction should probably be allocated to partners other than Karen, at least if the partnership's bookkeeping

---

12. Treas. Reg. § 1.721–1(b)(1). This section of the regulations contains a confusing and unnecessary discussion of partners who give up their rights under local law to be repaid their contributions of money or other property to the partnership. It now seems quite clear that recognition of income by a service partner who receives an interest in partnership capital does not depend upon whether the capital was contributed by the other partners or was amassed by the partnership during the course of its operations.

13. That is, transferable or not subject to a substantial risk of forfeiture. See Prop. Treas. Reg. § 1.721–1(b)(1).

14. This will be a "cost" basis under § 1012; see Philadelphia Park Amusement Co. v. United States, 126 F.Supp. 184 (Ct.Cl. 1954).

15. Conceivably, the partnership's outlay could be a non-deductible, non-capital expenditure. If, for example, a partnership gave a Government official an interest in the partnership (including an interest in partnership capital) as a bribe, the official would have income but the partnership would not be entitled to a deduction because of § 162(c) and the transfer would not increase the basis of any partnership property.

methods result in charging the expense to those partners.[16] If Karen performed capital services (if, for example, she is an architect who designed a building for the partnership) the partnership will have made a $25,000 capital expenditure.

Several commentators insist that a partnership which transfers an interest in itself to a service partner must recognize gains and losses on all of its assets. The theory behind this argument is that a transfer of an interest in the partnership to the service partner is economically identical to a transfer of an undivided interest in each of the partnership's assets to that partner, followed by the partner's recontribution of those assets to the partnership in a § 721 transaction. Because an actual transfer of an undivided interest in assets to someone who performed services would have been taxable to the partnership, so too, it is said, a transfer of an interest in the partnership should be taxable. However, one can plausibly equate the service partner's receipt of a partnership interest to the receipt of cash compensation, followed by a contribution of that cash to the partnership in exchange for an interest in partnership capital. The latter analogy suggests that the partnership does not recognize gains and losses.

Support for the position that a partnership does not treat the award of an interest in partnership capital to a service partner as a taxable event can be found in the rules governing a corporation's transfer of its own stock to an employee as compensation. As in the case of the partnership provisions, the Code provides (in § 1032) that a corporation recognizes no income when it exchanges its stock for property, but no Code provision says that a corporation recognizes no gain or loss when an employee receives stock for services. Nevertheless, the regulations under § 1032 say that a corporation does not have income in this case.[17] Those who drafted the regulations apparently determined that awarding corporate stock for services should be taxed like the economically identical case of paying cash to the employee, followed by the employee's using the cash to buy stock (a non-taxable event to the corporation under § 1032).[18] The partnership case is less clear than the corporate case because the partnership regulations are silent on the subject. However, the governing Code provisions are identical in all important respects.

---

16. This would typically be done by charging the expense to those partners' capital accounts. Capital accounts will be explained in Chapter 5.

17. Treas. Reg. § 1.1032–1(a).

18. Recognition of gain and loss by the corporation in cases like this would be extremely cumbersome. Consider the bookkeeping nightmare that would occur if an award of $1,000 worth of its stock by General Motors to a General Motors employee were taxed as if General Motors had transferred an undivided interest (a very, very small one) in every one of its assets to the employee. Somewhat similar considerations support nonrecognition in cases involving partnerships as well.

In practice, the Government seems never to have taken the position that a partnership recognizes gains and losses when a partner receives an interest in capital in exchange for services. In the many reported cases involving these transactions, the only issue the Government has raised is the amount of the service partner's income.[19] Significantly, Treasury and the Service have adopted this position in proposed regulations published in 2005.[20]

What if a taxpayer receives a partnership interest in exchange for services performed for a partner, rather than the partnership? In that case, the partner has made an actual transfer of property (the partnership interest) to the service provider, and both parties will recognize gain or loss.

Example 4–7: Lois is a one-third partner in the KLM partnership. Her basis for her partnership interest is $50,000 and its value is $70,000. To compensate Norm for services he performed for her, Lois transfers half her partnership interest to him. Norm has $35,000 income and a $35,000 basis for his partnership interest; Lois recognizes a $10,000 gain on the transfer.[21]

2. Receipt of an Interest in Partnership Profits

Very often, a partnership employee will be made a partner who has no interest in the capital of the partnership but who is entitled to a share of the partnership's profits. For example, an associate in a law firm may be made a partner who becomes entitled only to a share of whatever profits the partnership earns after the associate's elevation to partnership status. For many years, tax lawyers assumed that the

---

19. Furthermore, the Commissioner's argument in McDougal v. Commissioner, 62 T.C. 720 (1974) (discussed in Note 21, *infra*), assumed that a partnership asset's basis did not increase by reason of a service partner's becoming a partner and performing services for that partnership. The Commissioner's assumption appears to be based on the conclusion the transfer of a capital interest is not a recognition event for the partnership. The Tax Court did not reach this issue because it ruled that the services in question had been performed for the partner who had owned the asset, with the partnership being formed afterward.

20. Prop. Treas. Reg. § 1.721–1(b)(2), 70 Fed. Reg. 29,675 (May 24, 2005).

21. Unlike the case of a service provider who performs services for a partnership, the case of services performed for a partner does not require the transaction to be characterized as involving constructive transfers of property. The partner for whom the services were performed has actually transferred a partnership interest.

What if A performs services for B, and is compensated by being made a member of the new AB partnership, to which B contributes property? In this case, the Tax Court has held that the transaction should be taxed as if B had transferred an interest in the asset to A, followed by a transfer of A's and B's interests in the asset to the new partnership. McDougal v. Commissioner, 62 T.C. 720 (1974). The issue in *McDougal* was the asset's basis. The Commissioner argued that the partnership had been formed before the services were provided, and that no gain was recognized on its formation under § 721, making the asset's basis the same as it had been in B's hands.

service partner who received only a profits interest did not recognize income as a result of such receipt. This assumption (which found support in an offhand comment in a footnote in a Tax Court opinion[22]) was based more upon the language of the regulations than upon a close analysis of the problem. Section 1.721–1(b)(1) of the regulations, in requiring a service partner who receives an interest in capital to recognize income, says that § 721 of the Code does not provide for nonrecognition "[t]o the extent that any of the partners gives up any part of his right to be repaid his contributions (as distinguished from a share in partnership profits)."

In Diamond v. Commissioner,[23] the Tax Court and the Seventh Circuit held that a service partner who received an interest that both courts described as a profits interest[24] had income upon receiving the interest. Sol Diamond was a mortgage broker, who obtained financing for a building being purchased by Kargman. To compensate Diamond for obtaining this financing, Kargman made Diamond a partner in a venture that, in substance, owned the building. Under the partnership agreement, Diamond was to receive 60 percent of whatever profits remained from the sale of the building after Kargman had recovered all of the cash he had put up to buy the building. Very soon after making this arrangement, Diamond sold his interest in the partnership for $40,000. He reported a $40,000 capital gain from the sale of the partnership interest; this gain was offset by capital losses from unrelated transactions in which Diamond had engaged.

The Government argued that Diamond had recognized $40,000 of ordinary (compensation) income upon receiving the partnership interest, and the courts agreed. (Because Diamond's basis for the partnership interest was $40,000 if he had that amount of income upon receiving the interest, he had no further income when he sold the interest for $40,000.) The courts brushed aside the language of the regulations, the Tax Court's earlier approval of the inference which most commentators had drawn from that language, and the "startling degree of unanimity" among commentators.[25] They held that Diamond, having received "property" (his partnership interest) as compensation for services, recognized income upon that receipt, even though the interest was an interest only in the profits of the partnership.

---

22. Hale v. Commissioner, 24 T.C.M. 1497, 1502 n. 3 (1965).

23. 56 T.C. 530 (1971), affirmed, 492 F.2d 286 (7th Cir. 1974).

24. The interest may in fact have been an interest in partnership capital. The "profit" in which Diamond was entitled to share was the gain to be recognized on the sale of the partnership's building. If, as seems possible on the facts, the building was worth more than its basis when Diamond got his interest, that interest was at least partly an interest in partnership capital (the building) rather than a profits interest in the usual sense. See Martin B. Cowan, Receipt of an Interest in Partnership Profits in Consideration for Services: The *Diamond* Case, 27 Tax L. Rev. 161 (1972).

25. 492 F.2d at 289.

Some commentators have read the *Diamond* case as requiring all service partners who receive profits interests in partnerships in connection with the performance of services to recognize income if their profits interests are substantially vested under § 83. However, *Diamond* can be read more narrowly.

On its facts, *Diamond* reached an appropriate result. Diamond performed services for Kargman and was compensated by being given an interest in property. That the property was an interest in the profits of a partnership should not have made a difference in that case, and in many other cases. Suppose, for instance, that a divorce lawyer receives, as compensation for arranging a client's divorce, an interest in the profits of a real-estate partnership owned by the client. It is hard to argue seriously that the lawyer should have no income just because the property used as payment was a profits interest in a partnership rather than a share of the royalties of an oil well, or 100 shares of stock, or any other kind of property. In many cases, however, an interest in partnership profits received by a service partner should be viewed, not as compensation for services, but as the first step in an arrangement giving the service partner an opportunity to earn income. When that is the case, the service partner should not be seen as having engaged in a taxable transaction.

Consider a case in which two lawyers, Lloyd and Maria, form a partnership for the practice of law. Lloyd puts up $100,000 cash to buy essential supplies and pay expenses for the first few months of the operation. Both partners agree to perform services. Maria, who has put up no cash or property, will receive forty-five percent of the partnership's profits, if any, during its first year of operation, but she has no interest in the partnership's capital. Thus, if the partners change their minds about the venture tomorrow and unwind the partnership, Lloyd will get his $100,000 back and Maria will get nothing. On these facts, fundamental notions of what partnership taxation is all about show that Maria should not be treated as receiving "property" as compensation for services.[26] Recall that the central theme of partnership taxation is that

---

26. In many cases it will not matter whether the transaction is taxable to Maria or not. If the partnership's chance of making any money is remote, the value of Maria's profits interest may well be zero, so that the amount of income she reports would be zero even if, in theory, she has engaged in a taxable transaction. Furthermore, the partnership agreement will typically provide (at least by implication from the circumstances) that Maria will get nothing if she does no work, and one can argue that her interest is not substantially vested under § 83. (This argument, however, raises the embarrassing prospect that Maria is not a partner at all, since § 83 treats the recipients of substantially nonvested property rights as if they had received nothing.) In some cases, though, the partnership's prospects may be so bright that Maria would have to report income if *Diamond* controls this case. Suppose, for instance, that Lloyd has lined up a prosperous client who has promised the partnership lucrative work if Lloyd can induce Maria to join up. Maria's profits interest in this case could well have a value at the time she acquires it.

the existence of the partnership should, ideally, have nothing to do with the tax treatment of the partners. In practice, administrative considerations often make it necessary to treat the partnership as an "entity," distinct from its partners, but this practical reality does not mean that partners should be taxed differently from sole proprietors just because a partnership interest is "property." The new service partner whose "profits interest" in the partnership amounts, in substance, to the opportunity to earn income from the performance of services resembles a sole proprietor who is just beginning a business venture or an employee undertaking a new job. Sole proprietors and employees in that situation have no income (even though, in the case of the employee, the job may amount to a "property right" in the constitutional sense). Since that is so, a new service partner whose share of partnership profits amounts to compensation for the services that the partner will perform should not be taxed either. Taxing the service partner on the appropriate distributive share of income as it is earned is consistent with the taxation of those who are not partners and avoids serious administrative problems.[27]

Diamond is readily distinguishable from the typical service-partner case in three respects. First, Diamond rendered services to Kargman, not to the partnership. Second, Diamond received his partnership interest for past services, rather than for promising to perform services in the future. Finally, the profits in which Diamond was to share were profits attributable to partnership property that had accrued prior to the time Diamond joined the partnership. The profits were not attributable to Diamond's efforts for the partnership since the partnership sold the property shortly after Diamond joined. These features of the *Diamond* case made it clear that the transfer of the partnership interest to Diamond was compensatory. In the more-common case, the service partner receives a profits interest not as payment for work performed, but as the first step in creating an arrangement under which work will be done (and will be compensated by the partner's earnings). In the usual case there is no more reason to tax the service partner on the receipt of the profits interest than there is to tax a new employee on the "value" of the job the employee has "received."

The usual argument for taxing all service partners who receive profits interests uses a sort of syllogism: The receipt of property in connection with the performance of services is a taxable event; a profits interest in a partnership is "property"; and so any service partner who receives a profits interest must be taxed. The weakness of this argument lies in the too-facile assumption that anything that is "property" for

---

27. Taxing the service partner upon receipt of a profits interest would give the partner a basis which, presumably, would then be amortized over the partner's anticipated working life. Furthermore, it is not clear whether the partnership should receive an immediate deduction corresponding to the income recognized by the service partner.

some purposes must be "property" for all purposes, no matter what the context. Not everything that can be called "property" is property for purposes of applying § 83. For example, a legally binding promise to pay money is "property" for some purposes, but a cash-method taxpayer does not have income upon doing work and receiving a promise of payment. Indeed, the service partner's profits interest (an interest created by the partnership agreement) resembles a contract right to receive future payment quite closely.

For many years after *Diamond* was decided, neither the Service nor the courts did much to clarify its scope. A 1977 General Counsel's Memorandum proposed that the Service not invoke *Diamond* when a service partner receives an award of future partnership profits,[28] but no ruling to that effect was issued. Some courts avoided the issue by holding that the partnership interests in question had no value, so that the taxpayers had no income even if *Diamond* made their receipts of partnership interests taxable events.[29] Then, in Campbell v. Commissioner,[30] the Tax Court held a promoter of tax-shelter partnerships taxable on his receipt of limited partnership interests giving him rights to future partnership profits. The Tax Court's opinion in *Campbell* held that any award of a profits interest to a service partner was taxable, because a profits interest is "property." On appeal to the Eighth Circuit, the Government conceded that this reading of *Diamond* was too broad.[31] The Eighth Circuit's opinion in *Campbell*[32] found "some justification" for not taxing most service partners on their receipts of profits interests. Citing § 707(a)(1) of the Code (a provision almost certainly not drafted with the *Diamond* problem in mind) it suggested that taxability might be proper when the profits interest was awarded for services provided "other than in a partner capacity" (as in *Diamond*). Noting that Campbell's interests "were not transferable and were not likely to provide immediate returns," it expressed "doubt" that the Tax Court was right in taxing Campbell on the receipt of his interests. In the end, though, the Court of Appeals reversed the Tax Court on the narrow ground that the interests were so speculative that they had no fair market value when Campbell received them.

28. G.C.M. 36346 (1977).

29. Kenroy, Inc. v. Commissioner, 47 T.C.M. 1749 (1984); St. John v. United States, 84–1 USTC ¶ 9158, 53 AFTR2d 84–718 (C.D. Ill. 1983)

30. 59 T.C.M. 236 (1990), reversed, 943 F.2d 815 (8th Cir. 1991).

31. The Government argued that Campbell had received his partnership interests as compensation for services provided to his employer, rather than for services performed for the partnerships. This seems to have been an accurate description of the transactions. See Charles R. Levun & Michael J. Cohen, *Campbell's Quandary*, 68 TAXES 498, 502 (1990). But because the Tax Court had not specifically found that Campbell got his interests from his employer, the Eighth Circuit did not address this argument.

32. 943 F.2d 815 (8th Cir. 1991).

The *Campbell* case and the Government's concession in that case that not all service partners who receive profits interests are taxed made it imperative that the Service provide guidance for taxpayers. Revenue Procedure 93–27[33] announced that the Service will not generally treat as taxable the award of a "profits interest for the provision of services to or for the benefit of a partnership in a partner capacity or in anticipation of being a partner." The Revenue Procedure defines a "profits interest" by asking whether the partner would receive something if the partnership liquidated immediately after the award of the profits interest. The partner has a profits interest only if nothing would be distributed to that partner in the hypothetical liquidation. This definition suggests that Diamond did not receive a "profits interest" as defined in the Revenue Procedure. Diamond probably would have received something had the partnership liquidated immediately after he joined the partnership since he shared in profits from the partnership's sale of the building shortly after he joined the partnership. To ensure that a new partner is receiving a "profits interest," a partnership should amend its partnership agreement so that it allocates any gain existing in its assets at the time the service partner joins the partnership to the other partners.[34] Such an amendment will prevent the service partner from receiving anything in the hypothetical liquidation.

Even if a partner receives a "profits interest," there are three instances where the receipt of a profits interest will be taxable under the Revenue Procedure:

"(1) If the profits interest relates to a substantially certain and predictable stream of income from partnership assets . . . ;

(2) If within two years of receipt the partner disposes of the profits interest; or

(3) If the profits interest is a limited partnership interest in a 'publicly traded partnership' within the meaning of § 7704(b)."[35]

These exceptions do not reflect any coherent principle, and Revenue Procedure 93–27 is short on reasoned explanation, so much uncertainty in this area remains. It is at least clear, however, that the Service will not invoke *Diamond* in routine cases so long as the service partner receives a profits interest as defined in Revenue Procedure 93–27.

In 2005, in an attempt to reduce the uncertainty surrounding the tax treatment of partnership interests transferred in connection with performance of services, Treasury and the Service issued Proposed

---

33. 1993–2 C.B. 343.

34. Alternatively, the partnership can "book-up" capital accounts, a process discussed in Chapter 5.

35. Id.

Regulations under § 83 and subchapter K.[36] Among other things, the Proposed Regulations would authorize a partnership and its partners to elect a safe harbor under which they would treat the fair market value of a partnership interest issued in exchange for services as being equal to the liquidation value of the interest.[37] Under this approach, a person who received a profits only partnership interest in exchange for services would not recognize income on receipt of the interest, provided the person would receive no liquidating distribution if the partnership were liquidated immediately after issuance of the interest. At the same time, the Service issued Notice 2005–43,[38] which includes a proposed Revenue Procedure setting forth rules for the elective safe harbor authorized by the proposed regulations. Under the proposed Revenue Procedure, a "Safe Harbor Partnership Interest" is:

> any interest in a partnership that is transferred to a service provider by [a] partnership in connection with services provided to the partnership (either before or after the formation of the partnership), provided that the interest is not (a) related to a substantially certain and predictable stream of income from partnership assets, such as income from high-quality debt securities or a high-quality net lease, (b) transferred in anticipation of a subsequent disposition, or (c) an interest in a publicly traded partnership within the meaning of § 7704(b).[39]

The proposed Revenue Procedure explains that:

> [u]nless it is established by clear and convincing evidence that the partnership interest was not transferred in anticipation of a subsequent disposition, a partnership interest is presumed to be transferred in anticipation of a subsequent disposition for purposes of the preceding clause (b) if the partnership interest is sold or disposed of within two years of the date of receipt of the partnership interest (other than a sale or disposition by reason of death or disability of the service provider) or is the subject, at any time within two years of the date of receipt, of a right to buy or sell regardless of when the right is exercisable (other than a right to buy or sell arising by reason of the death or disability of the service provider).[40]

---

36. 70 Fed. Reg. 29,675 (May 24, 2005).

37. Prop. Treas. Reg. § 1.83–3(*l*). Legislation has been proposed that would confirm the approach of the proposed regulations. See § 411 of the proposed American Jobs and Closing Tax Loopholes Act of 2010, H.R. 4213, 111th Cong., 2d Sess.

38. 2005–1 C.B. 1221.

39. Prop. Rev. Proc. § 3.02(1).

40. Prop. Rev. Proc. § 3.02(1).

Notice 2005–43 provides that Revenue Procedure 93–27 will be "obsoleted" when the proposed regulations are issued in final form. Until that time, taxpayers may not rely on the safe harbor rule described in the proposed regulations and the proposed Revenue Procedure. Instead, "taxpayers may continue to rely upon current law, including Rev. Proc. 93–27...."[41]

C. CONTRIBUTIONS DISTINGUISHED FROM OTHER TRANSACTIONS

Because those who transfer property to partnerships seldom recognize gain, some people who, in the absence of tax considerations, would have sold property to partnerships will have an incentive to structure their transactions as contributions. The regulations have long provided that "the substance of the transaction will govern, rather than its form,"[42] and that "if the transfer of property ... results in the receipt by the partner of money or other consideration ... the transaction will be treated as a sale or exchange...."[43] Section 707(a)(2), which was adopted in 1984, deals with transfers of property to partnerships followed by related transactions in which the transferors receive money or other property. It provides that when a transaction of this kind is "properly characterized" as "a transaction occurring between the partnership and a partner acting other than in his capacity as a member of the partnership" or as "a sale or exchange of property" the transaction is to be treated in the appropriate way. Ample authority thus exists for recharacterizing purported contributions and related transactions as sales or exchanges. The hard part is distinguishing transfers that should be recharacterized from those that should not be.

1. Contribution vs. Sale to Partnership

It will sometimes be obvious that a purported contribution of property to a partnership followed by a distribution to the transferring partner should be recharacterized as a sale of the property.

Example 4–8: Neil, a 10–percent partner in NOP, owns a zero-basis machine worth $20,000. Neil transfers the machine to the partnership in exchange for a small increase in his percentage interest in the partnership. Two days later, the partnership distributes $20,000 cash to Neil, reducing his interest to 10 percent again. In the absence of a good reason to think that

---
41. Notice 2005–43.
42. Treas. Reg. § 1.721–1(a).
43. Id.

these two transactions were unrelated, they will be treated as a sale of the machine to the partnership.

Example 4–9: Ophelia transfers a capital asset worth $100,000 to the NOP partnership. She receives an interest in the partnership that entitles her to only a tiny portion of the partnership's profits, and, in addition, to an annual payment of $10,000 a year for the next 20 years. If Ophelia had sold her property for installment payments, the appropriate amount of those payments would have been about $10,000 a year for 20 years. The transaction is likely to be treated as a sale of the property.

Every contribution of property to a partnership by a partner creates an expectation that the partner will someday receive money or (occasionally) other property from the partnership. The size of the contributing partner's interest in the partnership typically depends in part upon the amount that the partner has contributed to the partnership, and the amount of money a partner can expect to take out of the partnership increases with the size of that partner's partnership interest. Therefore, we cannot say that a transfer in the form of a contribution must be recharacterized whenever the contributing partner expects that making the contribution will someday lead to a distribution of cash. Under the statute, the test is whether the purported contribution and related transactions are "properly characterized" as a sale or exchange.[44] The regulations under § 707 provide a number of rules and presumptions for distinguishing contributions from sales.

If a partner purportedly contributes property and later receives cash or other property, a key to determining whether the payment to the partner was consideration for the transfer of property is whether the payment depended on "the entrepreneurial risks of partnership operations."[45] Such factors as whether the transferring partner obtained an enforceable right to a payment, whether the right was to a fixed amount, and whether the partnership held liquid assets not needed for its business when the transfer was made tend to show that the payment was not subject to "entrepreneurial risk."[46] Furthermore, the regulations create a presumption that a transfer is part of a sale if the transferring partner receives a payment within two years of the transfer.[47] (Transfers more than two years apart are presumed not to be sales.[48]) However, the regulations provide some special rules to assure that routine kinds of

---

44. § 707(a)(2).

45. Treas. Reg. § 1.707–3(b)(1).

46. Treas. Reg. § 1.707–3(b)(2) lists these and seven other "facts and circumstances that may tend to prove the existence of a sale."

47. Treas. Reg. § 1.707–3(c)(1).

48. Treas. Reg. § 1.707–3(d).

partnership distributions are not treated as payments for transferred property, even if they are made within two years of a transfer.

Example 4–10: Ron contributes Blackacre, a tract of unimproved land worth $100,000, to the RST partnership. The partnership agreement is amended to provide that Ron will receive a fixed payment of $8,000 a year for the use of Blackacre. This amount is a reasonable amount to pay for the use of the land. The regulations will treat the $8,000 payments as "guaranteed payments" for the use of Blackacre rather than part of the purchase price of an interest in Blackacre.[49] If, by contrast, the partnership had made a one-time purported "guaranteed payment" of $50,000 in the year after the transfer, the regulations would tax the transaction as a sale of a one-half interest in Blackacre by Ron to the partnership.[50]

Ordinary distributions to a contributing partner of that partner's share of the partnership's operating cash flow are, like guaranteed payments, presumed not to be payments for contributed property. Similarly, reimbursements of expenses incurred by a partner in organizing the partnership are not part of a sale.[51]

The regulations deal at length with the question of when a partnership's assumption of or taking property subject to a partner's debt will be characterized as part of a sale of property to the partnership. Much of the regulations' emphasis is on whether the debt was incurred in anticipation of the transfer, as a means of giving the transferor cash. When a partnership assumes or takes property subject to that kind of debt, the reduction in the partner's debt is considered a payment to the partner for an interest in the property.

Example 4–11: Sarah owns real estate with a basis of $500,000 and a value of $1,000,000. Three weeks before transferring this property to the STU partnership, she borrows $800,000, secured by a nonrecourse mortgage on the property. She then transfers the property to the partnership. Assume that, for purposes of § 707, Sarah's share of the liability after the transfer is $200,000.[52] The transaction will be treated as a sale of an

---

49. Treas. Reg. §§ 1.707–4(a) and 1.707–4(a)(4) (Example 1). Chapter 9 examines the taxation of guaranteed payments.

50. Treas. Reg. § 1.707–4(a)(4) (Example 2).

51. Treas. Reg. § 1.707–4(d). A similar rule applies to reimbursements for some expenditures made by the partner in improving the contributed property. If the value of the contributed property is more than 120 percent of the property's basis in the partner's hands at the time of the contribution, the rule for improvements applies only to reimbursed capital expenditures not exceeding 20 percent of the property's value. Id.

52. Chapter 8 discusses the complex rules for sharing partnership nonrecourse debt under § 752. The regulations under § 707 use a method that is simpler than the method

interest in the property for $600,000 since Sarah's share of the debt encumbering the property has decreased by $600,000. Because the property as a whole is worth $1,000,000, Sarah has sold a sixty percent interest in it to the partnership. She will recognize a gain of $300,000 (60 percent of $500,000).[53]

Many liabilities incurred within two years of a transfer to a partnership are presumed to have been incurred in connection with the transfer. Liabilities incurred in the ordinary course of a business that is transferred to a partnership are not subject to this presumption. Liabilities incurred to improve transferred property also fall outside the presumption.[54]

2. Contribution vs. Sale or Exchange Between Partners

Sometimes the appropriate way to recharacterize a transaction will be as an exchange between two of the partners. If, for example, Ophelia transfers $50,000 worth of General Motors stock to the NOP partnership, Paul transfers a tract of land worth $50,000 to the partnership, and the partnership distributes the stock to Paul and the land to Ophelia, the "substance" of the transaction seems plainly to be an exchange between Ophelia and Paul.

Section 707 can recharacterize contributions as exchanges between partners.[55] Two other sections of the Code may also cause the partners to recognize gain or loss. If a partner contributes property and, within seven years, the property is distributed to another partner, § 704(c)(1)(B) may require the contributing partner to recognize gain or loss "built in" to the property at the time of the contribution. Furthermore, if a partner contributes property with a built-in gain to a partnership and the partnership distributes other property, which is not cash, to the contributing partner within seven years of the contribution, § 737 requires the contributing partner generally to recognize the built-in gain. Section 737 requires such gain recognition even though non-cash distributions of property are normally tax-free under § 731. Sections 704(c) and 737 operate mechanically, without regard to whether the transactions in question should be "properly characterized" as sales or exchanges. Sections 704(c) and 737 are examined in detail in Chapter 6.

Recharacterization under § 707 will sometimes be in order when partners perform services. This matter will be discussed in Chapter 9.

---

used under § 752. The regulations under § 707 allocate debt based solely on the partner's share of profits or deductions attributable to the debt. Treas. Reg. § 1.707–5(a)(2)(ii).

53. Treas. Reg. § 1.707–5(f) (Example 1).
54. Treas. Reg. § 1.707–5(a)(7).
55. § 707(a)(2)(B).

D. COMPARISON WITH SUBCHAPTER S

Transfers of property to S corporations are governed by the same rules as transfers of property to C corporations. These rules are considerably more restrictive than the partnership provisions. For example, transfers of property to corporations are tax-free under § 351 only if the transferors are "in control . . . of" the corporation immediately after the transfer.§ 351(a). By contrast, any partner, no matter how small that partner's interest in the partnership, can contribute property to a partnership tax-free under § 721.

Tax-free transfers accompanied by the receipt of boot are treated differently, depending upon whether the recipient is a corporation or a partnership. In transfers to corporations, gain is recognized to the extent of the amount of cash plus the value of the property received as boot. Boot received by a partner will generate income only if the amount of *cash* received exceeds the partner's outside basis. Thus, a transfer of property with a $10,000 basis and a $15,000 value to a controlled corporation in exchange for stock plus $4,000 cash would result in the transferor's recognizing a $4,000 gain under § 356. The same transfer to a partnership would be tax free, because the transferor's $10,000 of basis exceeds the amount of cash received. Roughly speaking, subchapter C treats boot as requiring the recognition of any income realized on the exchange, while subchapter K treats boot as requiring the recognition of income only when recognition is necessary to avoid giving the transferor a negative basis.

Both subchapter C and subchapter K sometimes treat a shift of debt from the transferor to the entity as a distribution of cash, but they do so in very different ways. Whenever a partnership assumes a transferor's debt, the partners other than the transferor increase their outside bases, because their increased shares of the partnership's debts are constructive cash contributions under § 752. The transferor is treated as receiving a cash distribution (which will often not be taxable) in the amount of the net decrease in the transferor's debt. In the case of debt assumptions by corporations in transfers subject to § 351, the entire amount of the debt reduces the transferor's outside basis, and any excess of debt over the basis of the transferred property is boot.[56]

Example 4–12: Rachel owns ninety percent of the stock of R Corporation. She transfers Greenacre, which has a basis of $100,000 and a value of $200,000, to R Corporation in a § 351

---

[56]. §§ 358(d) and 357(c). If the transferor's "principal purpose . . . with respect to the assumption or acquisition" was avoiding tax or otherwise "not a bona fide business purpose," § 357(b) will treat the corporation's assumption of the debt even less favorably than this.

transaction. If R Corporation assumes a $120,000 mortgage encumbering Greenacre, Rachel's basis for the stock received in the transaction will be zero[57] and she will recognize a gain of $20,000.[58] If Rachel had transferred Greenacre to the RS partnership, in which she had a ninety percent interest, her basis in the partnership would have increased by $88,000 (the $100,000 of new basis attributable to the basis of Greenacre minus the $12,000 cash distribution to Rachel under § 752(b)). She would have recognized no gain on the transfer.

---

57. § 358(d).

58. § 357(c).

Chapter Five

ALLOCATIONS OF PARTNERSHIP INCOME, DEDUCTIONS, AND CREDITS: AN INTRODUCTION

A. AN OVERVIEW OF THE CODE AND REGULATIONS

Up to this point we have not had to worry about how a partnership's income, deductions, and credits (the partnership's "tax items") are allocated among the partners. We have assumed, tacitly, that a "forty-percent partner" would report forty percent of all the partnership's tax items. In fact, however, a partnership may allocate different portions of its tax items to different partners. For example, partner A may report fifty percent of a partnership's ordinary income but only ten percent of its capital gains, or partner B may be taxable on half of the taxable income of a partnership's New York office but only ten percent of the taxable income of its Washington office.

Section 704 governs allocations of a partnership's tax items. Section 704(b) provides general rules, while § 704(c) contains special rules for allocating tax items attributable to property contributed to a partnership that has a tax basis different from its fair market value.[1]

Under the 1954 Code as originally enacted, § 704(b) said that a partner's distributive share of "any item of income, gain, loss, deduction, or credit" was determined by the partnership agreement unless the "principal purpose" of a special allocation was "avoidance or evasion of any tax."[2] The regulations, with support in the legislative history, did not take the reference to the tax-avoidance "purpose" of a special allocation very seriously. Indeed, they approved of a special allocation of tax-exempt interest, which is the sort of thing that only tax-conscious partners are likely to do.[3] Instead of inquiring only into the taxpayers' motives for a special allocation, the regulations listed "factors" to be considered in determining whether a special allocation was valid. By far the most important of these factors was whether the allocation had "substantial economic effect"; that is, whether the allocation might actually have affected "the dollar amount of the partners' shares of the total partnership income or loss independently of tax consequences."[4] In

---

1. Section 704(c) is explored in Chapter 6.
2. Former § 704(b).
3. Former Treas. Reg. § 1.704–1(b)(2) (Example (3)) (1956).

1976, Congress rewrote § 704(b) to add the "substantial economic effect" standard and to make clear that overall allocations (such as "half the partnership's income to A"), as well as special allocations (such as "ten percent of the partnership's capital gains to A"), are subject to the statutory standard.

Under today's version of § 704(b), an agreement allocating partnership taxable income or any item of partnership income, will be valid if the allocation has "substantial economic effect." If "substantial economic effect" cannot be found, either because an agreed-upon allocation lacks it or because there is no agreement at all, income is allocated according to the "partner's interest in the partnership," taking into account "all facts and circumstances."

B. THE "SUBSTANTIAL ECONOMIC EFFECT" TEST

1. Introduction

Roughly speaking, an allocation has economic effect if it will affect the wealth of the partners. Some kind of principle like this must control allocations of partnership income. It would be absurd to say that a partnership agreement allocating all of a partnership's *taxable* income to partner D should be respected if the agreement also makes it clear that D and E will share equally in all the money and property the partnership has and will get in the future. The regulations under § 704(b) have, however, gone far beyond this common-sense notion of "economic effect." They have taken that short statutory phrase and built upon it a remarkably elaborate, detailed, complex, and yet incomplete set of rules. These rules are so difficult that only a handful of partnership-tax specialists in large firms will be able to apply it. Garden-variety partnerships (small businesses advised by ordinary lawyers and accountants) will seldom make allocations that satisfy all the requirements for "substantial economic effect" in the regulations. Instead, their allocations will be judged by the "partner's interest in the partnership" standard, a very ambiguous standard that is supposed to take into account "all facts and circumstances."

No introductory book can cover all the details of the "substantial economic effect" regulations. Rather than attempt that task, we shall describe the so-called "capital account" version of the test as it was developed in the regulations and the case law under the former version of § 704. With an understanding of that relatively straightforward matter as background, you will be introduced to some of the more important ways in which the current regulations elaborate on that test.

---

4. Former Treas. Reg. § 1.704–1(b)(2) (1956).

First, however, a brief description of partners' capital accounts is necessary.

2. Capital Accounts

In many cases, the key to determining a partner's rights to the money and property of a partnership is the partner's capital account. In general, the capital account is supposed to reflect what a partner is entitled to receive upon the liquidation of a partnership. Capital accounts are created by the partnership agreement, and so the details of how they are kept will vary from partnership to partnership. The regulations under § 704(b), however, provide a lot of detail about how a partnership should maintain capital accounts in order for allocations to have substantial economic effect. What follows is a description of some key features of capital accounts.

When a partnership is formed the beginning balance of each partner's capital account will be the sum of money plus the fair market value (*not the income tax basis*) of the property the partner contributes.[5]

Example 5–1: Susan and Thomas form an equal partnership, ST. Susan contributes $50,000 in cash to ST; Thomas contributes property with a tax basis of $20,000 and a value of $50,000. The beginning balance of Susan's capital account in ST is $50,000. The beginning balance of Thomas's capital account is also $50,000.

A partner's capital account is often used as a measure of what that partner has put into the partnership. The tax basis of the contributed assets is irrelevant for capital accounts. It would not make sense to say that Thomas, in Example 5–1, had transferred less than half of what Susan had transferred, just because Thomas's basis in the transferred asset is only $20,000. Each partner contributed property of equal value, so the partners' capital accounts should be equal at the outset of their venture. The regulations under § 704(b) refer to the property's fair market value on the date of contribution as the property's "book value."[6] In example 5–1, the partnership's book value in the asset contributed by Thomas is $50,000. The book value of an asset is decreased to reflect depreciation. It is not, however, adjusted to reflect changes in the asset's fair market value except in certain circumstances, such as the admission or withdrawal of a new partner.[7]

Partners' capital accounts are increased by their additional contributions (if any) and by their shares of the partnership's income and gains.

---

5. Treas. Reg. § 1.704–1(b)(2)(iv)(*d*).
6. Treas. Reg. § 1.704–1(b)(2)(iv)(*g*).
7. See pages 48–49 *infra*.

These gains are measured by reference to the asset's book value, not its tax basis.[8] Partnership expenses and losses (also determined by reference to book values) and withdrawals from a partnership reduce the capital account balances of partners. To illustrate:

Example 5–2: The ST partnership (Example 5–1) earns $5,000 by performing services. Since this is an equal partnership, each partner is allocated $2,500 of income. The appropriate adjustment to capital accounts is an increase in each partner's account by $2,500, so that each partner will have a capital account balance of $52,500.

Suppose the partnership then sells the asset contributed by Thomas for $48,000. For tax purposes, this sale generates a $28,000 gain ($48,000 sales price less $20,000 tax basis). For partnership-accounting purposes, however, there is a $2,000 book loss ($50,000 book value minus $48,000 sales price). In effect, the partnership lost $2,000 by holding the asset from the time Thomas contributed it to the time it was sold. This book loss is allocated equally to each partner and reduces each partner's capital account balance by $1,000.

At this point, Susan and Thomas have capital account balances of $51,500 each. If Susan withdraws $500 from the partnership, her balance will decline to $51,000.

In practice, partnerships may maintain accounts other than capital accounts. For example, they may have "income accounts" and "drawing accounts" (records of partners' shares of income and withdrawals), which are closed out to the partners' capital accounts at the end of each year. To keep things simple, let us assume throughout this book that only capital accounts are kept and that earnings, losses, contributions and withdrawals credited or charged directly to them.

Some points to learn about capital accounts are:

(1) A capital account can have a negative balance. Suppose a partner contributes $10,000 to a new partnership and then withdraws $15,000 before the partnership has any earnings. This partner's capital account balance stands at minus $5,000. What this means in practical terms depends upon the partnership agreement (remember, capital accounts exist only because the partnership agreement creates them). Agreements sometimes make partners liable to make up deficits in their capital accounts, in which case this partner would owe the partnership $5,000 unless later events in-

---

8. Book gains and tax gains will be identical where the assets adjusted tax basis and book value are identical.

crease the balance. If the partnership agreement does not require that capital account deficits be restored, a $5,000 deficit in a partner's capital account balance could mean that the next $5,000 of that partner's share of earnings will be allocated to the partner. The partner, however, would not be entitled to receive that $5,000. The allocation would eliminate the partner's capital account deficit balance, but since the partner's capital account balance would then be zero, the partner would not be entitled to receive anything.

(2) The capital account is a partnership-accounting mechanism, not a tax concept. The Code does not refer to capital accounts at all, though the regulations under §§ 704 and 752 do. References in Code sections like § 705(a)(2)(B) to "expenditures ... chargeable to capital account" do not deal with partners' capital accounts: "Expenditure chargeable to capital account" is accounting jargon for "capital expenditure."

(3) Partners' shares of partnership liabilities are not ordinarily reflected in capital accounts.[9] Thus, if a partnership borrows $20,000 and later repays the debt, neither the borrowing nor the repayment will affect anyone's capital account, though each transaction will affect the partners' outside bases.

If property is valued accurately when contributed to a partnership and if the values of assets held by the partnership do not change, the balance of a partner's capital account will be the amount the partner is entitled to receive upon a sale of all the partnership's assets and a liquidation of the partnership. (A negative balance would show the amount the partner would have to pay in on an immediate liquidation if the partnership agreement makes partners liable to restore capital account deficits upon liquidation.) Capital accounts seldom reflect the true values of partners' interests, however. Increases and decreases in the value of partnership property will not usually affect capital accounts. Partnership agreements, however, usually provide that capital accounts and the book value of partnership assets must be written up or down to reflect the market values of partnership assets when property is contributed to or distributed from the partnership.[10] This write up or down is accomplished by increasing or decreasing the book value of the partnership's assets and allocating those increases and decreases among the

---

9. Treas. Reg. § 1.704–(b)(2)(iv)(c).

10. Although the regulations do not require partnership agreements to book-up capital accounts, they suggest that there will often be adverse tax results for failing to do this. Reg. § 1.704–1(b)(2)(iv)(F)(5) (last sentence).

partners in the same proportion that the partners share partnership gains and losses.

Example 5–3: Gloria and Henry form the GH partnership in which they are equal partners. Each contributes $100 cash and, therefore, each starts with an initial capital account of $100. The partnership uses the $200 of contributed capital to purchase an asset for which the partnership records a book value of $200. The asset subsequently appreciates in value to $300. Prior to the admission of a new partner, who is going to contribute cash, the partnership increases the asset's book value to $300 and allocates one half of the $100 appreciation to Gloria and one half to Henry. As a result, Gloria's and Henry's capital accounts are each $150 when the new partner joins GH. Note that the book-up insures that Gloria and Henry are credited with the asset's appreciation that occurred prior to the new partner joining the firm.[11]

3. The "Simple" Capital Account Test for Substantial Economic Effect: Orrisch v. Commissioner

In order for partnership allocations to affect the wealth of partners it is necessary that the partnership do more than merely maintain capital accounts. The capital accounts must also determine the amount each partner will receive upon leaving the partnership. The Tax Court's analysis in Orrisch v. Commissioner[12] demonstrates that merely maintaining capital accounts is not sufficient if the capital accounts do not reflect the economic expectations of the partners. In 1963, the Orrisches and the Crisafis formed a partnership, which engaged in the real-estate business. Each couple reported half of the partnership's income each year, in accordance with their oral agreement to create an equal partnership. Early in 1966 the parties orally agreed that all of the partnership's depreciation deductions would be allocated to the Orrisches, who had large amounts of income from other sources. All other income and deductions were to be shared equally except that, if property on which

---

11. A partnership will frequently book-up capital accounts when a service partner joins the partnership to insure that the service partner is receiving a profits interest. As discussed in Chapter 4, Revenue Procedure 93–27 says that a partner has received a profits interest if nothing would be distributed to that partner in a liquidation immediately after that partner joined the firm. Booking up the capital accounts to reflect any appreciation in the partnership's assets ensures that the service partner will not share in that appreciation. In Example 5–3, if the new partner contributed no property to the partnership, nothing would be distributed to the new partner in a liquidation occurring immediately thereafter because all of the appreciation in the partnership's assets would have been credited to the capital accounts of the other partners.

12. 55 T.C. 395 (1970), affirmed mem., 31 AFTR2d 73–1069 (9th Cir. 1973).

depreciation had been taken was sold at a gain, that gain, to the extent attributable to depreciation allocated to the Orrisches, would be "charged back" (i.e. allocated) to them. The Government challenged the allocation of the depreciation deductions to the Orrisches.

The Orrisches argued in the Tax Court that the special allocation of depreciation was valid under the pre–1976 regulations. They pointed out that the depreciation deductions allocated to them were reflected in their capital accounts since the depreciation expenses had reduced their capital account balance. Thus, they argued, the allocations had substantial economic effect. Their capital account balance, as of the end of 1967, was a $25,187.11 deficit, while the Crisafis' balance was a positive $405.65.

The Tax Court agreed with some of the Orrisches' reasoning. It held that the economic effect associated with depreciation deductions is to be found by asking who would bear the loss if the building in question should be sold for less than its original cost. It held also that the adjustments to the Orrisches' and the Crisafis' capital accounts were consistent with allocating all of the partnership's depreciation to the Orrisches. Nevertheless, the Tax Court found that the taxpayers had failed to show that the special allocation had substantial economic effect.

The Tax Court recognized that an allocation may have economic effect because it affects capital account balances, which in turn may determine the amount of money the partners will take out of the partnership. It held, however, that the special allocation of depreciation to the Orrisches lacked economic effect because, in its view, the parties did not intend that their capital accounts would control liquidating distributions by the partnership. Nor did it think that the Orrisches had agreed to pay in any capital account deficit upon liquidation of the partnership. Instead, it thought, the parties contemplated dividing the partnership's assets equally upon liquidation. Since the capital account adjustments were economically meaningless, the special allocation of depreciation deductions was disregarded.

The capital account version of the substantial economic effect test after the *Orrisch* decision was something like this: If allocations are reflected in the partners' capital accounts, and if those capital accounts control liquidating distributions, the allocations have substantial economic effect, at least if partners with deficit balances upon liquidation must pay in those balances. A refinement suggested by an influential commentator was that capital accounts would determine substantial economic effect even if some partners had no obligation to restore deficit balances, if the partnership's actual allocations did not reduce capital accounts below zero.[13] Thus, a reduction in a partner's capital account

---

13. William S. McKee, Partnership Allocations in Real Estate Ventures: *Crane, Kresser* and *Orrisch*, 30 Tax L. Rev. 1 (1974).

balance from $10,000 to $5,000 was seen as a serious measure of that partner's well being in all cases, while a reduction from zero to minus $5,000 would count only if the partner might someday have to restore the deficit.

Example 5–4: Theresa and Ulysses each contribute $100 to the TU partnership. The partnership pays $200 for a computer, which we will assume for purposes of simplicity is depreciable on a straight-line basis over a two-year period. The partnership will allocate all items equally, except that all depreciation is allocated to Theresa. At the end of the first year, each partner's capital account will appear as follows, assuming that TU has no income or expenses other than the computer's depreciation expense of $100.

	Capital Accounts	
	Theresa	Ulysses
Initial	$100	$100
Less: Year–One Depreciation	(100)	0
End of Year One	0	$100

The computer's book value at the end of year one is $100 (the initial book value of $200 minus the $100 of depreciation). If the partnership were to sell the computer for its book value of $100 at the beginning of year two and then liquidate in accordance with capital accounts, the partnership would have $100 to distribute. This $100 would be distributed to Ulysses because he has a $100 capital account balance and Theresa would receive nothing. In effect, Theresa would have borne the diminution in value of the computer that corresponds to the depreciation expense. In contrast, if the partnership distributed $50 each to Theresa and Ulysses, the allocation of all $100 of depreciation to Theresa would not have economic effect because Theresa would have borne only $50 of the asset's actual diminution in value.

If the partnership did not sell the computer at the end of year one it would allocate another $100 of depreciation to Theresa in year two. The capital accounts would now appear as follows:

Capital Accounts

	Theresa	Ulysses
Initial	$100	$100
Less: Year One Depreciation	(100)	0
Less: Year Two Depreciation	(100)	0
End of Year Two	(100)	$100

If the fair market value of the computer corresponded to its book value of zero at the end of year two, the partnership would have no assets to distribute upon liquidation. Observe, however, that Ulysses' capital account is still $100. In order for Theresa to bear the economic decline in value that corresponds to the $200 depreciation expense allocated to her, she should be required to contribute an additional $100 to the partnership. This will increase her capital account to zero and provide the partnership with $100 to distribute to Ulysses upon liquidation.

Orrisch itself made excellent sense. Allocations that are not reflected in capital accounts at all, or that are reflected in capital accounts but are meaningless because distributions will be made without regard to capital accounts, surely lack economic effect and should be disregarded. The converse of this proposition by no means follows, however. Allocations scrupulously reflected in the balances of accounts that will someday control distributions may or may not have a real bearing on the partners' economic welfare, depending upon the circumstances. For example, the distinction between positive and negative balances in the case of partners who do not have to restore deficits may mean very little: A negative balance can affect such a partner because the partner's share of future partnership gains may go toward reducing the deficit, rather than being available for distribution to the partner.[14] More basically, one's capital account balance today, whether positive or negative, will often say very little about one's chances of getting money if the partnership liquidates because the capital account may not reflect the current value of partnership assets. The partnership will normally book up capital accounts only at the time property is contributed to or distributed from the partnership. A fifty-percent partner in a partnership holding land worth millions more than it was worth when purchased may be wealthy, even if that partner's capital account shows a small deficit. A partner

---

14. Martin B. Cowan, Substantial Economic Effect: The Outer Limits for Partnership Allocations, 39 N.Y.U. Tax Inst. § 23 (1981).

with a positive capital account balance may be insolvent if the partnership holds assets on which substantial losses have not yet been, but inevitably will be, recognized.

4. The "Substantial Economic Effect" Regulations

The regulations under § 704(b) follow and expand the court's holding in *Orrisch*. They provide that an allocation of a tax item will have "economic" effect if (1) capital accounts are maintained in accordance with the regulations (as outlined above), (2) liquidating distributions are made in accordance with capital accounts, and (3) partners with deficit balances upon liquidation must restore those deficits. Whether that effect is "substantial" depends upon special "substantiality" rules discussed below.

Example 5–5: William and Yolanda each contribute $1,000 to the WY partnership. The partnership keeps capital accounts in accordance with the § 704 regulation, capital accounts control liquidating distributions, and any partner with a negative balance upon liquidation must pay in the amount of that negative balance. The partnership agreement provides that income and losses will be shared equally except that gains and losses from the sale of publicly traded stocks will be allocated sixty percent to Yolanda and forty percent to William. The partnership purchases publicly traded stock for $2,000, which it subsequently sells for $3,000, realizing a tax and book gain of $1,000. The partnership allocates $600 of the tax and book gain to Yolanda and $400 to William. The tax allocation has economic effect.

Note that in Example 5–5 the allocation of tax gain corresponded to the allocation of the book gain, which affected each partner's capital accounts. An allocation of tax gain that differs from the allocation of book gain cannot have economic effect under these rules because, as was the case in *Orrisch*, the tax allocation does not affect the partner's economic interest in the partnership. For example, if the WY partnership in Example 5–5 attempted to allocate the book gain on a sixty-forty basis to the partners' capital accounts, but allocated the tax gain fifty-fifty, the tax allocation would not have "economic" effect under the capital account test. Tax lawyers describe this by stating that "tax must follow book" under the substantial economic effect test. Sometimes, usually when property is contributed to a partnership, tax and book gain will differ. The special rules that apply in those situations are discussed in Chapter 6.

The substantial economic effect test provides a safe harbor. If the substantial economic effect test is satisfied, the allocation in question should almost always be valid. If the requirements for the safe harbor are not satisfied, the regulations say that the validity of the allocation depends on "all facts and circumstances" bearing on the "partner's interest in the partnership."[15]

a. Determining "Economic Effect" When Capital Account Deficits Need Not Be Repaid

The substantial economic effect test requires that partners restore deficits in their capital accounts. Most limited partners and members of limited liability companies do not want an unlimited deficit-restoration obligation. Such an obligation can impose significant liability on partners or members.

Example 5-6: Tom and Caroline are members of TC LLC. Under state law, members of a limited liability company are shielded from the liability of the company. The operating agreement of TC LLC, however, requires members to restore deficits in their capital accounts. Tom and Caroline each have capital accounts with positive balances of $10,000. TC is held responsible for the tortious act of an employee and becomes liable for a $2,020,000 judgment. Allocating the expense of paying the judgment to each member reduces each member's capital accounts to minus $1 million. Upon liquidation of TC, Tom and Caroline will each be required to contribute $1 million to TC under the LLC operating agreement. In effect, this obligation causes them to become liable for an obligation of TC from which they otherwise would have been shielded

Under the "alternate test for economic effect," an allocation can have economic effect even if partners with deficit capital account balances are not required to make contributions to the partnership to eliminate those deficits upon liquidation. Three requirements must be satisfied.[16]

(1) All of the usual requirements other than the obligation to restore deficits are met (i.e. the partnership maintains capital accounts and liquidates in accordance with capital accounts);

(2) The partnership agreement contains a "qualified income offset" (a kind of provision that will be explained below); and

---
15. Treas. Reg. § 1.704–1(b)(1)(i).
16. Treas. Reg. § 1.704–1(b)(2)(ii)(d).

(3) The allocation in question does not actually create or increase a deficit balance in the capital account of the partner to whom the deduction in question is allocated.

The reasoning behind the alternate test is that downward adjustments to a positive capital account balance will reduce, dollar for dollar, the amount the partner would be entitled to receive if the partnership were to liquidate. In contrast, adjustments that create or increase a deficit balance may not affect the amount of money a partner will get.

Example 5–7: The BCD partnership agreement allocates $12,000 of this year's tax and book loss to partner Bob. If none of the loss had been allocated to Bob, his capital account would have had a year-end balance of $5,000. The allocation reduces this balance to minus $7,000. Under the partnership agreement, Bob is not liable to restore a capital account deficit upon liquidation of the partnership. The partnership agreement contains a "qualified income offset" provision. The allocation of the first $5,000 of the loss in question to Bob will be treated as having "economic effect"; the allocation of the remaining $7,000 of the loss (the part that reduced Bob's balance to below zero) will not.

How should the portion of the loss that cannot be allocated to Bob be allocated? Bob may in fact bear the economic burden associated with that loss. For instance, suppose that the partnership had allocated the entire $12,000 loss to Bob so that Bob's capital account was negative $7,000. If the partnership then earns $20,000 the following year, allocates $12,000 of that income to Bob and liquidates, Bob would receive only $5,000, his capital account balance. Bob's capital account balance would be only $5,000 because the $12,000 income allocation raised that balance from minus $7,000 to plus $5,000. The full $12,000 year-one reduction in Bob's capital account affected his economic well-being, even though he was not required to restore any capital account deficit.

The regulations, however, do not take this possibility into account and do not permit an allocation to Bob to the extent it causes his capital account to become negative. According to the regulations, allocation of the portion of the loss that could not be allocated to Bob under the alternate test is made by examining what would happen if the partnership were to sell all of its assets for their book values (not adjusted to reflect current fair market value) and then liquidate.[17] One compares the results of a hypothetical sale and liquidation at the end of the previous

---

17. Treas. Reg. §§ 1.704–1(b)(3)(iii); 1.704–1(b)(5) (Examples (1)(iv), (1)(v), (1)(vi), (15)(ii) & (15)(iii)).

taxable year with the results of a hypothetical sale and liquidation at the end of the current year. The loss is then allocated to whatever partner would bear it under those circumstances. Usually, the excess loss is allocated to the partners whose capital accounts are still positive or have a deficit restoration obligation.[18]

Since partnerships cannot allocate losses that will create a negative capital account to partners who do not have deficit-restoration obligations, much depends upon the order in which events take place. If an allocation of a $10,000 loss to partner Carla leaves her with a capital account balance of zero, and a later distribution of $10,000 cash to Carla reduces her capital account balance to minus $10,000, we can say that the allocation did not create a negative balance. If the distribution had come before the allocation, the allocation would have created a negative balance, because the distribution would have reduced the balance to zero. The regulations deal with this problem in two ways. First, some adjustments for distributions and other things that are likely to occur are treated as already having taken place in determining whether an allocation takes a partner's capital account balance below zero.[19] Second, a partnership that wants to use the substantial economic effect test to support allocations to partners who do not have to restore deficits must have a "qualified income offset" provision in its agreement.

A "qualified income offset" provision deals with cases in which allocations reduce a partner's capital account balance, but not below zero, and then unexpected events, such as subsequent distributions, cause the capital account balance to become negative. The provision works by allocating partnership income to that partner so as to eliminate the deficit as quickly as possible.[20] The idea seems to be that negative capital account balances are tolerable if they are unlikely to persist for very long.

b. The "Substantiality" Rules

If the only test for the validity of an allocation were whether that allocation will determine the amount of money a partner will get from the partnership, many clearly improper allocations would pass muster. Consider these examples:

---

18. This approach by the regulations conflicts with the statute. The statutory rule for allocations that lack substantial economic effect requires taking into account "all facts and circumstances." § 704(b). The regulations ignore many relevant facts and circumstances (such as the real values of partnership assets and whether the partnership is likely to earn more income in future years). What would happen under hypothetical sets of facts not likely to arise hardly constitutes "all facts and circumstances."

19. Treas. Reg. § 1.704–1(b)(2)(ii)(*d*)(*4*),(*5*), & (*6*).

20. Treas. Reg. § 1.704–1(b)(2)(ii)(*d*).

Example 5–8: The three equal partners of ABC are Acme Widget Works, Inc., Beta Blasters Corporation, and Charlie. Acme and Beta are C corporations, whose capital gains are taxed at the same rate as their ordinary income. Charlie's capital gains are taxed at 15 percent; his ordinary income is taxed at a higher rate. The partnership maintains capital accounts as provided in the regulations under § 704, capital account balances control liquidating distributions, and any partner having a capital account deficit upon liquidation must pay in the amount of the deficit.

The partners discover early in the year that the partnership will recognize a capital gain of at least $100,000 from the sale of Orangeacre, a partnership asset. It will also have several hundred thousand dollars of ordinary income. The partners amend their partnership agreement to allocate the first $100,000 of partnership capital gains to Charlie. The first $200,000 of partnership ordinary income is allocated equally between Acme and Beta. All other income is allocated equally. These allocations are appropriately reflected in the partners' capital accounts.

The ABC partnership's allocations have economic effect, as they do determine the amount of money each partner will take out of the partnership. But the allocations' economic effect does not differ (except for intended tax consequences) from an allocation of one-third of all items of partnership income to each partner. Economically, the special allocation does not change the fact that this is an equal partnership in all respects. The special allocation should not be permitted. Taxpayers who are not partners cannot exchange different kinds of income with each other. If Acme, Beta, and Charlie were not partners, an agreement purporting to give Acme's and Beta's capital gains to Charlie in exchange for an equal amount of ordinary income would not be taken seriously. Taxpayers operating as partners should not be able to achieve tax results more favorable than those available to non-partners.

Example 5–9: Helmut and Inge are equal partners in HI. Helmut has a $50,000 net-operating-loss carryover from unrelated activities. This carryover will expire after year two. The HI partnership's agreement is amended to provide that, for year two only, all of the partnership's income (which the partners expect to be about $50,000) will be allocated to Helmut, with appropriate capital account adjustments. For the next five years, the first $10,000 of partnership income will be allocated to Inge, with the rest divided equally. Beginning in year eight, allocations will become fifty-fifty again. These special allocations will not affect the amount of current distributions the partners will receive.

As in the previous case, the partners are attempting to trade tax attributes with each other. They could not do this if they were not partners, and their being partners should not change that result.

To deal with problems like those presented by the examples, the regulations contain rules for determining whether an allocation that has "economic effect" has a *substantial* economic effect." This terminology is misleading, because these "substantiality" rules do not turn upon the meaning of the word "substantial" in any everyday sense of the term. Indeed, under the substantiality rules one allocation may be valid even though another allocation having exactly the same effect upon the partners' chances of making an economic profit would not be. For example, the substantiality rules would invalidate the ABC partnership's attempt in Example 5–8 to allocate $100,000 of capital gains to Charlie, but they would not invalidate the partnership's normal allocation of one-third of all items of income to each partner. Each of these allocations has the same effect on the partners' capital accounts, yet one is valid and the other is not. The difference between the two allocations is not a difference between their economic effects, for there is no such difference.[21] The regulations deal with abusive allocations like those described above by testing those allocations against three rules for determining whether an allocation's economic effect is "substantial." The rules are:

(1) The "general rules" of Treas. Reg. § 1.704–1(b)(2)(iii)(a). Under this provision, the economic effect of an allocation is not "substantial" if "the after-tax economic consequences" of the allocation to one partner are better than they would have been without the allocation, and "there is a strong likelihood that the after-tax economic consequences" to the other partners are no worse than they would otherwise have been. Determinations of whether allocations make partners better off, or no worse off, are made in terms of present value.

Under these "general rules," the allocations described in both Example 5–8 and Example 5–9 would lack "substantiality," because both would probably improve the after-tax position of at least one partner without making the other partners any worse off.

---

21. It may be tempting to think that the special allocation of capital gain to Charlie is invalid because it purports to allocate character. This would be wrong. True, the special allocation does allocate character, but so does the valid allocation which it replaced.

(2) The "shifting tax consequences" rule of Treas. Reg. § 1.704–1(b)(2)(iii)(*b*). This rule, which would cover the allocations described in Example 5–8, invalidates allocations which create a "strong likelihood" that (1) the changes in the partners' capital account balances under the allocations "will not differ substantially from" what they would have been without the allocations, and (2) The partners' total tax liability for the year in question will be less than it otherwise would have been.

Unlike the "general rules," the "shifting tax consequences rule" does not require that every partner's tax position under the allocation in question be as favorable as it would have been without that allocation. Rather, it looks at the partners' aggregate tax liability.

(3) The "transitory allocations" rule of Treas. Reg. § 1.704–1(b)(2)(iii)(*c*). This rule is virtually the same as the "shifting tax consequences" rule except that it covers periods of more than one year. The allocation in Example 5–9 of "this year's income to Helmut," combined with an allocation of about that much extra income to Inge over the next few years, is the sort of thing this rule was designed to prevent.

A serious weakness of the "substantiality rules" is that they test the validity of allocations by comparing actual allocations with the allocations that partnership agreements "would have" contained but for the allocations in question. In simple examples like those used so far, it has seemed easy to say what the hypothetical allocation would have been. When partners amend an agreement calling for a fifty-fifty split of all items to allocate a particular kind of gain in a special way, it may be reasonable to assume that the item in question would have been allocated fifty-fifty too, had it not received special treatment. Or when one formula allocates all but one of a partnership's income or deduction items, one can plausibly guess that that one item would normally have been allocated by the same formula. But some partnerships have no simple overall allocation at all. Some service partnerships make all of their allocations retroactively, after the year in question has ended and the partners know how things have worked out. In these cases, it is hard to see how the substantiality rules can be applied. An old joke ends with the punch line, "If you had a brother, would he like cheese?" Like the speaker in the joke, the drafters of the regulations have asked a question that cannot be answered. For all their apparent specificity, the "substantiality rules" rest on unstated assumptions about how to identify the hypothetical allocation with which an actual allocation must be compared. In cases involving allocation agreements more complex than those used in the regulations' examples, the rules provide little guidance.

c. Some Special Problems

Allocations of depreciation deductions and allocations attributable to nonrecourse financing have long been of special concern because partnerships have been used as vehicles for tax shelters.

i. Depreciation

Allocations of depreciation (or "cost recovery") deductions create difficulties for two reasons. First, the amount of these deductions is always known in advance. When property is placed in service, the partnership can calculate exactly how much depreciation will be deducted each year. Unlike allocations of items that are uncertain when the allocation is agreed upon, allocations of known items can be tailored to maximize tax benefits without risking unexpected non-tax consequences. Second, depreciation deductions for buildings are often deductions for an imaginary cost. Absent special and fairly unusual circumstances, well-maintained buildings rarely experience permanent declines in value, and they certainly do not become completely worthless after thirty-nine years. Furthermore, if gain on the disposition of a building is allocated in the same way as depreciation on that building, whatever effect the depreciation deductions had on the partners' capital accounts may be canceled out when the building is sold and gain is "charged back" to the partners who deducted the depreciation.

Example 5–10: The LMN partnership's agreement allocates all depreciation deductions on the partnership's building, which has a basis of $500,000, to partners Leonard and Margaret. Gain on the disposition of the building is also allocated half to Leonard and half to Margaret. Over the next thirty-nine years, the partnership deducts $500,000 in tax and book depreciation, allocating $250,000 to Leonard and $250,000 to Margaret. At this point, Leonard and Margaret have capital account balances of $100,000 each; if none of the depreciation had been allocated to them these balances would have been $350,000 each.

If the partnership sells the building for $500,000 it will recognize a tax and book gain of $500,000, which will be allocated $250,000 to Leonard and $250,000 to Margaret. At this point each of them will have a capital account balance of $350,000, just as if none of the depreciation had been allocated to them, or if it had been allocated ninety percent to Leonard and ten percent to Margaret (with a corresponding allocation of the first $500,000 of gain on the sale of the building).

The problem is that depreciation on a building does not usually correspond to any economic effect. But depreciation deductions must be allocated somehow. In the *Orrisch* case, the Tax Court said that the economic effect of a depreciation allocation must be found by asking "who is to bear the economic burden of the depreciation if the buildings should be sold for a sum less than their original cost."[22] The drafters of the regulations under § 704 adopted this principle,[23] though, as we shall see, they failed to apply it correctly to particular cases.

In Example 5–10, the allocation of depreciation would be treated as having economic effect, even though the gain chargeback would most likely offset the reductions in the balances of Leonard's and Margaret's capital accounts. The principle is that if the building should in fact decline in value to zero (an unlikely event, to be sure) the burden of that decline would be borne equally by Leonard and Margaret, and not at all by the other partner. The regulations provide that a gain chargeback does not invalidate an allocation of depreciation on "substantiality" grounds by creating a legal fiction. The regulations presume that the fair market value of a building equals its adjusted basis. This presumption means that there cannot be a "strong likelihood" that the effect of the depreciation allocations will be offset by the chargeback because the presumption means that there will be no gain.[24]

As long as an allocation of depreciation is accompanied by a "chargeback" of gain attributable to basis reductions caused by the depreciation deductions, it makes some[25] sense to say that the partners to whom the depreciation has been allocated bear whatever risk there is that the asset will decline in value. If, however, gain on the sale of the asset is allocated in a different way than depreciation was allocated, the partners to whom depreciation was allocated will not be the risk-bearing partners, even if we accept the proposition that capital accounts measure something important. The partners whose capital accounts will vary with the value of a depreciable asset are the partners whose capital accounts reflect gains and losses when the asset is sold, not the partners to whom depreciation has been allocated.

Example 5–11: The OPR partnership has just bought a small building for $200,000. The partnership agreement allocates the full $200,000 of the tax and book depreciation deductions to partner Oscar, but all gain on the disposition of the building is allocated to partners Phyllis and Roger. After the building has

---

22. 55 T.C. at 403.

23. Treas. Reg. § 1.704–1(b)(5) (Example (1)(i)) invalidates an allocation of depreciation because the partner to whom the depreciation was allocated "will not bear the full risk of the economic loss" corresponding to the depreciation deductions.

24. Treas. Reg. § 1.704–1(b)(2)(iii)(c)(2). See Examples (1)(iii), (1)(iv), (1)(vi), and (1)(vii) of Treas. Reg. § 1.704–1(b)(5).

25. "Some sense," rather than "excellent sense," because capital account balances are not a good measure of partners' economic welfare.

been fully depreciated, Oscar's capital account balance has been reduced by $200,000.

At first glance, the reduction in Oscar's capital account may seem to match a risk that the building will decline in value. If the building should happen to decline in value to zero, both the loss of value and the reduction in Oscar's capital account balance will be $200,000. In fact, however, the fate of Oscar's capital account balance is not tied at all to the value of the building. His balance will decline by $200,000 no matter what happens to the building. Suppose, for instance, that the building, when it has been fully depreciated, has lost half its value. It is then sold for $100,000. Oscar's capital account has still been reduced by $200,000, but now Phyllis's and Roger's capital account balances are $50,000 higher (each) than if the building had lost all its value. If the building's value had remained constant, Phyllis's and Roger's balances would each have been $100,000 more than if the building had become worthless.

Under the allocation in this example, the only partners whose capital accounts are affected by changes in the value of the building are Phyllis and Roger. This is not to say that the allocation of depreciation to Oscar does not affect him economically. It does, because it will reduce the amount that Oscar will ultimately get from the partnership. But the effect is not to subject Oscar to the risk that the building's value will decline. Therefore, the allocation should be viewed not as an allocation of depreciation to Oscar, but as a $200,000 reduction in his share of partnership income over the life of the building. Nevertheless, the regulations treat depreciation allocations not accompanied by gain chargebacks as valid allocations of depreciation deductions.[26]

The widespread belief that a depreciation allocation corresponds to risk of loss even if the allocation is not accompanied by a gain chargeback may derive from a misunderstanding of the regulations' assumption that changes in the basis of an asset are assumed to be matched by changes in the asset's value in applying the substantiality rule.[27] As we have seen, this assumption is needed to prevent the substantiality rules from invalidating depreciation allocations accompanied by gain chargebacks.[28] It cannot sensibly be used in asking who bears the risk that an asset's value will fall. That inquiry requires comparing partners' economic positions if the asset declines in value with their positions if it

---

26. See examples (1)(iii), (1)(iv), (1)(vi), and (1)(vii) of Treas. Reg. § 1.704–1(b)(5).
27. Treas. Reg. § 1.704–1(b)(2)(iii)(c).
28. See page 61.

does not. Partners who are to share risks that depreciable assets will decline in value should always be subject to gain chargebacks corresponding to the depreciation allocated to them.

ii. Deductions Attributable to Nonrecourse Debt

Suppose that Serena and Ted form the ST equal partnership by contributing $100,000 each. The partnership buys a depreciable building for $1,000,000, paying $200,000 in cash and taking the building subject to a nonrecourse mortgage. For simplicity, assume that the partnership has no income and no expenses (other than depreciation), and that it does not pay off any of the principal on the mortgage. Over the years, the partnership will deduct $1,000,000 in depreciation. Of this amount, $200,000 can be thought of as corresponding to an economic risk borne by the partners, for if the building declines in value to $800,000 by the time it is sold, Serena and Ted will be out their (combined) $200,000. But what if the building falls in value by $300,000? In that case, the decline in value will still cost Serena and Ted $200,000. The mortgagee will have lost the other $100,000.

The fact that some of the economic risk associated with depreciation on property financed by nonrecourse debt is borne by the mortgage lender rather than by the partners gives us no reason to deny the partners the full deductions for depreciation on the property. An individual who owns property having a basis attributable in part to nonrecourse debt can deduct full depreciation on the property even though that individual does not bear the full risk that the property's value will fall. However, a system of allocations based on tracing the "economic effects" associated with the items being allocated to the partners breaks down when the economic effect in question will be felt by someone who, like the mortgage lender, is not a partner. Special rules are therefore needed to handle this case.

Because the economic effect corresponding to allocations based on nonrecourse debt is an effect on the mortgage lender, rather than on the partners, the regulations treat allocations of these "nonrecourse deductions" under the "partner's interest in the partnership" standard.[29] They provide a complicated safe-harbor method for making allocations that meet this standard. Partners who fail to create allocations that come within the safe harbor get little guidance. The regulations say that nonrecourse deductions must be allocated according to the partners' "overall economic interests in the partnership" if the safe-harbor provisions do not apply.[30] In this case, as elsewhere, the drafters of the

---

29. Treas. Reg. § 1.704–2(b)(1).

30. Treas. Reg. § 1.704–2(b)(1), incorporating by reference Treas. Reg. § 1.704–1(b)(3). Sometimes a debt may be nonrecourse as to the partnership, but a particular partner bears

regulations provided detailed guidance for tax specialists (who will draft agreements satisfying the safe-harbor tests for sophisticated investors) while slighting questions of how the law should apply to ordinary taxpayers. The following explanation outlines the safe harbor.

An examination of the safe harbor for nonrecourse allocations must begin with a look at a new concept—the concept of "minimum gain." Consider a partnership that owns a depreciable asset with a basis of $1,000,000, of which $800,000 is attributable to nonrecourse purchase-money debt. So long as the property's basis stays higher than the unpaid balance of the mortgage, we cannot know how much gain or loss a sale of the property will produce unless we know the property's value. Indeed, we cannot even know whether a sale will result in a gain or a loss. Suppose, however, that the property's basis is reduced by depreciation deductions to a figure lower than the unpaid balance of the debt. If the property is sold, the outstanding balance of the debt will be includable in the seller's amount realized under the *Crane* rule. Therefore, we know that a sale of the property will generate a gain, and we know also that the amount of the gain must be at least the excess of the balance of the debt over the property's basis. This amount (which corresponds to deductions taken by the property's owner but financed by the nonrecourse lender) is the "minimum gain."[31]

Example 5-12: Arnold and Belle form the AB partnership. They agree that they will share income and expenses equally, except that Arnold will be allocated twenty percent and Belle eighty percent of all depreciation expenses. The partnership pays $200,000 cash to buy a depreciable asset subject to an $800,000 nonrecourse purchase money debt. No principal is payable on the debt for ten years and the depreciation expense for the asset is $50,000 per year.

The depreciation expenses in the first four years do not result in partnership minimum gain. At the end of year four, the property's basis of $800,000 just equals the $800,000 nonrecourse debt. The depreciation expense in year five, however,

---

the risks associated with that debt, as where a partner guarantees payment of a partnership's nonrecourse debt. In that kind of case, nonrecourse deductions associated with the debt must be allocated to the partner who bears the risk of loss; Treas. Reg. § 1.704–2(i).

31. Treas. Reg. § 1.704–2(d)(1). Minimum gain is calculated by reference to the asset's book value, rather than its tax basis if the asset's book value differs from its tax basis; Treas. Reg. § 1.704–2(d)(3). For example, if a partner contributes property with a basis of $200,000 and a value of $500,000, the book value of the property is $500,000 and the partnership's minimum gain is calculated by reference to that book value, rather than by reference to the $200,000 basis. The reason for this is that § 704(c) (discussed in Chapter 6) provides special rules for allocating gains, losses, and depreciation attributable to differences between book value and basis for contributed property.

reduces the basis to $750,000, creating $50,000 of partnership minimum gain ($800,000 nonrecourse debt less $750,000 basis).

Partnership deductions that increase the partnership's minimum gain are called "nonrecourse deductions." In Example 5–12, the $50,000 depreciation expense in year five was a nonrecourse deduction because it increased partnership minimum gain from $0 to $50,000.

One requirement for making an allocation of nonrecourse deductions is that the partnership agreement contain a "minimum gain chargeback" provision.[32] This provision requires that, when the partnership's minimum gain is reduced, income equal to the minimum gain be allocated to the partners who took the deductions which created the minimum gain. If the allocation of $10,000 (twenty percent of $50,000) of the nonrecourse deduction to Arnold and $40,000 (eighty percent of $50,000) to Belle in year five is to be valid, the minimum gain created by those deductions must be charged back to them when the partnership minimum gain decreases.[33] Suppose, for example, that the AB partnership transfers the asset encumbered by the $800,000 nonrecourse debts in the beginning of year six. The partnership would experience a decrease in partnership minimum gain of $50,000 as a result of the transfer since it no longer owns the property and would also recognize $50,000 of gain ($800,000 debt minus $750,000 basis). The minimum gain chargeback provision would allocate $10,000 of that gain to Arnold and $40,000 to Belle. In this respect, the regulations correspond to the rules for individual taxpayers, because an individual property owner who takes nonrecourse deductions will report the corresponding gain upon selling the property.

In technical terms, the regulations require that the minimum gain chargeback provision in the partnership agreement allocate income to partners when there is a "decrease in partnership minimum gain" to the extent of their "share" of the decrease.[34] A sale of the property is usually the event that triggers the decrease in minimum gain. A decrease in partnership minimum gain may also occur when principal on the loan is paid or when the debt is converted from nonrecourse to recourse. Each partner's "share" of minimum gain is usually equal to the amount of nonrecourse deductions allocated to that partner.[35]

Example 5–13: John and Kara form the JK partnership. Neither partner contributes capital. The JK partnership purchases

---

32. Treas. Reg. §§ 1.704–2(e)(3); 1.704–2(f).

33. Treas. Reg. §§ 1.704–2(e)(3); 1.704–2(f)(1); 1.704–2(f)(6).

34. Treas. Reg. § 1.704–2(f)(1).

35. Treas. Reg. 1.704–2(g)(1)(i). A partner's share of minimum gain also equals the amount of any proceeds of partnership nonrecourse debt distributed to that partner if the debt created partnership minimum gain when incurred. Id.

real estate for a $390,000 nonrecourse note for which no principal is payable for ten years. Sixty percent of the depreciation expenses are to be allocated to John and forty percent to Kara. After two years, John has been allocated $12,000 of depreciation expenses and Kara $8,000. The partnership minimum gain is $20,000 ($390,000 nonrecourse debt minus $370,000 real estate basis). John's share of the partnership minimum gain is $12,000 and Kara's is $8,000.

If the partnership sells the real estate at the beginning of year three for the $390,000 nonrecourse debt encumbering it, the partnership experiences a decrease in partnership minimum gain of $20,000. John's share of the decrease is $12,000 and Kara's is $8,000. Pursuant to the minimum gain chargeback provision, John will be allocated $12,000 of the partnership gain and Kara $8,000.

Suppose that the partnership did not sell the real estate, but instead converted the debt from nonrecourse to recourse. The partnership would still experience a decrease in minimum gain from $20,000 to $0. As a result, the partnership would allocate $12,000 of income to John and $8,000 to Kara. Note that the partnership would not have any gain attributable to the real estate to allocate in the chargeback since it did not sell the real estate. The regulations direct in that situation that a pro rata portion of the partnership's other items of income and gain be used.[36]

Finally, assume that the partnership did not sell the real estate or refinance the debt, but instead that Kara contributed $390,000 to the partnership that the partnership then used to pay off the nonrecourse loan. The partnership's minimum gain would decrease to zero and the minimum gain chargeback would be triggered. The chargeback would allocate $12,000 of income to John. Although Kara would normally also be allocated income because her share of partnership minimum gain decreased by $8,000, the regulations save her. The regulations say that a partner will not be subject to a chargeback to the extent that the partner made a contribution that was used to decrease partnership minimum gain by paying off the debt or increasing the asset's basis.[37] The rationale is that Kara has assumed the risk of loss previously held by the lender as a result of contributing the amount used to pay the loan.

---

36. Treas. Reg. § 1.704–2(j)(2)(i).

37. Treas. Reg. § 1.704–2(f)(3). Other exceptions to the chargeback are also included in Treas. Reg. § 1.704–2(f).

The regulations' other principal requirements for creating an allocation of nonrecourse deductions that are within the safe harbor are (suppressing some details and qualifications):

(1) Throughout the life of the partnership, capital accounts must be properly maintained and must control liquidating distributions.[38]

(2) The allocation of nonrecourse deductions must be "reasonably consistent with" the allocation of "some other significant ... item attributable to the property securing the nonrecourse liabilities," and the allocation of that other item must have substantial economic effect.[39]

(3) "All other material allocations and capital account adjustments" must satisfy the regulations' rules for valid allocations.[40]

A debt that is nonrecourse with respect to partners generally may be recourse in the sense that some partner or partners bear the "economic risk of loss" associated with that debt. For example, if a partner guarantees a nonrecourse loan to the partnership, that partner bears the economic risk of loss. Nonrecourse deductions attributable to these "partner nonrecourse liabilities" must be allocated to the partners who bear the economic risk of loss.[41]

Application of the rules for nonrecourse deductions to LLCs is not clear. Suppose a partnership that is an LLC incurs debt for which the LLC is personally liable. This debt is not a nonrecourse debt in the traditional sense because the LLC itself is liable.[42] However, none of the LLC's members will be liable if the LLC defaults and its assets are insufficient to satisfy the debt. It is far from clear how the rules discussed above apply in this kind of case. It is as true of an LLC's "recourse" liability as of traditional nonrecourse liabilities that some risks of loss are borne by the creditor, rather than by the owners of the entity. These liabilities therefore seem to be nonrecourse. But questions like how to calculate minimum gain when a "nonrecourse liability" is not secured by a particular asset have no clear answers. What is needed is a way of calculating nonrecourse liabilities and minimum gain on an

---

38. Treas. Reg. § 1.704–2(e)(1). In addition, either partners must be obliged to pay in capital account deficits upon liquidation or the partnership agreement must contain a qualified income offset; id.

39. Treas. Reg. § 1.704–2(e)(2).

40. Treas. Reg. § 1.704–2(e)(4).

41. Treas. Reg. §§ 1.704–2(b)(4); 1.704–2(i)(1). The regulations then apply a minimum gain chargeback to those partners when the minimum gain attributable to such debt is reduced.

42. This means that, if the LLC defaults, any of its assets, not just the particular asset that secures the liability, can be used to obtain money to pay the debt.

overall basis, rather than asset-by-asset, as the current regulations do. At present, practitioners have little guidance in this area.[43]

iii. Interaction of Nonrecourse Deductions With the Alternate Test for Economic–Effect Test

Recall that one of the guiding principles for allocations to have economic effect is that partners should bear the economic burden for expenses and losses allocated to them. The economic burden for losses is imposed on partners by requiring them to restore deficits in their capital accounts or, under the alternate test for economic effect, requiring that they not be allocated items that will create a negative capital account.

Application of these rules to nonrecourse deductions is difficult because no partner bears the economic burden for nonrecourse deductions; only the nonrecourse lender bears the economic burden. Two approaches are theoretically possible. The first approach would prohibit allocations of nonrecourse deductions to the extent that the allocation created or increased a negative capital account. The problem with this first approach is that there is no reason to distinguish between nonrecourse deductions that cause or increase negative capital accounts and those that do not. Partners do not bear the risk of loss associated with nonrecourse deductions regardless of the balance in their capital accounts—only the nonrecourse lender bears that risk. The second approach would permit allocations of nonrecourse deductions that created or increased a negative capital account so long as the nonrecourse lender (and not any partner) bore the risk of loss. The regulations adopt the second approach and permit partners who do not have deficit restoration obligations to have deficit balances in their capital accounts so long as the deficit is attributable to nonrecourse deductions and the partnership satisfies the requirements of the alternate test for economic effect. Technically, the regulations accomplish this by saying that, under the alternate test, a partner can have a deficit capital account equal to any limited amount of the deficit that the partner has agreed to restore.[44] The regulations then create a legal fiction by treating a partner's share of partnership minimum gain as being the equivalent of a limited deficit restoration obligation.[45]

---

43. In one narrow situation, the calculation of minimum gain under § 704(c) (discussed in Chapter 6), Treas. Reg. § 1.752–3(b) allows partnerships to allocate nonrecourse debts encumbering more than one asset by using any "reasonable" method.

The difficulties presented by recourse debts of LLCs are discussed in Karen C. Burke, Exculpatory Liabilities and Partnership Nonrecourse Allocations, 57 Tax Law. 33 (2003).

44. Treas. Reg. § 1.704–1(b)(2)(ii)*(d)(3)*.

45. Treas. Reg. § 1.704–2(g)(1) (penultimate sentence).

Example 5–14: Mike and Nancy form the MN partnership. Neither contributes capital to the partnership and neither has a deficit-restoration obligation. The partnership agreement satisfies all the requirements for the alternate test for economic effect (see pages 54–56, above) and for nonrecourse deductions (see pages 63–68, above). Thus, the agreement includes qualified income offset and minimum gain chargeback provisions. The partnership purchases real estate for $100,000 by delivering a nonrecourse note to the buyer for which no principal is payable for five years. The partnership deducts $2,000 of depreciation in year one that is allocated equally to the partners.

The allocation of $1,000 to Mike and Nancy will create a negative capital account of $1,000 for each. Although neither Mike nor Nancy has an obligation to restore a deficit capital account balance, the allocation is deemed to have economic effect under the alternate test for economic effect and the requirements for nonrecourse deductions. The depreciation deduction of $2,000 created partnership minimum gain of $2,000 since the partnership's $100,000 nonrecourse debt now exceeds the real estate's basis by $2,000. Since each partner was allocated $1,000 of this nonrecourse deduction, each has a $1,000 share of the partnership's minimum gain. This share of partnership minimum gain qualifies as a limited deficit restoration obligation (Treas. Reg. § 1.704–2(g)(1)) and the alternate test for economic substance allows a capital account to be negative to the extent of a limited deficit restoration obligation. Treas. Reg. § 1.704–1(b)(2)(ii)*(d)(3)*.[46]

iv. Allocating Credits

An allocation of a tax credit cannot have any economic effect in the usual sense, as there is no reason to adjust any partner's capital account balance by the amount of whatever tax credits the partners are allowed. As a rule, the regulations allocate tax credits by looking to the allocation of the deduction or income items associated with the outlays or receipts that gave rise to the credits.[47] The foreign tax credit (§ 901) is claimed separately by each partner; it is not computed at all at the partnership level.[48] Foreign tax expenditures by the partnership, which may allow a

---

46. This approach also permits a partner's capital account to become negative as a result of certain distributions. A partner's share of minimum gain includes (in addition to nonrecourse deductions) the amount of any proceeds of nonrecourse debt distributed to that partner if the debt created partnership minimum gain when incurred (see note 35, above). Treas. Reg. § 1.704–1(b)(2)(ii)*(d)(3)*.

47. Treas. Reg. § 1.704–1(b)(4)(ii).

48. § 703(b)(3).

foreign tax credit, must be allocated in direct proportion to allocations of foreign income to which the foreign tax relate.[49]

C. COMPARISON WITH SUBCHAPTER S

Allocations of the income and deductions of S corporations are much simpler than partnership allocations because S corporations cannot make "item allocations." An S corporation's income and deductions are allocated to its shareholders in proportion to the number of shares of stock they own.[50]

---

49. Temp. Treas. Reg. § 1.704–1(b)(4)(viii)(*a*).

50. §§ 1366; 1377(a).

Chapter Six

ALLOCATIONS ATTRIBUTABLE TO CONTRIBUTED PROPERTY: SECTION 704(c)

A. ALLOCATIONS OF GAIN OR LOSS

In Chapter 5 we saw that the substantial effect test requires that tax allocations correspond to book allocations made to a partner's capital account. Special considerations apply to allocations attributable to property contributed to a partnership when the property's fair market value (i.e. its book value) differs from its tax basis. If property contributed to a partnership in a transaction subject to §§ 721, 722, and 723 has a tax basis that differs from its book value, the tax consequences attributable to that difference should be borne (or, if they are favorable, enjoyed) by the contributing partner. Suppose that a new partner contributes unimproved land with a tax basis of $30,000 and a value of $40,000 in exchange for an interest in a partnership. The contributing partner has a capital account of $40,000 and the partnership's book value for the asset is $40,000. The partnership later sells the land for $44,000. The contributing partner should report all of the $10,000 tax gain that was "built in" at the time of the contribution. Only the $4,000 increase in the property's value that took place after the contribution (i.e. the book gain of $4,000) corresponds to an increase in the partnership's wealth; the first $10,000 of the gain represents an increase in value that took place while the contributor held the property.

Section 704(c)(1)(A) requires that taxable income and deductions "with respect to property contributed to the partnership by a partner shall be shared among the partners so as to take account of" any basis/value difference at the time of the contribution. On the facts of the example in the previous paragraph, $10,000 of the $14,000 tax gain recognized by the partnership would be taxed to the contributing partner under § 704(c)(1)(A). The balance of the tax gain of $4,000 (which is also the amount of book gain) would be allocated under § 704(b), in the same manner that the book gain is allocated.

Example 6–1: Helen and Ike form an equal partnership. Helen contributes unimproved land with a basis of $20,000 and a fair market value of $30,000. Ike contributes $30,000 cash. Both have initial capital accounts of $30,000. During the partnership's first year, the land appreciates in value to $32,000 and the partnership sells it. The partnership has a tax gain of $12,000 ($32,000 sales price minus $20,000 tax basis) and a book gain of $2,000

($32,000 sales price minus $30,000 book value). The first $10,000 of the tax gain is allocated to Helen because it is attributable to appreciation that occurred prior to Helen's contribution of the land to the partnership. There is no capital account adjustment for this allocation to Helen because her $30,000 capital account already included the land's built-in appreciation.

The remaining $2,000 of tax gain is allocated in the same manner as the $2,000 book gain. Helen and Ike are each allocated $1,000 of the tax gain and $1,000 of the book gain. Their capital accounts are each adjusted upward by $1,000.

Here is an example involving a built-in loss:

Example 6–2: Claire and Dennis form an equal partnership. Claire contributes land with a basis of $50,000 and a value of $40,000; Dennis contributes $40,000 in cash. Each has an initial capital account balance of $40,000. During the partnership's first year, the land declines in value to $38,000 and the partnership sells it for that amount. Economically, the partnership's $12,000 loss is attributable to a $10,000 decline in value that took place while Claire owned the property and a $2,000 decline that took place while the property was held by the CD partnership. Therefore, $10,000 of the tax loss is allocable to Claire under § 704(c)(1)(A). The other $2,000 tax loss (which is also the amount of the book loss) is allocable half to Claire and half to Dennis, under § 704(b). The appropriate capital account adjustment is minus $1,000 for each partner.

A complication arises if the gain or loss recognized by the partnership is less than the gain or loss that was built in at the time of the contribution. Suppose that the property Claire contributed to the CD partnership (Example 6–2) had increased in value to $41,000 between the contribution and the sale. The purpose behind § 704(c) would be served by treating the sale as producing a $10,000 tax loss (allocable to Claire under § 704(c)) and a $1,000 tax gain (allocable $500 to Claire and $500 to Dennis under § 704(b)). However, the regulations under the pre–1984 version of § 704(c) created a "ceiling rule," under which a partnership-level loss cannot be divided up in that way.[1] Because the partnership recognized a $9,000 loss on the sale, neither partner can be allocated a tax gain, according to these regulations. Therefore, the correct allocation is $9,000 of the tax loss to Claire. This comes as close as possible to the ideal allocation without "dividing" a $9,000 loss into a $10,000 loss and a $1,000 gain.

---

1. Former Treas. Reg. § 1.704–1(c)(2)(i). The current version of the ceiling rule is found in Treas. Reg. § 1.704–3(b)(1).

The ceiling rule makes little sense either in theory or in practice.[2] Economically, the parties' dealings with the property in the previous paragraph enriched Dennis by $500 and made Claire poorer by $9,500. Neither limiting Claire's loss deduction to $9,000 nor failing to tax Dennis on the $500 economic gain he enjoyed can be defended persuasively. The drafters of the current regulations appreciated this point. The regulations retain the ceiling rule, but they allow the partners to make "curative allocations" or "remedial allocations" of income and deductions to offset the ceiling rule's effects. In some cases, a curative allocation (or some other way of offsetting the ceiling rule) will be required. A curative allocation works by allocating other items of partnership income or deduction in a way that makes up for the distortions caused by the ceiling rule. (The items allocated in this way must have the same character as the items affected by the ceiling rule: a partnership cannot make a curative allocation of capital gain to make up for a misallocation of ordinary income or loss.) Remedial allocations resemble curative allocations except that the items allocated to compensate for the ceiling rule's distortions are imaginary (or, as the regulations call them, "notional").[3]

Example 6–3: The facts are the same as in Example 6–2, except that the property contributed by Claire increases in value to $41,000 and is sold for that amount, producing a partnership-level tax loss of $9,000 and a book gain of $1,000. As discussed above, the ideal allocation would be an allocation of a $500 tax gain to Dennis and a $9,500 tax loss to Claire, but the ceiling rule prevents this. If the partnership has at least $1,000 of taxable income of the same sort that it would have recognized had it sold the land at a gain, it may make a curative allocation to Dennis of the $500 portion of that other income that would have been taxed to Claire under the partnership's normal practice of sharing gains equally. This curative allocation increases Dennis's share of taxable income by the $500 and reduces Claire's share by the same amount. As a result, the sale of the property causes Dennis to recognize $500 more taxable income than if it had not been sold, and Claire to recognize $9,500 less taxable income (her $9,000 loss on the sale of the property plus $500 of income that would have been taxed to her but which has been allocated to Dennis).

If the CD partnership chooses to overcome the ceiling rule's distortion by using a remedial allocation, it will make the following allocations:

---

2. For a history of the ceiling rule, see Marich, Hortenstine & Penick, The Remedial Allocation Method: A Viable Cure for the Ceiling Rule, 65 Tax Notes 1267 (Dec. 5, 1994).

3. Curative allocations are described in Treas. Reg. § 1.704–3(c); Remedial allocations in Treas. Reg. § 1.704–3(d).

(1) The $9,000 tax deduction for the loss on the sale of the land will be allocated to Dennis.

(2) The rest of the partnership's taxable income or loss will be allocated equally between Claire and Dennis.

(3) The partnership will allocate a "notional" tax gain of $500 to Dennis and a "notional" deduction of $500 to Claire. This is the remedial allocation, which results in Claire's total allocation of gain or loss on account of the sale of the property being a $9,500 tax loss, just as if there had been no ceiling rule. The character of these notional tax gains and losses must be the same as the character of the gain or loss from the sale of the property in questions, so if the land is a capital asset, the notional gains and losses will be capital rather than ordinary.[4]

(4) Each partner's capital account would be increased by one-half of the book gain.

According to the regulations, the traditional method, the traditional method with curative allocations, and the traditional method with remedial allocations are "generally reasonable." "Other methods" may be reasonable too.[5] A de minimis rule allows partnerships to ignore § 704(c) in cases involving small disparities between book value and basis.[6] Although § 704(c) allocations must generally be done on an asset-by-asset basis, the regulations allow some kinds of properties contributed by a partner during the same taxable year to be aggregated.[7]

In some cases, partnerships may not use the traditional method, and in others, use of curative allocations is prohibited. As many of these cases involve allocations of depreciation and of gains from the sale of depreciable property, they will be examined below.

B. ALLOCATIONS OF DEPRECIATION

A basis/value difference existing when a partner contributes property to a partnership will affect the allocation of depreciation deductions as well as the allocation of gains and losses. In applying § 704(c) to depreciation allocations, it is helpful to approach § 704(c) as dealing with the difference between "book" and "tax" figures. As a general rule, book depreci-

---

4. Treas. Reg. § 1.704–3(d)(3); cf. Treas. Reg. § 1.704–3(d)(7) (Example 2).

5. Treas. Reg. § 1.704–3(a)(1).

6. Treas. Reg. § 1.704–3(e)(1). A "small disparity" exists if (1) the book value of all the properties contributed by one partner during the year does not differ from the tax basis by more than 15 percent of that basis and (2) the "total gross disparity" for all property contributed by that partner is $20,000 or less.

7. Treas. Reg. § 1.704–3(e)(2).

ation is calculated by scaling tax depreciation up or down according to the basis/value difference at the time of the contribution. For example, if contributed property has a value of $50,000 and a basis of $10,000, book depreciation is five times whatever tax depreciation is.[8] As the partnership takes depreciation on the property, the tax basis of the asset is reduced by the tax depreciation deductions,[9] while the property's book value is reduced by the depreciation that would have been taken if there had been no book/basis disparity.[10] Eventually the book/basis disparity is eliminated.

1. The Traditional Method

Here is an example showing how depreciation deductions are allocated under the traditional method.

Example 6–4: Elaine contributes depreciable property having a basis of $6,000 and a value of $10,000 to the EF equal partnership. The property has two years of depreciation remaining. Frobisher contributes $10,000 in cash. The partnership's tax depreciation deductions will be $6,000 over the remaining two-year depreciation period. The basis/value difference in this case will cause the partnership to have $4,000 less in tax depreciation deductions than it would have had if the property's basis had been equal to its value. This consequence ($4,000 too little partnership tax depreciation) must be borne by Elaine under § 704(c)(1)(A). Therefore, Elaine should be allocated $1,000 of the tax depreciation over the asset's remaining life; Frobisher should be allocated $5,000. Both partners, however, will be allocated equal amounts of book depreciation over the two-year period. This allocation of book depreciation will reduce each partner's capital account by $5,000. At the end of the two-year period, the book/basis disparity will have been eliminated because book value and tax basis will both be zero.

The disparity between the partners' outside bases and their capital accounts is also eliminated. When the partnership was formed, Elaine's outside basis and capital account were $6,000 and $10,000, respectively, and Frobisher's outside basis and capital account were $10,000. At the end of the two-year period both partners have an outside basis and capital account of $5,000, as shown below.

---

8. Treas. Reg. § 1.704–1(b)(2)(iv)(g)(3).

9. § 1016.

10. Treas. Reg. § 1.704–3(a)(3).

	Elaine		Frobisher	
	Outside Basis	Capital Account	Outside Basis	Capital Account
Initial	6,000	10,000	10,000	10,000
less	(1,000) tax depreciation	(5,000) book depreciation	(5,000) tax depreciation	(5,000) book depreciation
Ending	5,000	5,000	5,000	5,000

The result of the allocation described in Example 6–4 is sometimes explained by saying that Frobisher, having put up cash, should compute depreciation as if he had bought a 50–percent interest in the asset. Section 704(c)(1)(A) falls considerably short of doing that. If Frobisher had bought a depreciable asset for $5,000, his depreciation deductions would have been spread out over the full depreciation period for that asset under § 168. When a partner contributes depreciable property to a partnership, the partnership continues depreciating the property on the schedule the partner was using. Therefore, if an asset depreciable over five years is contributed to a partnership when two years' worth of depreciation is left, the partnership writes off the remaining basis over that two-year period. Frobisher will therefore be better off in the example than he would have been if he had bought a half-interest in an identical asset for $5,000: He will get his deductions sooner.

Under the regulations' "traditional method" of making allocations under § 704(c), the ceiling rule applies (on a year-by-year basis) to allocations of depreciation under § 704(c).[11]

Example 6–5: The facts are the same as in Example 6–4 except that the property's basis is $4,000. The partnership's tax depreciation deductions (on a straight-line basis) will be $2,000 for year one and $2,000 for year two.

Ideally, Frobisher should deduct $5,000 in tax depreciation over the asset's life, or $2,500 a year. There is only $2,000 a year to allocate, though, so Frobisher will deduct that. Were it not for the ceiling rule, Frobisher would deduct $2,500 a year, with Elaine reporting $500 a year in taxable income to make the total work out right.

Suppose that the EF partnership (Example 6–5) sells the depreciable property for $10,000 in year three. How is the $10,000 tax gain to be allocated? The gain built in when Elaine contributed the property was $6,000, so one might think that at least $6,000 of the gain on the sale

---

11. Treas. Reg. § 1.704–3(b)(2) (Example 1).

should be allocated to Elaine. The "traditional method" does not do that, however. The regulations reason that, once the asset's basis has been reduced to zero by depreciation deductions, there is no longer a disparity between book and tax figures: each is zero. Since the $10,000 book gain is shared equally, the $10,000 tax gain is allocated equally between Elaine and Frobisher under the traditional method.[12] The regulations' slavish adherence to book/tax disparities as a method of analyzing § 704(c) problems compounds the distortions created by the ceiling rule. In the example, not only is Frobisher allowed less depreciation than he would have gotten without a book/tax disparity, he is taxed on half of the gain that was built in to the property when Elaine contributed it.

2. The Traditional Method With Curative Allocations

To correct the ceiling rule's distortions of not allocating sufficient tax depreciation expenses to Frobisher in Example 6–5, the regulations allow curative allocations.

Example–6: The facts are the same as in Example 6–5, except that the partnership has other depreciable assets, not contributed by either partner. The partnership may make up for its inability to allocate tax depreciation of $2,500 a year to Frobisher by allocating to him $500 a year of depreciation on its other assets for tax purposes only.[13] This allocation will increase Elaine's taxable income by $500 a year, because the depreciation allocated to Frobisher is not allocated to her.

In some cases, using the traditional method without curative allocations (or other methods of correcting the distortions of the ceiling rule) is not allowed. The principal concern here is that the ceiling rule may, as we have seen, shift income from one partner to another. When the partners do that on purpose, by shifting income from a high-bracket to a low-bracket partner, the regulations say that the traditional method is not appropriate.

Example 6–7: Fred is in a high tax bracket; his partner, Ethel, has a net operating loss carryover and expects to pay no tax for years. Fred owns a tugboat which will be fully depreciated in one more year. The boat's basis is $10,000 and it is worth $150,000. Fred contributes the property to the EF equal partnership. To keep the partnership equal, economically, Ethel contributes $150,000 cash.

---

12. Treas. Reg. § 1.704–3(b)(2) (Example 1). The earlier regulations also used this method.

13. That is, the allocation will not be reflected in either partner's capital account. For partnership-accounting purposes, only the book depreciation will affect capital accounts.

Under the traditional method, the $10,000 depreciation deduction for year one is allocated entirely to Ethel. This does not in itself help Fred's tax position. But when the partnership sells the boat for $150,000 in year two, half of the $150,000 gain on the sale is allocated to Ethel, who pays no tax on that gain because of her NOL carryover. At least if the contribution was made "with a view to" shifting a substantial amount of taxable income from Fred to Ethel, use of the traditional method is not reasonable.[14]

According to the regulations, curative allocations will not be permitted in some circumstances. For example, when the ceiling rule limits the allocation of depreciation to the non-contributing partner, a curative allocation works by allocating income to the contributing partner or depreciation on other assets to the non-contributing partner. If the contributing partner pays tax at a lower rate than the non-contributing partner, the curative allocation shifts taxable income away from a high-bracket taxpayer.

Example 6–8: Edsel Corporation, which has a net operating loss carryover that is about to expire unused, contributes depreciable property worth $200,000 to the EFGH equal partnership, the other members of which pay tax at high rates. The property's basis is $10,000 and there is one more year of depreciation to be taken on the property, though the property will in fact last much longer than that. Book depreciation on the property is $200,000, of which $150,000 would be allocated to partners other than Edsel Corporation.

Under the traditional method, the partners other than Edsel Corporation would deduct $10,000 of depreciation and Edsel Corporation would deduct none. Edsel would, however, deduct one-fourth of the depreciation on other partnership assets (not subject to § 704(c)). A curative allocation would work by allocating $140,000 of depreciation deductions on that other property away from Edsel and to the other partners, or by allocating $140,000 of income of the kind generated by the property contributed by Edsel away from the other partners to Edsel. The combined effect of the contribution of the property, the use of the traditional § 704(c) allocation, and the curative allocation is to reduce the other partners' tax liabilities without increasing that of Edsel Corporation. If the transaction was entered into to achieve this result, use of the curative allocation will not be allowed.[15]

---

14. Treas. Reg. § 1.704–3(b)(2) (Example 2).
15. Treas. Reg. § 1.704–3(c)(4) (Example 3).

The distortion which the regulations sometimes attribute to curative allocations is one that can occur even when § 704(c) does not apply. The problem is not that the basis and the value of the contributed property differ, it is that the non-contributing partner gets depreciation deductions over the property's remaining useful life.

Example 6–9: Elmer owns a four-year-old depreciable asset having a useful life under § 168 of five years. Its basis and its value are $100,000. If Elmer sells a half interest in this asset to Frances for $50,000, Frances will recover her $50,000 outlay over the next five years. If Elmer and Frances form an equal partnership, with Elmer contributing the asset and Frances contributing $100,000 cash, Frances will recover the $50,000 which she has, in effect, used to buy a half interest in the asset, over one year. If Frances is subject to tax at a higher rate than Elmer, forming the partnership leads to a lower combined tax burden for Elmer and Frances than either a sale of a half interest in the asset or Elmer's continuing to own all of it.

The distortion illustrated by Example 6–9 was not caused by a basis/value difference in the contributed property. When it occurs in a context other than that of § 704(c), the anti-abuse regulations under § 701 may sometimes allow the Commissioner to override the usual rules. If Elmer and Frances are related and if the asset in question could have been used as effectively outside the partnership as inside, or if the partnership was formed only to accelerate Frances's depreciation deductions, the Commissioner might insist on calculating depreciation as if Frances had bought a half interest in the asset.[16]

3. The Remedial Allocation Method

The regulations also allow remedial allocations to offset ceiling-rule distortions.[17] Remedial allocations resemble curative allocations except that the income or deduction items allocated to the contributing and non-contributing partners are not actual items of partnership income or deduction: they are imaginary. If, for example, a depreciation allocation under the traditional method would give non-contributing partners $20,000 too little depreciation, a partnership using the remedial allocation method would allocate $20,000 of non-existent depreciation to those partners and, to offset that, would allocate $20,000 of non-existent income to the contributing partner. Because the regulations use a different method of calculating book depreciation when remedial alloca-

---

16. Cf. Treas. Reg. § 1.701–2(d) (Example 8) (formation of partnership by related taxpayers followed by transfer of a depreciated asset to the partnership in order to duplicate losses).

17. Treas. Reg. § 1.704–3(d).

tions are used,[18] a partnership's decision to use remedial allocations can affect the timing of depreciation deductions as well as their allocation. The example that follows, based on one in the regulations,[19] illustrates the point.

Example 6–10: Edward contributes a depreciable asset having a basis of $4,000 and a value of $10,000 to the EF equal partnership. Fiona contributes $10,000 cash. The contributed asset is depreciable on a straight-line basis over a 10–year recovery period. At the time of the contribution, the asset has four years of depreciation deductions to go ($1,000 a year). Under the usual rules for applying § 704(c) to depreciation, this asset would have book depreciation of $2,500 a year for four years.

But if the partnership chooses to use remedial allocations in connection with this asset, book depreciation is calculated in a different manner. The remedial allocation calculates book depreciation by depreciating $4,000 of the $10,000 book value over a four-year period (the remaining tax depreciation period) and depreciating the remaining $6,000 book value over a ten-year period. Thus, for each of years one through four book depreciation is $1,600, which represents the sum of $4,000 book value depreciated over a four year period ($1,000 per year) plus $6,000 book value depreciated over a ten-year period ($600 per year). In years five through ten, book depreciation is $600 a year, which is just the $6,000 book value being depreciated over a ten-year period. These figures result from an approach that makes the excess of book depreciation over tax depreciation ($6,000) recoverable as if the partnership had bought the property at the time of the contribution and had started a new 10–year depreciation period. Accordingly, only the amount of book depreciation that does not exceed tax depreciation ($4,000 in this example) is recovered over the property's four-year remaining life; the rest ($6,000) is recoverable over a ten-year period.[20]

The partnership's $1,600 book depreciation for each of years one through four is allocated equally (i.e., $800) to each partner. The partnership's $1,000 tax depreciation deduction for each of the first four years is allocated $200 to Edward and $800 to Fiona. That is, Fiona, the non-contributing partner, takes tax depreciation equal to half the $1,600 book depreciation; Edward takes the rest.[21]) In years five through ten, tax depreciation is

---

18. See Treas. Reg. § 1.704–3(d)(2).

19. Treas. Reg. § 1.704–3(d)(7) (Example 1).

20. Treas. Reg. § 1.704–3(d)(2).

21. Note that if the partnership had not chosen remedial allocations, the ceiling rule would have applied. Under the usual rule, annual book depreciation for years one through

zero (the property's $4,000 basis having been recovered by the end of year four). The $600 of book depreciation for each of years five through ten is allocated $300 to each partner. In order to give Fiona tax depreciation equal to her $300 a year of book depreciation, a remedial allocation, consisting of a $300 tax deduction for Fiona and $300 of taxable income for Edward, must be made. This is not an allocation of taxable income or depreciation that the partnership actually has: these items are imaginary, but are treated for tax purposes as real.

In the long run, Fiona will deduct $5,000 in tax depreciation (just as if the property had had a basis equal to its $10,000 value at contribution) and Edward will deduct $800 in tax depreciation and report $1,800 in taxable income. If the partnership had used curative allocations, rather that remedial allocations, the total amounts of income and deductions for each of the partners would have been the same. However, curative allocations could have given Fiona her deductions sooner, with Edward reporting his "extra" income sooner as well.

As if all this were not complex enough, the regulations contain a special anti-abuse provision for allocations under § 704(c). It provides:

> An allocation method (or combination of methods) is not reasonable if the contribution of property ... and the corresponding allocation of tax items with respect to the property are made with a view to shifting the tax consequences of built-in gain or loss among the partners in a manner that substantially reduces the present value of the partners' aggregate tax liability[22]

It is hard to find any meaning in this rule, apart from the usual vague suggestion that bad outcomes are not allowed no matter what the rest of the regulations may seem to say. In order to determine whether an allocation "substantially reduces the present value of the partners' aggregate tax liability" one must have some idea of what that aggregate tax liability would have been without the particular allocation. There is no "normal" or "baseline" system of allocations under § 704(c): all three methods (and other "reasonable" methods as well) have equal status. Therefore, the fact that an allocation under one method provides better overall results than some other method does not mean that the

---

four would have been $2,500, and the ceiling rule would have prevented allocating more than the tax depreciation of $1,000 to Frances. In this example, the choice of remedial allocations avoids triggering the ceiling rule for years one through four *by delaying much of the book depreciation to years later than year four.*

22. Treas. Reg. § 1.704–3(a)(10). If a partner is itself a flow-through entity, the regulation requires that the impact of the allocation on the partner's owners also be taken into account to determine whether aggregate tax liability has been reduced.

first method is improper.[23] How, then, can one possibly determine whether an allocation method leads to a substantially reduced tax liability: substantially reduced compared to what? This particular anti-abuse rule seems more an expression of suspicion about aggressive tax planning than a rule seriously meant to be applied by the courts and the Service.[24]

C. "REVERSE § 704(c) ALLOCATIONS" UNDER SECTION 704(b)

Section 704(c) applies only to basis/value differences existing when property is contributed to a partnership. In some cases, principles similar to those of § 704(c) should control allocations when basis/value differences arise while a partnership holds property.

Example 6-11: Golda and Henri contribute $50,000 cash apiece to the GH partnership, which buys farmland for $100,000 and rents that land to farmers. Three years later the land, now worth $200,000, still has a basis of $100,000; the land is the partnership's only asset. Isabel joins the partnership, becoming a one-third partner in exchange for contributing $100,000. Somewhat later, the partnership sells the farmland for $230,000.

The events described above have enriched Isabel by only $10,000 (one third of the increase in the value of the land since she became a partner). Her distributive share of the gain should therefore be $10,000. The first $100,000 of the gain corresponds to the amount by which the land increased in value while being held by Golda and Henri (as partners) and should be taxed to them. This situation is similar in principle to that covered by § 704(c)(1)(A), but that section does not apply because the basis/value difference when Isabel joined the partnership was not a difference "at the time of contribution"—indeed, the property was never contributed to the partnership.

The regulations under § 704(b) endorse two ways of dealing with the kind of problem illustrated by Example 6-11. The partners may write up (or down) the capital accounts of the old partners to market value when the new partner is admitted. In Example 6-11, this would

---

23. See Treas. Reg. § 1.704-3(a)(1) ("An allocation method is not necessarily unreasonable merely because another allocation method would result in a higher aggregate tax liability").

24. The general anti-abuse regulations under § 701 ask whether the present value of the partners' tax liability is substantially less than it would have been had the partners owned the assets and conducted the activity directly; Treas. Reg. § 1.701-2(c)(1). Perhaps that is what was intended here as well. If so, the particular anti-abuse rule of Treas. Reg. § 1.704-3(a)(10) merely restates the general rule in a rather cryptic fashion.

mean that Golda and Henri's capital accounts would increase from $50,000 to $100,000. In effect, Golda and Henri would be treated as though they had actually contributed the appreciation in the land to the partnership with a zero tax basis. When the property is sold, the tax gain that has already been reflected in the old partners' capital accounts (i.e., the first $100,000 of the tax gain) will be taxed to them "in accordance with section 704(c) principles."[25] As an alternative, the partnership agreement can be amended to allocate the "built in" gain to the old partners when the property is sold.[26] If this is done, the capital account write-ups will await the sale of the property.

What if the partners in Example 6-11 take neither of the approaches approved by the regulations and instead try to allocate a full one-third of the gain on the sale of the property to the new partner, Isabel, even though much of that gain represents appreciation that took place before Isabel became a partner? The regulations recognize the issue but avoid resolving it; they say that the partners "should consider" the applicability to this case of a variety of Code sections and "common-law" tax doctrines.[27] Some of those doctrines will be described in the next chapter.

D. DISTRIBUTIONS OF SECTION 704(c) PROPERTY

Section 704(c)(1)(A) requires the contributing partner to bear the tax consequences of basis/value differences whenever the partnership sells the contributed property or calculates depreciation on that property. But what if the partnership distributes contributed property to another partner? Until 1989, a distribution of contributed property to some partner other than the contributing partner would often shift tax burdens or benefits to the distributee. This happened because a partnership generally recognizes neither gain nor loss when it distributes property to a partner, and because the distributee usually takes the distributed property with the partnership's basis.[28]

> **Example 6-12:** Jack contributes stock with a basis of $40,000 and a value of $55,000 to the JKL partnership. Under § 704(c)(1)(A), Jack will be taxed on all of the gain if the partnership sells the stock for $55,000. Three years later, when the stock is worth $90,000, the partnership distributes it to

---

25. Treas. Reg. § 1.704-1(b)(5) (Example (14)).

26. Id.

27. Treas. Reg. § 1.704-1(b)(5) (Example (14)(iv)). Under the anti-abuse regulations, it would seem clearly improper to allocate any of the gain that accrued before Isabel became a partner to her.

28. See Chapter 11.

Kirsten, who takes it with a $40,000 basis and sells it for $90,000. Under pre-1989 law, the $15,000 gain that would have been taxed to Jack if the partnership had sold the stock was taxed to Kirsten (as part of the $50,000 gain she recognized when she sold the stock).

Section 704(c)(1)(B) limits the ability of partnerships to shift built-in gains and losses to someone other than the contributor. If the partnership distributes contributed property to someone other than the contributor within seven years of the contribution, gain or loss that would have been allocated to the contributor under § 704(c)(1)(A) upon a sale by the partnership is taxed to the contributor. In Example 6–12, Jack would be taxed on a $15,000 gain, as if the partnership had sold the property for $55,000. (Kirsten will now ordinarily take the stock with a basis of $55,000, so that the gain that was taxed to Jack will not be taxed to her as well; § 704(c)(1)(B)(iii).)

What if the partner who contributed property with a built-in loss has already left the partnership at the time that property is distributed? Section 704(c)(1)(C), which applied to property contributed to a partnership after October 22, 2004, eliminates the loss. The statute defines the term "built-in-loss" as "the excess of the adjusted basis of property . . . over its fair market value at the time of contribution." The statute further provides:

> (i)Such built-in-loss shall be taken into account only in determining the amount of items allocated to the contributing partner, and (ii) except as provided in regulations, in determining the amount of items allocated to other partners, the basis of the contributed property in the hands of the partnership shall be treated as being equal to its fair market value at the time of contribution.

Example 6-13: Karen contributes undeveloped land with a fair market value of $100,000 to the KLM partnership in exchange for a one-third interest in KLM. The land has a basis of $120,000 in Karen's hands. Two years later, KLM makes a distribution to Karen in complete liquidation of her interest in KLM. Subsequently, KLM sells the land for $100,000. Under § 704(c)(1)(A), KLM has no loss on the sale of the land because KLM must use the fair market value of the land on the date of the contribution ($100,000) as its basis. If KLM had sold the land for $100,000 while Karen was still a partner, KLM would have had a $20,000 loss, which it would have allocated entirely to Karen under § 704(c)(1)(A).

Ch. 6   *PROPERTY TO A PARTNER*

E. DISTRIBUTIONS OF PROPERTY TO A PARTNER WHO HAS CONTRIBUTED SECTION 704(c) ASSETS

Distributions of property by a partnership to a partner are often tax free to the partner (see Chapter 11). This rule creates an opportunity to dispose of appreciated property without recognizing gain by contributing the property to a partnership and later receiving other property from the partnership. Some transactions like this will be characterized as sales by § 707 (Chapter 4), but some will not. Section 737 deals with the problem by requiring some partners who would have recognized gains under § 704(c) if property they had contributed to the partnership had been sold to recognize gains when they receive property from their partnerships.

> **Example 6–14:** Four years ago, Irving contributed Puceacre, a tract of unimproved land, to the IJK partnership. At that time, Puceacre had a basis of $50,000 and a value of $75,000; it is now worth $200,000. The partnership distributes Roseacre, a capital asset worth $100,000, to Irving, reducing his interest in the partnership. Irving's basis for his partnership interest just before the distribution was $90,000.
>
> Under § 731, partners do not recognize gain when their partnerships distribute property to them, even if the value of the property exceeds their outside basis. In this case, however, Irving would have recognized a $25,000 gain under § 704(c)(1)(B) if the partnership had distributed Puceacre to another partner. Section 737(a) requires Irving to recognize gain equal to the lesser of (1) this $25,000 gain, or (2) the excess of the value of the property he received in the distribution over the basis of his partnership interest. Irving will therefore recognize a gain of $10,000 on the distribution. If Irving's outside basis had been only $20,000, he would have recognized a gain of $25,000 under § 737.

Section 737 covers only distributions within seven years of the contribution of § 704(c) property to the partnership, and it exempts distributions of property to the partner who contributed that property to the partnership.

Section 737 (unlike § 704(c)(1)(B)), applies to gains that would have been recognized had the partnership sold the property, but not to losses. This omission permitted the duplication of built-in losses prior to the adoption of § 704(c)(1)(C).

> **Example 6–15:** The facts are the same as in Example 6–13 except that Puceacre has a basis of $200,000 and a value of

$100,000 at all times. When Irving contributed Puceacre to the partnership, his outside basis became $200,000. Three years later, the partnership distributes property worth $100,000 (and having a basis in the partnership's hands of $100,000) to Irving, liquidating his interest. Irving takes this property with a basis of $200,000. Soon after, the partner-ship sells Puceacre to an unrelated buyer, and Irving sells the property he received for his interest in the partnership. Both Irving and the partnership recognize a $100,000 loss. Although the taxpayers in this example started out with one loss asset, having a built-in loss of $100,000, a total of $200,000 in losses has been recognized.[29]

Under § 704(c)(1)(C), the partnership now cannot recognize the loss if Irving contributed Puceacre after October 24, 2004. Section 704(c)(1)(C) treats Puceacre as having a basis equal to its fair market value at the time of its contribution to the partnership.

F. COMPARISON WITH SUBCHAPTER S

Subchapter S contains nothing corresponding to § 704(c). If an individual holding appreciated property contributes that property to an S corporation in a § 351 exchange, and if the corporation then sells the property, the gain will be taxed to all of those who owned stock in the corporation during the year in which the asset is sold. This simple but crude system will certainly encourage taxpayers to try for tax savings by channeling sales through S corporations, and courts faced with schemes that produce tax outcomes too good to be true may find ways around these simple principles.

---

29. The distortion will be corrected, in a sense, if the partners sell or liquidate their partnership interests before they die, because their losses reduce their outside bases. But this may not happen for years, or they may hold their interests until they die.

Chapter Seven

PARTNERSHIP ALLOCATIONS: ASSIGNMENT-OF-INCOME PROBLEMS

Some of the rules examined in Chapter 5 and Chapter 6 dealt with aspects of the "assignment of income." For example, the "substantiality rules" of the regulations under § 704(b) deal with cases in which partners attempt to allocate income having a particular tax character to the partners who can benefit most from that kind of income. Those rules, however, focus upon attempts to allocate tax character without affecting the amount of money the partners take out of a partnership. In some cases, particularly those involving family members, partners may be willing to allocate both income (in the tax sense) and money to someone who would not be considered the person taxable on the income under general tax principles. For example, partners might be willing to make their children partners and to allocate to those children shares of the income that would normally be taxed to the parents. Even if the allocations result in the children's getting large sums of cash, so that the allocations have "substantial economic effect," the allocations should not be (and will not be) respected.

This Chapter will address two assignment-of-income problems that have led to legislation: allocations of income to partners' relatives and allocations of deductions to persons who became partners after the economic events corresponding to the deductions had occurred. In addition, the applicability of the anti-abuse regulations under § 701 and of the assignment-of-income doctrine in the partnership context will be discussed.

A. FAMILY PARTNERSHIPS

The Code's "family partnership" provision, § 704(e), is of surprisingly little practical importance. For the most part, § 704(e) requires the same outcomes as the courts had reached before that section was adopted. Let us therefore begin by considering how attempts at using partnerships to funnel income to relatives should be treated under general tax principles.

Earned income is usually taxed to whoever earned it, whether or not the earner receives the money in question.[1] Income from property is usually taxed to the owner of that property. Thus, a parent who works at

---

[1] Lucas v. Earl, 281 U.S. 111 (1930).

a $100,000–a-year job and who owns income-producing property that generates another $100,000 a year can easily "assign" income from the property to lower-bracket children (by giving them some or all of the property) but will remain taxable on the salary even if it is paid to the children. These outcomes should not change if the parent's work consists of work done as a partner or if the income-producing property in question is partnership property. A law partner's diversion of legal fees to children or other relatives who are licensed attorneys (by making them partners and giving them unreasonably high distributive shares) should have no more effect on taxation than a similar attempt by a salaried lawyer. But a gift of an interest in a partnership that derives its income from interest, dividends, and rents on unimproved land differs very little from a gift of an interest in the partnership's assets. A gift of the assets themselves would shift taxability to the donee, so a gift of a partnership interest should also make the donee taxable so long as the donee would be entitled to receive those assets upon liquidation of the partnership.

One approach to determining whether the distributive shares of family members should be taken at face value is to ask whether those family members should be treated as being partners. To answer this it becomes necessary to distinguish between partnerships that derive income from services and from capital. Section 704(e) does not address when donees should be treated as partners in a partnership that derives its income from services. It does, however, address when a person will be treated as a partner in a partnership for which capital is a material income-producing factor.

Where capital is not a material income-producing factor, case law controls the determination of whether a taxpayer will be treated as a partner. In Commissioner v. Culbertson,[2] the Court said that the test for determining whether a taxpayer is a partner is to ask whether "the parties in good faith and acting with a business purpose intended to join together in the present conduct of the enterprise." Application of this test prevents many attempts to assign income from services to persons who have not earned it. A lawyer's children who are made partners in a law firm so that they can be taxed on some of the lawyer's income, even though they earn none of it, will not be treated as partners for tax purposes under the *Culbertson* test, even if, under state law, they are technically partners.

What if a donee receives a genuine (though small) interest in a service partnership and is then allocated a higher share of partnership income than the donee's services would justify? Section 704(e)(2) does address this problem. It provides that a donee partner's distributive

---

2. 337 U.S. 733, 742 (1949).

share is includable in the donee's income "except to the extent that such share is determined without allowance of reasonable compensation for services ... [of] the donor." This rule prevents allocating an excessively high distributive share to a donee partner who is overcompensated. A family member who purchases a partnership interest is a "donee" for purposes of this rule.[3]

Example 7–1: Tanous, Zaira, and their son, Paul, are lawyers and partners in TZP partnership. Tanous and Zaira gave Paul his interest in TZP shortly after Paul passed the bar exam. TZP earns $300,000 during the taxable year, which represents reasonable compensation of $125,000 each for work performed by Tanous and Zaira and $50,000 for work performed by Paul. Tanous and Paul would like to allocate $100,000 of TZP's income to Paul.

Under the *Culbertson* test, Paul is treated as a partner in TZP because he is participating in TZP's business. Section 704(e)(2) prevents the allocation of $100,000 to Paul, however, because that allocation would result in less than reasonable compensation being allocated to Tanous and Zaira for their services. Even if Paul had purchased his partnership interest in TZP, § 704(e)(2) would still apply because a family member who purchase a partnership interest is treated as a donee. § 704(e)(3).

If "capital is a material income-producing factor" in a partnership, section 704(e)(1) provides that a taxpayer who owns a capital interest in that partnership is to be recognized as a partner, even if the interest was acquired by gift. This statutory rule rejects the holding of some earlier court decisions that suggested that donees could not be partners unless they contributed their own capital.[4] But statutory recognition of the

---

3. § 704(e)(3).

4. Section 704(e)(1), however, adds little, if anything, to the law. Under the earlier law, the Supreme Court had held in Commissioner v. Culbertson, 337 U.S. 733 (1949), that a donee who was really a partner would be treated as a partner for tax purposes, and § 704(e)(1) says no more than that. Congress enacted § 704(e)(1) in 1951 because some courts had held that family members would be recognized as partners only if they had contributed "vital services" or "original capital" (i.e., capital of their own, as opposed to capital acquired from the donor). The "original capital" doctrine would have prevented donees from being partners, even if their interests were in partnerships having only income from property, a result inconsistent with assignment-of-income notions. The Supreme Court's 1949 *Culbertson* decision had rejected the "original capital" doctrine even before § 704(e)(1) was adopted. Section 704(e)(1) is more an endorsement of the *Culbertson* outcome than a provision with any real effect on the law. Today's cases often discuss the question whether capital is a "material income-producing factor" under § 704(e)(1), but a careful reading of the opinions suggests that nothing turns on the answer to this question. The distributive share of a donee who is a genuine partner will be taxed to the donee (except to the extent attributable to the donor's services), whether or not capital is a material income-producing factor. The distributive share of a donee who is not a genuine partner will not be taxed to the donee, even if capital is a material income-producing factor.

donee as a partner in a capital partnership does not mean that additional income can be shifted to the donee. Section 704(e)(2) provides that the donee's share of income cannot be proportionately greater than the donor's share of income attributable to the donor's capital. The partner's respective interests in capital are determined by asking what each partner would receive upon liquidation of the partnership.

Example 7-2: Uri and Victoria are equal partners in the UV partnership, in which capital is a material-income producing factor. Uri received his interest as a gift from Victoria. Uri's capital account is $50 and Victoria's is $100. Both capital accounts were recently booked up to reflect the fair market value of UV's assets, and UV's partnership agreement provides that liquidating distributions are to be made in accordance with capital accounts. Under § 704(e)(2), the partnership cannot allocate more than one-third of income from the partnership's assets to Uri.

Suppose in Example 7-2 that Uri is Victoria's son and that Uri had purchased his interest from Victoria instead of receiving it as a gift. The result would be the same. A family member who purchases an interest is treated as a "donee" for purposes of this rule.[5]

B. LAST–MINUTE PARTNERS: SECTION 706(d)

A problem that raised some Congressional concern during the 1970's was this: A tax-shelter partnership, which was certain to have large losses because of nonrecourse deductions, would transfer interests to investors late in the year (the last week of December, for example). The partnership agreement would allocate a share of the full year's losses to these last-minute investors. Because a partner ordinarily reports partnership income and deductions for the partnership year ending "within or with" the partner's taxable year,[6] the investor would deduct all of these losses, even though the investor was a partner for only a tiny fraction of the period during which the losses were generated. In substance, a high-bracket taxpayer could buy a whole year's worth of deductions in December.

Whether buying tax-shelter deductions at the last minute is a more serious social problem than buying tax-shelter deductions early in the year may be debatable, but it certainly looks bad. Congress's response was § 706(d). This provision, while highly technical in some respects, is simple in principle: It requires that each partner's distributive share of partnership items take into account the partner's varying interest in the

---

5. § 704(e)(3).
6. § 706(a).

partnership during the partnership's taxable year. In general, this is accomplished by the interim closing-of-books method or the proration method.[7] Under the interim-closing-of book method, the partnership closes its books on the date of the ownership change. Income and losses occurring before that date are allocated based on each partner's old share in the partnership. Items occurring after that date are allocated based on the new ownership interest. Under the proration method, the partnership waits until the end of the year and then allocates all its total income and expenses on a pro rata basis among partners based on their varying interests in the partnership throughout the year. A special rule in § 706(d)(2) prevents a partnership that uses the cash method of accounting from using the interim closing-of-book method and postponing the payment of its expenses until after the last-minute partner arrives. The rule requires the partnership to prorate such expenses over the entire year.[8] The result is that the last-minute partner can only deduct an amount of the expense that is proportional to the portion of the year that the last-minute partner was a partner.

C. ASSIGNMENTS OF INCOME NOT DEALT WITH BY SPECIFIC CODE PROVISIONS: THE ANTI-ABUSE REGULATIONS

All attempts to allocate partnership income raise questions of who is to be taxed. A little-noted provision of the regulations under § 704(b) provides that determinations of distributive shares under the many specific and extremely detailed provisions of those regulations are "not conclusive as to the tax treatment of a partner."[9] Allocations that pass the tests of the § 704(b) regulations may be invalid under other Code sections (such as the family-partnership provisions or § 706(d)), or they may fail under "related assignment of income principles."[10] In addition, the anti-abuse regulations under § 701 prohibit use of the partnership provisions to achieve favorable tax results that are "inconsistent with the intent of subchapter K,"[11] even if the transaction is "within the

---

7. The regulations say that when a partner sells his entire partnership interest, the partnership year closes for that partner and the partner's share of partnership income and loss can be determined by using the interim-closing-of-books method or proration method. Treas. Reg. § 1.706–1(c)(2). The regulations are silent as to the method to be used where the partner does not sell his entire interest but the partner's interest in the partnership changes. The legislative history for § 706(d), says that the interim closing of or proration method may be used. S. Rep. No. 938, 94th Cong., 2d Sess. 98 (1976).

8. § 706(d)(2).

9. Treas. Reg. § 1.704–1(b)(1)(iii).

10. Id.

11. Treas. Reg. § 1.701–2(b).

literal words of a particular statutory or regulatory provision."[12] These provisions seem to make the bulk of the § 704(b) regulations potentially irrelevant. All allocation questions are questions of who is to be taxed, and therefore of assignments of income. Allocations which give income or deductions to the wrong partner are "inconsistent with the underlying economic arrangements of the parties." In practice, therefore, an application of the substantial-economic-effect rules that seems to result in the wrong person's being taxed may be disregarded under the assignment-of-income doctrine or the anti-abuse regulations. Some allocations are, however, allowed even if they produce undesirable results, on the ground that those results were "clearly contemplated" by the provision in question.[13] In short, improper allocations allowed by the regulations under 704(b) will be disallowed under the anti-abuse regulations unless those improper results were "clearly contemplated."[14]

Example 7–3: The AB partnership has, until now, been an equal partnership. The partnership needs a new warehouse, which will cost $500,000, for its business. Archie's taxable income is high; Bob's is low. The partnership buys the warehouse and allocates depreciation deductions entirely to Archie. Gain attributable to depreciation on the warehouse will be charged back to Archie when the warehouse is sold.

In practical terms, Bob and Archie have nearly equal interests in the warehouse. Chances are that Archie's special allocation of depreciation will be made up for by a chargeback of gain when the warehouse is sold. The money used to buy the warehouse came from partnership profits, earned by and taxed to Bob and Archie equally. Furthermore, Bob and Archie will share equally in whatever increase in profits the partnership makes because it has the warehouse. Archie does bear the risk, however small, that the warehouse will decline in value. (It is Archie's assumption of this risk that makes Bob willing to give up his share of depreciation.)

Can the Service successfully challenge the allocation of depreciation in Example 7–3? Probably not. The example comes directly from the regulations under § 704,[15] though that is not in itself determinative. But

---

12. Id.

13. Treas. Reg. § 1.701–2(a)(3).

14. The trick is to figure out how to tell the difference between an allocation just allowed by the "literal words" of the § 704(b) regulations and an allocation "clearly contemplated" by the words of those regulations. Factors to be considered are listed in Treas. Reg. 1.701–2(c). Cases in which all partners affected by an allocation are related and cases in which an allocation gives income to partners who are not subject to income taxation because they are foreigners or tax-exempt entities may be particularly susceptible to attack under the anti-abuse regulations.

15. Treas. Reg. § 1.704–1(b)(5) (Example (1)(xi)).

a somewhat-similar example in the anti-abuse regulations describes the assumption that basis will equal value as a "safe harbor" and concludes that the kind of distortion present in this example was "clearly contemplated" by the regulations under § 704(b).[16]

The anti-abuse regulations' only example of an allocation that meets the requirements of the § 704(b) regulations but is "abusive" involves a stripping transaction, in which income from property is allocated to a foreign partner not subject to U.S. taxation, while deductions attributable to the property are taken by U.S. partners.[17] The partnership in the example buys equipment and leases it for a substantial period. The partnership then sells its right to receive rentals under the lease, and allocates all the income from that sale to the foreign partner, whose interest is then liquidated. The partnership then buys other property subject to debt; this transaction increases the outside bases of the U.S. partners. Finally, the partnership sells the leased equipment (for a low price, since most of the equipment's income stream has already been sold), recognizing a loss. The example concludes that the partnership is not bona fide, that the transactions cannot be respected under substance-over-form principles, and that the income of the U.S. partners is not clearly reflected.

Why are the transactions in the regulations' example less worthy of respect than those in Example 7–3? In both cases, the application of the § 704(b) regulations leads to a division of income and deductions from the same property that could not have been obtained without using a partnership; in that sense, both transactions are "abusive."[18] "Factors" that may have led the drafters to conclude that only the stripping transaction is invalid seem to include the fact that the foreign partner in the example was a partner for only a short time[19] and the fact that the arrangement shifted income to a person not subject to U.S. taxation.[20] Perhaps, if the stripping transaction had assigned the income to a long-term partner, who had other interests in the partnership's business, or if it had assigned the income to a low-bracket but not completely nontaxa-

---

16. Treas. Reg. § 1.701–2(d) (Example 6).

17. Treas. Reg. § 1.701–2(d) (Example 7).

18. In each case, the abuse consists of allocating deductions to a taxpayer who can use them to get a tax benefit, while income is taxed to someone else. Taxpayers who are not partners cannot divide income and deductions from property in this way.

19. See Treas. Reg. §§ 1.701–2(c)(2) (partner whose participation was needed to get the result would be a partner only temporarily); 1.701–2(c)(3) (foreign partner faced little risk of loss and participated in partnership gains only by getting a return on capital).

20. Treas. Reg. § 1.701–2(c)(5). The regulations' example lists as another relevant factor the fact that the present value of the partner's aggregate federal tax liability is substantially less than if they had owned the property directly; Treas. Reg. § 1.701–2(d) (Example 7), referring to Treas. Reg. § 1.701–2(c)(1). This "factor" is useless in determining whether a favorable result was "clearly contemplated" by the rules of subchapter K, as it merely shows that the result in question was favorable.

ble partner, the result would have differed. Or maybe stripping transactions just look worse than special allocations of depreciation.

Another example from the § 704(b) regulations seems to violate assignment of income principles. In the example, two partners operate a travel agency. One of them, T, works in a foreign country; the other works in the United States. T is not subject to U.S. taxation on his share of income arising from operations in the foreign country. The partnership agreement provides that all gains and losses will be shared equally. This sharing is reflected in the partners' capital accounts, which are maintained according to the substantial economic effect rules. According to the example, each partner is taxed on half the income from the partnership's foreign operations and half the income from its U.S. operations, even if the partnership agreement purports to allocate foreign income to T up to the amount of T's fifty-percent share of total partnership income.[21] The example says that the allocation of foreign income up to the amount of this 50 percent share lacks substantiality because there is a strong likelihood that the capital accounts will be the same as they would have been without the special allocation (i.e., each partner is allocated 50 percent of income) and the tax liability of the partners is reduced.

If the foreign and domestic operations of the partnership in the regulations' example are conducted largely independently, viewing T as earning most or all of the partnership's foreign-source income seems not only desirable but required by the assignment-of-income principle, as T's services earn most of the foreign-source income. Perhaps the § 704(b) regulations have concluded that the substantiality rules of § 704(b) should trump the assignment of income doctrine where the taxpayer will not be allocated all the income he earned in the foreign country. Here, the fact that T's income from the foreign country was capped at fifty percent of the partnership's total income meant that T would not be allocated income from the foreign country in excess of fifty percent of the partnership's income. The problem is that the § 704(b) regulations rely on mechanical tests having little to do with the assignment-of-income doctrine. Those regulations therefore encourage allocations designed to reduce taxes. The § 701 regulations and the brief reference in the § 704(b) regulations to the assignment-of-income doctrine seek to tax partners according to the economic reality of their ventures. The regulations as a whole endorse two inconsistent goals: mechanical bright-line rules and taxation based on all the circumstances of particular transactions. Rather than rewrite the § 704(b) regulations to align them with fundamental tax principles (at the cost of losing the appearance of certainty which is the goal of mechanical rules), the Government's

---

21. Treas. Reg. § 1.704–1(b)(5) (Example(10)(ii)).

current approach is to keep the § 704(b) rules in place, while providing that those rules will not control in some (largely unspecified) cases.

D. COMPARISON WITH SUBCHAPTER S

Section 1366(e) resembles the family-partnership provisions. Moreover, § 1377(a)(1) applies the proration method to allocate the S corporation's income and expenses among stockholders where stock ownership changes during the year. Section 1377(a)(2) allows the S corporation to elect to use the interim-closing-of books method when a stockholder terminates her interest. There is no anti-abuse rule comparable to § 706(d)(2), however.

Chapter Eight
ALLOCATION OF PARTNERSHIP DEBT
A. INTRODUCTION

As discussed in Chapter 3, partners include their shares of partnership debt in their outside bases because § 752(a) treats increases in partners' shares of partnership debt as cash contributions to their partnerships. This rule matters to partners because § 704(d) limits a partner's deductions to the amount of that partner's outside basis.[1] In addition, cash distributions to a partner do not result in gain recognition except to the extent such distributions exceed the partner's outside basis.[2]

This Chapter discusses the rules that determine each partner's share of partnership debt under the § 752 regulations. The threshold issue is whether the partnership's debt is the type of liability that the regulations permit to be included in the partner's outside basis. After that issue is resolved, it is next necessary to classify the debt as recourse or nonrecourse. The regulations contain very different rules for allocating debt depending on whether it is recourse or nonrecourse.

B. WHAT IS A PARTNERSHIP LIABILITY UNDER § 752?

Prior to 2005 amendments, the § 752 regulations provided little guidance on the question of the type of partnership debt that would qualify as a "liability" for purposes of § 752. The current regulations[3], however, provide that an obligation will qualify as a "liability" for purposes of § 752 only if (1) it creates or increases the partnership's basis in its assets (including cash), (2) it results in an immediate deduction when incurred, or (3) it is attributable to an expenditure that is not deductible and does not qualify as a capital expenditure.[4] This approach comes from Rev. Rul. 88–77,[5] which notes that under this approach an obligation that will result in a deduction when paid (rather than when incurred) will not qualify as a "liability" for § 752 purposes.

---

1. See page 19, above.
2. See page 17, above.
3. Treas. Reg. §§ 1.752–1(a)(4), 1.752–6 and 1.752–7.
4. Treas. Reg. § 1.752–1(a)(4)(i).
5. 1988–2 C.B. 128.

Ch. 8   RECOURSE & NONRECOURSE DEBT

The need for this treatment stems mainly from problems that occur in transferring accounts payable of a cash-method taxpayer to a partnership, a matter that will be examined below in Section F.

Example 8–1: The YZ partnership employs the cash method of accounting and incurs the following obligations:

1. It borrows $10,000 cash from a bank.
2. It purchases a used truck, giving the seller a note for $4,000, and taking the truck with a $4,000 tax basis.
3. It promises to contribute $5,000 to a political candidate. Political contributions are not deductible.
4. It owes an employee $800 for services performed last week.

Obligations 1 and 2 qualify as "liabilities" to be allocated to partners under § 752. The partnership obtained a tax basis in cash and in the truck as a result of the loans.

Obligation 3 also qualifies as a "liability" for purposes of § 752 because it is a nondeductible expenditure that is not a capital expenditure.

Obligation 4 does not qualify as a liability because it did not result in a deduction when incurred but instead will be deductible when paid.

Suppose that YZ uses the accrual method of accounting instead of the cash method. In that situation, Obligation 4 *would* qualify as a "liability" because the incurrence of the obligation to pay the salary results in an immediately deductible expenditure.

C. THE DEFINITION OF RECOURSE AND NONRECOURSE DEBT

1. Introduction

Because the § 752 regulations adopt different rules for allocating partnership liabilities based on the debt's character, it is important to determine whether the debt is recourse or nonrecourse. Before focusing on the approach of the § 752 regulations, it is helpful to survey the general landscape for nonrecourse and recourse debt. In general, nonrecourse debt is debt for which the lender's only remedy upon default is to foreclose on the property that secures the debt. If the value of the property securing the debt is too low, the lender cannot seek to recover the difference from the borrower. In contrast, if the debt is recourse debt, the lender can look to all the assets of the borrower for payment. Recourse debt may or may not be secured by collateral. But regardless of whether it is, the lender can use all remedies permitted by law, such as garnishment of the borrower's wages or taking other assets of the borrower, to obtain payment.

A partner may be held personally responsible for recourse debt of the partnership either by operation of law or by agreement. If a creditor makes a recourse loan to a general partnership, all the partners will be held personally liable for the loan by operation of law.[6] If a lender makes a recourse loan to a limited partnership, only the general partners are personally liable for the loan. The limited partners are shielded from liability unless they agree to become liable. Members of an LLC are also not personally liable for recourse loans to their LLCs unless they agree to be.

2. Economic Risk of Loss and Constructive Liquidation

The § 752 regulations focus on the personal liability of partners for partnership debt in determining whether the debt is recourse or nonrecourse. Debt is recourse for purposes of § 752 if a partner (or person related to a partner) bears the economic risk of loss with respect to that debt.[7] If no partner or related person bears the risk of loss, the § 752 regulations classify the debt as nonrecourse. To determine whether a partner or related person bears the risk of loss, the § 752 regulations assume a doomsday scenario in which the partnership assets become worthless and the partnership liquidates. Those partners who would be required to pay the partnership's creditors directly or make a contribution to the partnership that would be used to pay the partnership's creditors are deemed to bear the economic risk of loss for the liability.

The constructive-liquidation method for determining whether a partner bears the economic risk for a partnership liability method uses the capital account approach discussed in Chapter 5. Specifically, the regulations say that the following is deemed to occur in the doomsday scenario:

1. All partnership liabilities become fully payable;
2. All partnership assets, including cash, become worthless;
3. The partnership transfers all its assets in a fully taxable transaction for no consideration other than relief from nonrecourse debt secured by the property;

---

6. Uniform Partnership Act § 15 (1914); Revised Uniform Partnership Act § 306 (1997).

7. Treas. Reg. § 1.752–1(a)(1).

4. All items of partnership gain and loss are allocated to the partners' capital accounts;
5. The partnership liquidates; and
6. The loan becomes due and payable.[8]

If, in the constructive liquidation, a partner would be obligated to pay a creditor or make a payment to the partnership (such as restoring a capital account deficit) that would be used to pay a creditor, the partner is deemed to bear the risk of loss for the liability and the loan is treated as a recourse liability.[9]

Example 8–2: Judy and Kate are equal partners in the JK partnership, which is a general partnership. Each contributes $50 cash to the partnership. The partnership borrows $200 cash and purchases an asset for $300. The loan to the partnership is recourse so that the lender is not limited to a particular asset for repayment. The partnership agreement requires the partnership to maintain capital accounts in accordance with the regulations and to liquidate in accordance with capital accounts. In addition, each partner is required to restore any deficit in that partner's capital account.

The loan is a liability for purposes of § 752 since the partnership obtained a basis in an asset with the borrowed proceeds. To determine whether it is a recourse loan, we engage in a constructive liquidation. We assume that the partnership's asset, which has a book value of $300, becomes worthless. The partnership then transfers it for zero consideration, generating a $300 loss which is allocated equally to each partner. As a result of the allocation, each partner's capital account is reduced to negative $100 (initial capital account of $50 minus $150 loss). The partnership still owes $200 to the creditor, which is entitled to seek payment from any asset of the partnership. Each partner is required to restore a $100 deficit in her capital account and the $100 paid by each partner to the partnership will be used to pay the creditor. Thus, the § 752 regulations classify the liability as recourse.

Note that the result in Example 8–2 would be the same even if the partners do not have a deficit restoration obligation. Under the Uniform Partnership Act and the Revised Uniform Partnership Act, partners in a general partnership are personally liable for the recourse debts of the partnership. Since the partners would still be obligated to pay the creditor, the loan would be treated as a recourse liability for purposes of

---

8. Treas. Reg. § 1.752–2(b)(1)(i)–(v).

9. Treas. Reg. § 1.752–1(a)(1).

§ 752. Similarly, if a lender makes a recourse loan to a limited partnership, the loan will be "recourse" for purposes of § 752 because the general partners in a limited partnership are personally liable for the loan by operation of law, regardless of whether they have agreed to restore deficits in their capital accounts.

The focus of the regulations on whether a partner bears the economic burden of partnership debt means that loans to an LLC will be classified as nonrecourse even if the lender can look to all the assets of the LLC to force repayment. Since no LLC member can be compelled to pay the creditor directly or to make a contribution to the LLC that will in turn be used to pay a creditor, no member bears the economic burden for the debt. A loan to an LLC will only be classified as recourse under the § 752 regulations if a member agrees to be personally liable for the loan.

D. ALLOCATION OF RECOURSE LIABILITY

1. In General

Once debt is determined to be a recourse liability, it is allocated among partners based upon the extent to which they are deemed to bear the economic burden of the liability in the constructive liquidation.[10] In determining who bears the burden, all arrangements among the partners, such as guarantees and indemnifications, are considered.[11] The regulations assume that all partners will fulfill their obligations, regardless of their net worth, unless the facts and circumstances indicate a plan to circumvent or avoid the obligation.[12]

In Example 8–2, above, each partner was obligated in the constructive liquidation to contribute $100 to the partnership, which would then be paid to the creditor. Because it is assumed that partners will satisfy their contribution obligations, each partner in Example 8–2 is deemed to bear $100 of the economic burden of the loan. Accordingly, each partner would include $100 of the debt in her outside basis.

Although each partner in Example 8–2 included one-half of the partnership recourse liability in her outside basis, it cannot always be assumed that equal partners in a general partnership will share recourse debts equally. Because the constructive liquidation approach looks to capital accounts to determine how much each partner will contribute in the doomsday scenario, equal partners who have different capital account balances will be allocated different amounts of debt.

---

10. Treas. Reg. § 1.752–2(a).
11. Treas. Reg. § 1.752–2(b)(3).
12. Treas. Reg. § 1.752–2(b)(6).

Example 8–3: Laura contributes $100 and Mike contributes $50 to the LM general partnership. Laura and Mike will share all gains and losses equally. The partnership also borrows $200 cash. The lender can look to all assets of the partnership for payment. The partnership agreement requires the partnership to maintain capital accounts in accordance with the § 704 regulations and to liquidate in accordance with capital accounts. In addition, the partnership agreement requires each partner to restore capital-account deficits upon liquidation.

To determine how the partners will share the partnership's debt, which qualifies as a "liability" because the partnership obtained a tax basis in cash as a result of incurring the obligation, we engage in the constructive liquidation. In the doomsday scenario, all partnership assets ($350 cash) become worthless and are transferred for zero consideration. The $350 loss is then allocated to the partners. Laura's capital account becomes negative $75 ($100 initial capital account minus $175 loss). Mike's capital account becomes negative $125 ($50 initial capital account less $175 loss).

As a result, Laura is required to contribute $75 and Mike $125 to the partnership. These contributions will be paid to the creditor, who is entitled to obtain payment from all partnership assets. Laura will therefore include $75 of the partnership liability in her outside basis; Mike will include $125 of the partnership liability in his outside basis.

As Example 8–3 demonstrates, it is not clear that the constructive litigation approach adopted by the regulations makes sense.[13] Despite their repeated use of the phrase "economic risk of loss," the regulations do not really allocate debt in accordance with risk. As Stephen G. Utz has pointed out, "the regulations evince no serious interest in the reality of economic risk of loss": instead, they allocate liabilities according to "ultimate legal responsibility for a loss."[14] Most debts are paid out of partnership receipts in the ordinary course of a partnership's operations or the partnership's assets. Since Laura and Mike are equal partners in Example 8–3, they share equally the burden of making routine payments of principal and interest on the debt if partnership operations proceed normally. In addition, Laura arguably has more at risk than Mike,

---

13. See Richard A. Epstein, The Application of the *Crane* Doctrine to Limited Partnerships, 45 So. Cal.L. Rev. 100 (1972); Glenn E. Coven, Limiting Losses Attributable to Nonrecourse Debt: A Defense of the Traditional System Against the At–Risk Concept, 74 Cal. L. Rev. 41 (1986).

14. Stephen G. Utz, A Comment on Disproportionate Loss Allocations and Other Matters, 49 Tax Notes 1025, 1029 (1990). See also Stephen G. Utz, Partnership Taxation in Transition: Of Form, Substance, and Economic Risk, 43 The Tax Lawyer 693 (1990).

because she contributed more capital. Mike's obligation to contribute additional capital is triggered only if the capital already held by the partnership becomes worthless. The chance that all the partnership's assets (including cash) will become worthless is remote.[15] By requiring a calculation based on all assets of the partnership becoming worthless, the regulations introduce unnecessary complexity.

2. Effect of Guarantees and Indemnifications of Recourse Debt

Since the § 752 regulations take into account all arrangements among partners in determining who will bear the risk of loss, indemnifications and guarantees can change the allocation of recourse partnership liabilities.

Example 8–4: Belinda and Carlos form the BC general partnership as equal partners. Each contributes $100 cash. The partnership agreement requires the partnership to maintain capital accounts in accordance with the § 704 regulations and to liquidate in accordance with capital accounts. In addition, all partners are required to restore capital account deficits. Belinda agrees to indemnify Carlos for any payments that Carlos will have to make directly or indirectly to a creditor. The partnership borrows $300 from a lender. Pursuant to the loan agreement, the lender can look to all the partnership's assets. The partnership uses the $200 contributed by the partners and the borrowed $300 to purchase a building for $500.

In a constructive liquidation, the partnership will transfer the building, which has a book value of $500, for zero consideration. Thus, each partner would be allocated a $250 loss. Although this results in each partner's having a negative $150 capital account balance, all the debt will be allocated to Belinda and included in her outside basis. Since Belinda indemnifies Carlos for the $150 contribution he makes, she, not Carlos, bears the ultimate burden for the entire $300 loan. Thus, Belinda includes the entire $300 loan in her outside basis.

One might think that the same result would occur in Example 8–4 if Belinda had guaranteed the partnership's recourse debt instead of agree-

---

15. What, for instance, could cause nearly all of a partnership's assets, including cash, to become worthless, while leaving the partners' individual assets intact? Death rays from Mars, perhaps. See Joseph A. Snoe, Economic Reality or Regulatory Game Playing?: The Too Many Fictions of the § 752 Liability Allocation Regulations, 24 Seton Hall L. Rev. 1887 (1994), rejecting the label "atom bomb rule" at p. 1899, n. 62: "Dare we imagine a world where an atomic bomb destroys all assets except the partners' personal assets not held in the partnership, and kills all people except for partners, their creditors, and the Internal Revenue Service?"

ing to indemnify Carlos. As a guarantor, Belinda would have to pay the lender in the event the partnership failed to make payment. However, as illustrated in Example 8–5 below, the result is quite different because the regulations' assumption that all partners fulfill their obligations means that the need for the guaranty will never arise.

Example 8–5: Assume the same facts as in Example 8–4 except that Belinda guarantees the loan rather than agreeing to indemnify Carlos. Pursuant to the guaranty, Belinda will have to pay the loan if the partnership fails to pay.

As in Example 8–4, the constructive liquidation results in each partner having a negative capital account of $150, which they have to restore. Because the regulations assume that Belinda and Carlos will fulfill their obligations and contribute $300, which will be used to pay the loan, Belinda will never have to make good on the guaranty.[16] As a result, the loan is allocated equally between the two partners.

3. Contributions of Property Encumbered by Recourse Debt

The rules for allocating recourse debt can often result in an unpleasant surprise for a partner contributing property encumbered by recourse debt. As shown in Example 8–6 below, there is a significant risk of income recognition when a partner contributes property encumbered by recourse debt and the partnership assumes the debt.

Example 8–6: Otto and Penelope form the OP equal partnership. Otto is contributing property in which his tax basis is $200 and which is encumbered by $500 of recourse debt. The property has a fair market value of $800. Penelope contributes $300 cash. The partnership assumes Otto's liability for the $500 recourse debt.

As a result of the contributions, each partner will have an initial capital account balance of $300 (the net fair market value of the assets contributed by each). Under the constructive-liquidation method, the $500 recourse debt will be allocated equally to Otto and Penelope. This means that Otto's share of the debt will have decreased from $500 (his liability for the debt before his contribution) to $250. Section 752(b) says that a decrease in liabilities is treated as a cash distribution. Before taking into account this constructive cash distribution, Otto's outside basis under § 722 was $200 (the tax basis of the property he contributed). The deemed cash distribution of $250

---

16. Treas. Reg. § 1.752–2(f) (Example 3).

reduces his basis to zero (§ 705(a)(2)) and causes him to recognize $50 of gain (§ 731(a)(1)).

E. ALLOCATION OF NONRECOURSE LIABILITY

Because no partner is personally liable for nonrecourse debt, that kind of debt cannot be allocated based on who bears the economic burden. As a result, the § 752 regulations adopt a different approach that uses multiple tiers to allocate the debt. The regulations provide that a partner's share of partnership nonrecourse liabilities equals the sum of:

1. the partner's share of partnership minimum gain;
2. the partner's share of any taxable gain that would be allocated to the partner under § 704(c) if the partnership disposed of property that is encumbered by nonrecourse debt (i.e. "§ 704(c) minimum gain"); and
3. the partner's share of "excess nonrecourse liabilities." (i.e. the nonrecourse liabilities not allocated under 1 and 2 above).[17]

1. The First Tier of Nonrecourse Debt Allocation

a. *Sufficient Basis for Nonrecourse Deductions*

The regulations' multi-tiered approach, although complex, is surprisingly taxpayer friendly. Recall that a partner's share of minimum gain equals the amount of nonrecourse deductions allocated to that partner.[18] The first-tier allocation, which allocates an amount of nonrecourse debt to a partner equal to the partner's share of partnership minimum gain, in effect ensures that all partners will have sufficient basis for their nonrecourse deductions.

Example 8–7: Qiu and Rick form the QR partnership, but contribute no capital to the partnership. They agree that all income and expenses will be shared equally except that all depreciation expenses will be allocated to Qiu.

The partnership purchases a depreciable asset for $100, giving the seller a $100 nonrecourse note for which no principal will be due for two years. The partnership takes a $100 tax and book basis in the asset and allocates the first year's depreciation (which we will assume unrealistically to be $100) to Qiu.

---
17. Treas. Reg. § 1.752–3(a).
18. See page 65, above.

At the end of the first year, the partnership has $100 of partnership minimum gain because the partnership's nonrecourse debt exceeds its basis of zero in the asset by $100. Qiu's share of the partnership minimum gain is $100 because all the depreciation expenses (i.e., nonrecourse deductions) were allocated to her.[19]

Pursuant to the first tier allocation, all $100 of the nonrecourse debt is allocated to Qiu at the end of the partnership's first taxable year. This means that Qiu will have an outside basis of $100. That basis will enable her to deduct the $100 depreciation expense allocated to her during the partnership's taxable year.

b. Refinancing

The first tier allocation permits a partnership to borrow on a nonrecourse basis and distribute the proceeds tax-free to its partners. This is a major benefit because it allows partners to benefit from the appreciation in partnership assets without recognizing taxable gain.

Example 8–8: Helen and Ignatius are partners in the HI partnership. Both have an outside basis of zero in their partnership interests. The partnership has real estate with a fair market value of $1 million and a tax basis of zero.

The partnership borrows $1 million on a nonrecourse basis, using the real estate as collateral, and distributes $500,000 to Helen and $500,000 to Ignatius.

Although both partners had a zero tax basis in their partnership interests prior to the partnership's borrowing, neither recognizes gain on the distribution. The reason is that a partner's share of partnership minimum gain includes the amount of proceeds from nonrecourse debt that is distributed to the partner where the debt resulted in an increase in partnership minimum gain. (Treas. Reg. § 1.704-2(g)(1)(i).) The partnership minimum gain increased from zero to $1 million when the partnership incurred the nonrecourse debt and the proceeds were distributed to the partners equally. Thus, each partner's share of partnership minimum gain is $500,000. Pursuant to the first tier allocation of partnership debt, each partner includes $500,000 of the debt in that partner's outside basis. The distribution then reduces each partner's outside basis to zero, but since the distribution does not exceed their outside basis, Helen and Ignatius do not recognize any gain.

---

19. See page 65, above.

2. The Second Tier of Nonrecourse Debt Allocation

a. *No Gain Recognized When Contributing Property Encumbered by Nonrecourse Debt*

The second tier allocation, which allocates an amount of nonrecourse debt equal to § 704(c) minimum gain, is also quite taxpayer friendly. It prevents a partner from recognizing gain upon contributing property encumbered by nonrecourse debt. This stands in stark contrast to the gain frequently recognized by a partner contributing property encumbered by recourse debt, as illustrated in Example 8–6, above.

Example 8–9: Tina contributes property in which she has $100 of basis and which is encumbered by $300 of nonrecourse debt to a new partnership she is forming with Uday.

Since the partnership is newly formed, there is no partnership minimum gain and, therefore, the first tier for allocating nonrecourse debt will not apply. Pursuant to the second tier, Tina is allocated $200 of the nonrecourse debt, which is the § 704(c) minimum gain (the amount of gain that would be allocated to her under § 704(c) if the partnership disposed of the property encumbered by the debt). This allocation of debt insures that she will not recognize gain on the contribution. Even if she is allocated zero debt in the third tier of the allocations, her allocation of $200 of the debt under tier two will mean that she has experienced a reduction in debt of only $100 (her $300 initial debt minus $200 allocated share). This reduction, which is treated as a cash distribution under § 752(b), would reduce her outside basis from the initial amount of $100 (§ 722) to zero, but would not result in gain recognition.

3. The Third Tier of Nonrecourse Debt Allocation

The third tier allocates any remaining nonrecourse liabilities not accounted for in tiers one and two. The regulations permit significant flexibility in making the third tier allocation. The remaining liabilities may be allocated in accordance with the partners' share of partnership profits or a significant item of partnership profits.[20] Alternatively, the remaining liabilities may be allocated in the same manner as the deductions attributable to the nonrecourse debt, such as depreciation expenses.[21]

---

20. Treas. Reg. § 1.752–3(a)(3).

21. Id. The regulations also permit the remaining debt to be allocated to a partner to the extent of gain that would be allocable to that partner under § 704(c) that was not accounted for in the second tier allocation of § 704(c) minimum gain.

Ch. 8 NONRECOURSE LIABILITY

Example 8–10: Dixon and Ellen are equal partners in the DE partnership, except that all depreciation expenses are allocated to Ellen.

The partnership borrows $900 on a nonrecourse basis and purchases a depreciable asset for $1,000, giving the lender a security interest in the asset. No principal is payable on the debt for five years. The asset will generate $100 of depreciation expense per year.

In Year One, tiers one and two of the nonrecourse-debt allocation rules will not apply. Tier one does not apply because there is no partnership minimum gain at the end of year one since the amount of nonrecourse debt ($900) just equal's the partnership basis ($900). Tier two does not apply because the property's book value equals its tax basis.

Thus, all the debt is allocated according to tier three at the end of year one. The partnership can allocate the debt equally to the partners since they share profits equally. This would result in each partner's including $450 of the debt in outside basis. Alternatively, the partnership can allocate all the debt to Ellen since Ellen will be allocated all the depreciation expenses attributable to the debt.

The partnership should be advised that if it allocates the debt equally at the end of Year One, it will have to recalculate the way in which that debt is shared in subsequent years. This is illustrated in Example 8–11.

Example 8–11: The facts are the same as in Example 8–10. The partnership elects at the end of Year One to allocate the excess nonrecourse debt under tier three equally to the partners in the same manner that they share partnership profits.

At the end of Year Two, the partnership once again allocates its liabilities between Dixon and Ellen. Tier one of the allocations applies at the end of Year Two because the partnership now has partnership minimum gain of $100.[22] Ellen's share of the minimum gain includes all $100 because she was allocated all the nonrecourse deductions that generated the minimum gain.[23] Thus, tier one allocates $100 of the $900 debt to Ellen. Tier two does not apply because there is no § 704(c) gain. Tier three allocates the remaining $800 debt equally between the partners. Consequently, at the end of Year Two, Ellen's share of

---

22. At the end of year two, the nonrecourse debt of $900 exceeds the partnership's $800 basis in the asset by $100.

23. See page 65, above.

partnership debt is $500 and Dixon's is only $400. Because Ellen's share of debt increases by $50 at the end of Year Two, her outside basis also increases by $50 (§ 752 (a)). In contrast, since Dixon's share of debt decreases by $50, his outside basis decreases by $50 (§ 752 (b)).

At the end of Year Three, the same analysis would result in $550 of the debt being allocated to Ellen and only $350 to Dixon. Once again, Ellen's outside basis would increase by $50 and Dixon's would decrease by $50. Every year more debt will be allocated to Ellen and less to Dixon. At the end of Year Ten, all $900 of the debt will be allocated to Ellen.

Rather than deal with the complexity of calculating each partner's debt share every year, the partnership can allocate all the debt to Ellen in Year One by electing to make the tier three allocation consistently with her share of nonrecourse deductions. Ellen will then continue to be allocated all the debt in subsequent years. She will be allocated some of the debt under tier one as her share of partnership minimum gain increases and the remainder of the debt under tier three.[24]

4. Effects of Guarantees of Nonrecourse Debt

We saw earlier that the guaranty of recourse debt does not affect the allocation of recourse debt.[25] The result is very different for nonrecourse debt. A partner who guarantees nonrecourse debt will generally be allocated the nonrecourse debt to the extent of the guaranty. The reason is that the guarantor bears the economic risk of loss for the portion of the guaranteed nonrecourse debt.

Example 8–12: Gloria and Henry form the GH partnership as equal partners. The partnership borrows $100,000 on a nonrecourse basis to purchase a building, which is used as security for the loan. Henry guarantees the $100,000 nonrecourse debt.

Without the guaranty, the lender could look only to the building for payment. With the guaranty, the lender can recover any deficiency from Henry, if the building does not have sufficient value to cover the debt. Since the loan is nonrecourse, Henry cannot recover the amount he would have to pay on the loan as guarantor, even if he is subrogated to the rights of the

---

24. Dixon may prefer to share in the debt so that he will have sufficient basis to deduct other partnership expenses that might occur during the partnership's early years. This is fine so long as Dixon remembers that the decrease in his share of partnership debt each year is treated as a cash distribution to him under § 752(b). If his basis is reduced sufficiently by other expenses, the reduction in his share of debt each year will result in gain to the extent that the deemed distribution exceeds his outside basis.

25. See page 102, above.

lender after paying the guaranty. The regulations conclude, therefore, that the guaranty causes Henry to bear the risk of loss for the loan and allocate the amount of debt guaranteed ($100,000) to Henry.[26]

F. OBLIGATIONS THAT ARE NOT "LIABILITIES" UNDER § 752

As noted earlier in this chapter, a partnership (or a partner) can be subject to an obligation that is not a "liability" for purposes of § 752. For example, a cash-method taxpayer's obligation to pay an amount that will give rise to a deduction upon payment is not a "liability" in the § 752 sense because incurring the obligation gave the taxpayer no basis in cash or property, did not allow the taxpayer a deduction, and was not incurred in connection with a non-deductible expenditure that was not a capital expenditure.[27] To see why it makes sense to treat some obligations as not being "liabilities," consider the transfer of a going business to a partnership by a cash-method taxpayer.

When a going business is transferred to a partnership, the partnership may assume the transferor's debts. If the transferor used the cash method of accounting, some of those debts may be debts on account of which the transferor would have received a deduction upon payment. Suppose, for example, that a cash-method sole proprietor owes an employee money for services performed, and suppose that the proprietor will be allowed a deduction upon payment. Absurd tax consequences would result if this kind of debt were treated as a "liability" under § 752.

> **Example 8–13:** Imelda, a cash-method sole proprietor, forms an equal partnership with John. Imelda contributes a business asset with a basis of $40,000 and a value of $70,000; the partnership assumes a $10,000 debt for salary owed to one of the business's employees. John contributes $60,000 in cash.
>
> If the $10,000 debt were treated as a liability, Imelda would be overtaxed. Suppose, for instance, that the partnership engages in only two transactions: It pays the employee and it sells the asset contributed by Imelda for $70,000. If the debt is a "liability" in the statutory sense, Imelda's outside basis immediately after the partnership was formed becomes $35,000 ($40,-

---

26. Treas. Reg. §§ 1.752–2(f) Ex. 5 and 1.752–2(e)(1). There is an exception to this result. A special rule will treat the debt as still being allocable under the regular nonrecourse rules if the partner who guarantees the nonrecourse debt has an interest of no more than ten percent in partnership items. Treas. Reg. § 1.752–2(e)(4).

27. See page 96, above.

000 under § 722 less $5000 because of the constructive cash distribution resulting from the reduction in her liabilities). John's outside basis becomes $65,000 ($60,000 for his actual cash contribution plus $5,000 for his constructive cash contribution). Upon selling the asset, the partnership has a gain of $30,000, while payment of the $10,000 salary gives it a $10,000 deduction; its income is therefore $20,000. Under § 704(c) (see Chapter 6); all of this income should be taxed to Imelda. This taxable income increases Imelda's outside basis from $35,000 to $55,000 (§ 705). Payment of the $10,000 salary also reduces each partner's share of the liabilities from $5,000 to zero. This reduction—a constructive cash distribution under § 752—reduces Imelda's outside basis to $50,000 and John's to $60,000.

After all of the events described above, the partnership's only asset is $120,000 in cash. If it then liquidates, distributing $60,000 to each partner, Imelda will recognize a $10,000 gain because the liquidating distribution exceeds her outside basis by $10,000. John has no gain because the amount of his liquidating distribution equals his outside basis.

For John, the result described above makes sense: He went in with $60,000 cash, came out with $60,000 cash, and has had no income. Imelda, however, has been overtaxed. She began the series of transactions with property having a $40,000 basis, with an obligation to pay $10,000, and with the prospect of a $10,000 deduction upon payment of that obligation. If she had sold the property herself and paid the $10,000 debt, she would have ended up with $60,000 in cash and with net income of $20,000 ($30,000 gain from the sale of the property and a $10,000 deduction for payment of the salary). The partnership-tax calculations, however, give her $10,000 more income ($30,000 distributive share of gain on the sale of the property, $10,000 distributive share of the deduction for the salary payment, and $10,000 gain on the liquidation of the partnership).

The bizarre result reached in Example 8–13 is avoided by treating a cash-method transferor's obligation to pay for a deductible outlay as not being a "liability."

Example 8–14: The facts are the same as in Example 8–13. Because Imelda's obligation to pay the salary is not a "liability," for purposes of § 752, her outside basis when the partnership is formed is $40,000 (the basis of the contributed property). John's outside basis is $60,000. When the partnership sells the asset and pays the salary, its income (all allocable to Imelda) consists of a $30,000 gain and a $10,000 deduction, and so Imelda's outside basis increases by $20,000 to $60,000. Neither partner has a gain when the partnership is liquidated. In the long run, Imelda recognizes a $30,000 gain and a $10,000 deduction for business expenses, just as if the partnership had never been formed.

It may be worth noting that the differences between the accounts receivable of cash-method and accrual-method taxpayers create no particular problem under § 722. Like payables, receivables have different tax consequences when they are incurred, depending on the taxpayer's accounting method: A cash-method taxpayer has no income upon acquiring an account receivable, while an accrual-method taxpayer has income equal to the face amount of the receivable. Because this difference in tax treatment is mirrored in the taxpayers' bases for the receivables—cash-method taxpayers have a zero basis, while accrual-method taxpayers have a basis equal to the amount includable in income—§ 722 distinguishes between the two kinds of receivables by setting the transferor's outside basis equal to the basis of the transferred property. For payables, however, there is no convenient tax concept like basis to distinguish payables that will give rise to deductions from those that will not. It is therefore necessary to give the term "liabilities" a special and somewhat counterintuitive definition, which distinguishes between different kinds of obligations.[28]

Obligations that are not "liabilities" for purposes of § 752 cannot always be ignored, as their existence does reduce the value of interests in partnerships that owe them. Consider a taxpayer who acquires a partnership interest by contributing land with a basis and gross value of $300,000. The owner of the land must someday incur environmental cleanup expenses before using it, so the net value of the land is only $200,000, taking into account the expected cost of the cleanup. Therefore, the contributing partner would receive a partnership interest worth $200,000 for the contribution. The obligation to incur the cleanup cost, which will give rise to a deduction when it is incurred, is not a liability for § 752 purposes. Therefore, the owner's contribution of the land would give the owner a $300,000 basis for the partnership interest. Absent a special rule for this situation, which is discussed in the following paragraph, a sale of that partnership interest would generate a $100,000 loss, in effect accelerating the owner's deduction for the cleanup cost.[29]

---

28. See William D. Andrews & Alan L. Feld, Federal Income Taxation of Corporate Transactions 264–265 (3d ed. 1994).

29. Similar transactions involving contributions to corporations were used to accelerate and duplicate deductions for contingent liabilities, a practice countered by the enactment of § 358(d) in 2000. Under § 358(d), many tax-free contributions to corporations of property subject to obligations that are not liabilities result in a reduction of the basis of the stock

Regulations under § 752 call obligations that are not liabilities for purposes of § 752 "§ 1.752–7 liabilities."[30] The regulations provide that the contributing partner will be allocated the partnership's deduction associated with a § 1.752–7 liability when the deduction is allowed. If the contributing partner has been "separated from" that liability by the time it becomes allowable (for instance, if the contributing partner in the preceding paragraph had sold the partnership interest before the partnership cleaned up the land), that partner's outside basis will generally be reduced by the amount of the § 1.752–7 liability. This basis reduction prevents accelerating the deduction. When the partnership eventually incurs the cost, the contributing partner, rather than those who are partners at the time, is allowed the deduction.

G. COMPARISON WITH SUBCHAPTER S

Subchapter S does not include rules for allocating the S corporation's liabilities to the shareholders because the corporation's liabilities are not attributed to the S corporation's shareholders. Section 357 provides rules for determining when an S corporation's assumption of a shareholder's liabilities can cause the shareholder to recognize gain. Section 358 describes the effect of an S corporation's assumption of a shareholder's liabilities on the shareholder's stock basis.

---

received in exchange by the amount of the obligations. This basis reduction eliminates the potential shareholder level loss. The legislation that enacted § 358(d) authorized the Treasury to adopt regulations dealing with similar transactions involving partnerships.

30. Treas. Reg. § 1.752–7.

Chapter Nine

TRANSACTIONS BETWEEN PARTNERSHIPS AND THEIR PARTNERS

Sometimes the Code treats a transaction between a partnership and one of its partners just as if the partner were an outsider. For example, if a partnership buys property from a partner, the partnership's basis and the amount of the partner's gain on the sale will be calculated exactly as if the partner were an unrelated person. Section 707(a) provides that, subject to exceptions to be noted later:

> If a partner engages in a transaction with a partnership other than in his capacity as a member of such partnership, the transaction shall ... be considered as occurring between the partnership and one who is not a partner.

Section 707(c) deals with "guaranteed payments" by partnerships to partners "for services or the use of capital." Like § 707(a) payments, these guaranteed payments are treated as made to non-partners, but only in some respects: Section 707(c) payments are "considered as" made to non-partners *only* in determining whether the payments are includable in the partners' gross incomes and whether the payments are deductible as business expenses under § 162(a).

As a (minor) illustration of the difference between § 707(a) payments and guaranteed payments, consider a case in which partner Jean receives $10,000 cash for services performed for the JK partnership. If the partnership had paid an outsider for these services, it would have deducted the $10,000 as an ordinary and necessary business expense under § 162(a). The payment, being a flat fee for services rather than a share of the partnership's income, is probably either a § 707(a) payment or a guaranteed payment, but without more information we cannot tell which. (Even if we had more information we might not be able to tell; the distinction, as we shall see, is fuzzy.) What difference does it make? In either case, the partnership can deduct the payment and Jean must include it in income.

One difference between treating the payment to Jean as a guaranteed payment and treating it as a § 707(a) payment involves the timing of her income and the partnership's deduction. If the payment is a guaranteed payment, Jean will include it in her income for her taxable year "within or with" which the partnership's taxable year ends.[1] This is the same timing rule that governs the inclusion of a partner's distribu-

---

1. § 706(a).

tive share. Suppose that the partnership, which uses a calendar year and an accrual method of accounting, accrues the payment in 2010. Jean, a cash-method taxpayer, does not receive the payment until 2011. The "within or with" rule of § 706(a) requires that Jean include the $10,000 in her 2010 income (the partnership year 2010, in which the partnership accrued the item, ends with Jean's 2010 taxable year). Therefore, the timing of a partner's income from a guaranteed payment will depend upon the partnership's method of accounting, rather than upon the partner's method.

If Jean's $10,000 payment is a § 707(a) payment (one made to her in a non-partner capacity), the timing of her income will depend upon her accounting method, just as if she had received the payment from an unrelated third party. In the example, she would have income for 2011. If § 707(a) were the whole story, the partnership would deduct the payment in 2010, under its accrual method. However, § 267(a)(2) will delay the partnership's deduction until the payment is includable in Jean's income. Although § 707(a) treats Jean as a sort of non-partner, she and the partnership are "related" under § 267(b).[2]

Many payments by partnerships to partners for services or for the use of capital are neither § 707(a) payments nor guaranteed payments. A third possible classification is "distributive share." If Jean's work for the JK partnership entitles her to ten percent of the partnership's income for the year, and if that income is $100,000, her $10,000 payment is probably (but not necessarily) a distributive share. (Technically, it is a distribution attributable to her having a distributive share of $10,000. Tax lawyers have fallen into the sloppy but understandable practice of referring to the *payment* as a distributive share in cases like this. For convenience, we will follow the practice of the tax lawyers.)

To summarize, a payment by a partnership to a partner who has performed services or furnished property may be one of three things:[3]

(1) A distributive share of partnership income;

(2) A guaranteed payment, subject to § 707(c); or

(3) A § 707(a) payment.

The first question to ask in deciding how a particular payment should be labeled is whether the partner performed services or furnished property in the partner's "capacity" as a partner. Payments made for something done in a non-partner capacity are § 707(a) payments, no matter what their form. Partnership-capacity payments, however, are classified according to how they are measured. If the amount of those

---

2. See § 267(e).

3. There are other possibilities, too, but these three may be enough to think about at this point.

payments depends on the amount of the partnership's income, the payments are distributive shares; if the amount of the payments doesn't depend on partnership income, they are guaranteed payments.

The following table depicts the statutory pattern. Each box contains the appropriate label for a payment having the characteristics noted above and to the left of that box.

	Measured by Income	**Not Measured by Income**
Partner Capacity	Distributive Share	Guaranteed Payment
Non–Partner Capacity	§ 707(a) Payment	§ 707(a) Payment

Sometimes it is hard to say whether a payment depends upon a partnership's income; we shall look at some examples in section C, below. Often, however, the answer to this question will be obvious, and the only question will involve the partner's "capacity."

A. INCOME–RELATED PAYMENTS: DISTRIBUTIVE SHARES AND SECTION 707(a) PAYMENTS

Classifying a payment to a partner as a distributive share has much the same effect, from the point of view of the other partners, as allowing a deduction for the payment. The question whether a particular payment is a distributive share or a § 707(a) payment thus becomes important in cases in which a payment to a non-partner would not be deductible by the partnership.

Example 9–1: The LMN partnership has $100,000 of ordinary income and no deductions. Partner Lewis is an architect. Lewis's partnership activities for the year have consisted entirely of designing a building that the partnership will build in the near future. Under the partnership agreement, Lewis is entitled to a distributive share of twenty percent of the partnership's taxable income. If this distributive share is really what it purports to be, the total income of the other partners, Mairead and Nigel, will be $80,000; Lewis will report income of $20,000. If Mairead and Nigel had been the only owners of the business, and if they had earned $100,000 and paid Lewis $20,000 for designing the building, their combined incomes would have been $100,000, rather than $80,000. Lewis's income would still have been $20,000.

If the purported distributive share of such a partner can be recharacterized as a § 707(a) payment, the result will be less favorable for the other partners.

Example 9–2: The Service challenges the characterization of Lewis's payment in Example 9–1 as a distributive share and convinces a court that the payment was really a § 707(a) payment. The partnership must capitalize the payment. Since the partnership's income is still $100,000, and since Lewis's distributive share is zero, the combined distributive shares of Mairead and Nigel are $100,000. Lewis has $20,000 of income from the performance of services.

How does one tell whether the payment in the examples is a distributive share or a § 707(a) payment? Section 707(a)(2)(A) says that the matter turns upon whether Lewis's performance of services and the related allocation and distribution to him are "properly characterized" as a § 707(a) payment. According to the legislative history of this provision, we should look to whether the calculation of Lewis's "distributive share" exposes him to the kinds of risks faced by the other partners.[4] In other words, the issue is whether (with respect to his distributive share) he is genuinely a partner, economically speaking. Someone who designs a building and, as a result, becomes entitled to one percent of the partnership's bottom-line income[5] for the indefinite future would have a distributive share. Someone who performed the same services, receiving in exchange 30 percent of the income of a specific partnership activity for one year only, might well have a § 707(a) payment, especially if the amount of that income was readily determinable when the agreement was made.[6]

The approach described above differs from that of the cases decided before § 707(a)(2) was enacted in 1984. Those cases looked more at whether the activities performed by the partner were the kinds of activities that the partnership normally carried on, or whether they were something unusual.[7] Under that test, a lawyer who is a member of a cattle-raising partnership would be regarded as receiving § 707(a) payments if someone sued the partnership and the lawyer/partner handled the case.

---

4. Deficit Reduction Act of 1984, Explanation of Provisions Approved by the Committee on March 21, 1984, S. Prt. 98–169 (Vol. 1) (1984), says at p. 227:

> The first, and generally the most important, factor is whether the payment is subject to an appreciable risk as to amount. Partners extract the profits of the partnership with reference to the business success of the venture while third parties generally receive payments which are not subject to this risk.

5. § 702(a)(8).

6. See the Senate Finance Committee's explanation (cited in Note 4) at pp. 228–229.

7. E.g., Pratt v. Commissioner, 550 F.2d 1023, 1026 (5th Cir. 1977) ("in order for the partnership to deal with one of its partners as an 'outsider' the transaction dealt with must be something outside the scope of the partnership. If, on the other hand, the activities constituting the 'transaction' were activities which the partnership itself was engaged in, compensation for such transaction must be treated as [a distributive share]").

A payment's being a distributive share or a § 707(a) payment may affect character, as well as timing.

Example 9–3: The NOP partnership has $50,000 of ordinary income (net of expenses) and $50,000 of capital gains. Partner Omar receives ten percent of all partnership income (net of deductions other than those, if any, attributable to payments to Omar). If Omar's $10,000 payment is a distributive share, he has $5,000 ordinary income and a $5,000 capital gain. The other partners report a total of $45,000 ordinary income and $45,000 capital gain. If Omar's $10,000 is a 707(a) payment for services, and if it is deductible by the partnership as a business expense, Omar has $10,000 ordinary income. The partnership's income, after taking into account the payment to Omar, is $40,000 of ordinary income (net of deductions) and $50,000 of capital gain.

B. FIXED PAYMENTS: GUARANTEED PAYMENTS AND SECTION 707(a) PAYMENTS

The 1984 amendments to § 707(a) addressed mainly the problem of distinguishing § 707(a) payments from distributive shares. The legislative history's focus upon whether a purported distributive share represents a genuine long-term interest in the partnership or is merely a mechanism for paying a fee for services (in the form of a distributive share) is hard to apply to the problem of distinguishing a guaranteed payment from a § 707(a) payment. Both fixed-amount payments under § 707(a) and guaranteed payments under § 707(c) resemble fees for services or for the use of capital (property). The distinction must be sought not just in the form of the payment but also in other aspects of the transaction.

When payments for services are involved, classification as § 707(a) payments or guaranteed payments may turn upon whether the payments are a regular part of the partner's compensation and whether the services consist of the partner's usual activities. A partner who receives $10,000 plus thirty percent of the partnership's income, year after year, would normally be thought of as having a guaranteed payment and a distributive share. A partner who usually gets thirty percent of the partnership's income, but who gets an additional $10,000 for extra work done in 2010, might well be treated as having a $10,000 § 707(a) payment for 2010, especially if the additional work was something the partner did not ordinarily do for the partnership.

A minimum payment combined with a distributive share will probably create a guaranteed payment, at least if a "pure" percentage-interest distributive share would have been treated as a partner-capacity payment and if the percentage interest is not so low as to be practically meaningless.

> **Example 9–4:** The PR partnership agreement provides that Priscilla is to receive ten percent of partnership income or $30,000, whichever is more, for services she performs. If the partnership's income is very unlikely to exceed $300,000, the "ten percent" portion of this agreement may be meaningless, and Priscilla may not even be a partner. But if the partnership's income is likely to be well over $300,000 in most years, Priscilla's payments may well be treated as being made to her in her capacity as a partner, even if in one particular year the partnership earns nothing.

As an example of a § 707(a) payment for the use of capital, the regulations use interest on a loan made by the partner to the partnership.[8] A fixed annual payment of a percentage of the capital contributed by a partner to a partnership would normally be a guaranteed payment. A loan would ordinarily give the partner a right to repayment on a fixed date and priority over returns of capital contributions to the other partners; a capital contribution would not.

C. DETERMINING WHETHER A "PARTNER CAPACITY" PAYMENT IS A DISTRIBUTIVE SHARE OR A GUARANTEED PAYMENT

A payment to a partner in that partner's "capacity" as a partner must be either a distributive share or a guaranteed payment, depending upon whether the amount of the payment is determined with regard to the partnership's income. § 707(c). Deciding whether a payment is determined with regard to partnership income presents difficulties when (1) the amount of the payment may or may not depend upon partnership income, depending on how much income the partnership has, or (2) the payment is a fraction of a partnership's gross income, rather than its taxable income.

1. Minimum Payments

If a partnership agreement calls for a guaranteed minimum payment to a partner, the agreement "fixes" the amount of the partner's payment in the sense that the partner will get at least the minimum, but the partner's payment also depends in part upon how much income the partnership has. Section 707(c)'s definition of "guaranteed payment" is ambiguous as applied to this case.

---

8. Treas. Reg. § 1.707–1(a).

Example 9–5: The ST partnership's agreement provides that Sandra will receive a distributive share of forty percent of the partnership's bottom-line income or $20,000, whichever is more. Assume that this payment is to Sandra in her capacity as a partner. If the partnership has no bottom-line income for year one, Sandra's $20,000 payment is plainly a guaranteed payment in full. If the partnership has $100,000 in bottom-line income for year two, Sandra will get $40,000. At least $20,000 (the excess over the minimum amount) must be a distributive share, but the status of the first $20,000 is unclear. Sandra would have received that first $20,000 even if the partnership had had no income, so in that sense the payment is determined without regard to the partnership's income. On the other hand, Sandra would have received $40,000 even if the agreement had not guaranteed her a minimum amount, so calling the entire $40,000 a "distributive share" is not wildly implausible.

The regulations deal with the problem presented in Example 9–5 by treating any "overlap" between the guaranteed minimum and the percentage figure as a distributive share. In the example, Sandra's entire $40,000 for Year Two would be a distributive share because she would have received $40,000 even if the agreement had contained no minimum. But suppose that the partnership's bottom-line income for Year Three turns out to be $30,000, so that the minimum comes into play by raising Sandra's payment from the $12,000 it would have been on a straight "forty percent of bottom-line income" basis. Now, according to the regulations, $12,000 (the amount Sandra would have received without the minimum) is a distributive share; the rest ($8,000 on these figures) is a guaranteed payment.[9]

One reason for distinguishing between guaranteed payments and distributive shares has to do with the character of the partners' incomes.[10] For instance, suppose that Sandra is entitled to 40 percent of the partnership's income from all sources, with a guaranteed minimum of $20,000. The partnership's total income is $50,000, consisting of $25,000 ordinary income and $25,000 capital gains. If Sandra's $20,000 is a guaranteed payment, on the theory that she gets that much even if the partnership earns nothing, her $20,000 income for the year will all be ordinary income. If she has performed ordinary and necessary services for the partnership, so that any salary paid to her would be deductible, the partnership will deduct the $20,000 payment, leaving it with $5,000 of ordinary income (the $25,000 less the $20,000 deduction for the payment to Sandra). This leaves $5,000 of ordinary income and

---

9. Treas. Reg. § 1.707–1(c) (Example (2)); see also Rev. Rul. 69–180, 1969–1 C.B. 183.

10. This is also true of the distinction between distributive shares and § 707(a) payments. See Example 9–3, above.

$25,000 of capital gain as the distributive share of the other partner, Terry. If, following the regulations, the entire $20,000 is a distributive share, Sandra's distributive share consists of forty percent of the partnership's ordinary income, or $10,000, and forty percent of its capital gain, also $10,000. Terry's distributive share also consists of equal amounts of ordinary income and capital gain.

Another important difference between a distributive share and a guaranteed payment arises because guaranteed payments, if made for capital-expenditure-type services, must be capitalized.[11] When capitalization is in question, the important dividing line lies between guaranteed payments and § 707(a) payments on the one hand and distributive shares on the other. Both guaranteed payments and § 707(a) payments must be capitalized in appropriate cases, while distributive shares are never capital expenditures.

The regulations' method for determining what portion of a minimum payment is a guaranteed payment is controversial. A statement in the legislative history of § 707(c) contradicts the regulations' approach to the minimum-payment problem.[12] Furthermore, the regulations will sometimes create computational embarrassments:

Example 9–6: Wendy is entitled to fifty percent of the WX partnership's income (calculated before taking any payments to her into account) or $10,000, whichever is more. The partnership earns $3,000, so Wendy receives the $10,000 minimum payment. According to the regulations, $1,500 of this (the amount Wendy would have gotten without the minimum) is a distributive share and only the balance of $8,500 is a guaranteed payment. If this is right, the partnership's taxable and bottom-line income is a $5,500 loss: $3,000 of gross income less a deduction of $8,500 for Wendy's guaranteed payment. Thus, although the partnership reports a loss for the year, Wendy's distributive share for the year is $1,500 of ordinary income.

These considerations suggest that the regulations' approach may be unwise, perhaps even invalid. It may be worth noting, though, that the oddity of having one partner report a positive distributive share even though the partnership has a loss can occur even in cases not involving guaranteed payments. Suppose that partner Tobias is entitled to fifty percent of the profits of the partnership's New York office—a distributive share by anybody's definition. If the New York office makes money but the

---

11. § 707(c).

12. S. Rept. No. 1622, 83d Cong., 2d Sess. (1954), says at p. 387, "A partner who is guaranteed a minimum annual amount for his services shall be treated as receiving a fixed payment in that amount."

partnership, on an overall basis, has more deductions than income, Tobias's distributive share is positive although the partnership has a loss.

2. Payments Measured by a Partnership's Gross Income

Whether a payment measured by a partnership's gross income (or by some particular kind of gross income) can be a guaranteed payment is unclear. Section 707(c)'s reference to "income" is broad enough to include "gross income" if doing so makes sense; but the term "income" in § 707(c) could also be interpreted as meaning "taxable income" (or some portion of taxable income) if that reading produces better results.

The main argument for reading "income" in § 707(c) as meaning "taxable income" is that calling a fraction of gross income a "distributive share" can cause a partner's distributive share of income to exceed the partnership's total income. If Viola is entitled to ten percent of a partnership's gross rental income from renting out Blackacre, for instance, her "distributive share" will be positive if the partnership has any gross income at all, even though the partnership will have a loss if its deductions exceed its gross income. Section 707(c) was adopted in 1954 just to avoid this kind of mess by treating guaranteed payments as not being distributive shares.[13] Therefore, the argument goes, the definition of "guaranteed payment" should be as broad as the statutory language allows. In response to this argument, note that, as long as the Code allows any kind of item allocation, the possibility that a partner's distributive share will exceed the partnership's total income remains.[14] Furthermore, the only harm done by this kind of outcome is that uncertainty over how to report the income may arise. The Service, apparently confusing § 707(c) and § 707(a), has ruled that payments measured by gross income or gross receipts can be either guaranteed payments or distributive shares.[15] The Tax Court has held that payments measured by gross income are measured by "income" and so can never be guaranteed payments.[16]

D. SOME OTHER ASPECTS OF TRANSACTIONS BETWEEN PARTNERS AND PARTNERSHIPS

Section 707(b)(1) disallows deductions for losses on sales or exchanges of property between partnerships and those who own, actually

---

13. See William S. McKee, William F. Nelson & Robert L. Whitmire, Federal Taxation of Partnerships and Partners ¶ 14.03[1] (4th ed. 2007).

14. See Example 9–6, above.

15. Rev. Rul. 81–300, 1981–2 C.B. 143.

16. Pratt v. Commissioner, 64 T.C. 203 (1975). The Fifth Circuit affirmed *Pratt* without deciding what kind of payments the fees were; 550 F.2d 1023 (5th Cir. 1977).

or constructively, interests of more than fifty percent of the capital or profits of the partnership. It also disallows deductions for losses on sales or exchanges between partnerships in which the same persons have interests of more than fifty percent in capital or profits. Section 707(b)(2) treats gains on sales or exchanges of property between related (in the more-than-fifty-percent sense) partnerships or between partnerships and controlling partners as ordinary income if the property is not a capital asset in the recipient's hands. Thus, if someone who owns a fifty-five-percent interest in the capital of a partnership sells a capital asset to the partnership and recognizes a $10,000 gain, the gain will be ordinary income if the asset is not a capital asset in the partnership's hands. Section 1239 can also apply to sales between partners and their partnerships.

E. COMPARISON WITH SUBCHAPTER S

Subchapter S contains nothing comparable to § 707(c); there is no such thing as a "guaranteed payment" to an S corporation's shareholder. An S corporation may pay a salary to one or more of its shareholders; when it does, the tax treatment does not differ from that given a C corporation's salary payments. (For purposes of taxing fringe benefits, however, § 1372 treats many shareholder-employees of S corporations as if they were partners, rather than employees. Code provisions granting favorable treatment to employee fringe benefits do not extend to an S corporation employee who owns more than two percent of the corporation's stock on any day during the taxable year.[17]) Because S corporations may have only one class of stock, many of the problems that arise in the partnership area when purported "distributive shares" are created to compensate persons who have no genuine long-term interest in the business should seldom arise under subchapter S: Someone who gets stock should be treated as a shareholder; someone who doesn't shouldn't be.

---

17. See page 14, above.

Chapter Ten

SALES OF PARTNERSHIP INTERESTS

This Chapter will examine sales of partnership interests from the point of view of the seller, the buyer, and the other partners. We are concerned here only with cases in which one partner sells an interest in the partnership. That interest may be all of the seller's interest or only a part of it, and the buyer may be either an outsider or someone who has been a partner all along and is becoming a bigger partner by acquiring another partner's interest. Transactions in which one "buys" a partnership interest from the partnership itself are not "sales" for tax purposes; they are acquisitions subject to §§ 721, 722, and 723, covered in Chapter 4. A transaction in which a partnership "buys" an interest in itself from a partner is not a "sale" either; it is a liquidation of the partner's interest. Chapters 11, 12 and 13 deal with liquidations.

A. TAXATION OF THE SELLER

The tax treatment of someone who sells a partnership interest differs in three ways from that of someone who sells a share of stock or a tract of land. First, the partnership's liabilities will enter into the calculation of the seller's amount realized. Second, if the partnership has any "§ 751 property" (and nearly every partnership will) the seller must calculate gain and loss separately on the sale of the interest attributable to that kind of property and on the sale of the balance of the interest. Third, if a sale of all the partnership's assets would result in an allocation of "collectibles gain" or "unrecaptured section 1250 gain" to the selling partner, the seller will recognize that kind of gain upon selling a partnership interest.

1. The Seller's Amount Realized

A partner's outside basis depends in part on the partner's share of the partnership's liabilities. (Recall that § 752 treats an increase in a partner's share of partnership liabilities as a cash contribution to the partnership. This constructive cash contribution increases the partner's outside basis.[1]) Just as a liability (such as a purchase-money mortgage) to which property is subject is included in the seller's amount realized when the property is sold, a partner's share of partnership liabilities is included in the partner's amount realized when a partnership interest is sold. The Code authorizes this result by providing in § 752(d) that

---

1. See Chapter 3.

"partnership liabilities shall be treated in the same manner as liabilities in connection with the sale ... of property not associated with partnerships" whenever a partnership interest is sold. (This phrasing is opaque, but the meaning of the provision is clear.)

Example 10–1: Antje, a thirty percent partner in ABC, sells her interest in the partnership to Dwight for $50,000 cash. The partnership owns a building subject to a nonrecourse mortgage of $100,000; Antje's share of this liability under the § 752 regulations was $30,000 just before the sale. Antje's amount realized on the sale is $80,000, consisting of the $50,000 cash and her $30,000 share of the debt.

Because a partner's share of partnership liabilities is part of the amount realized upon the sale, there will be few cases in which a transfer of a partnership interest is not a "sale or exchange," at least in part. If a partner makes a gift of an interest in a partnership, the "gift" will be a part-gift, part-sale transaction if the transfer reduces the donor's share of partnership liabilities. Or consider a partner who abandons a partnership interest in the hope of claiming that the loss on the disposition of the interest was ordinary for lack of a "sale or exchange."[2] If this partner had a share of partnership liabilities, which disappeared as a result of the "abandonment," the partner will have an amount realized and so the transaction will be a "sale."

2. Section 751(a)

Section 741, which provides that gains and losses from sales of partnership interests are treated as capital gains and losses, is limited by § 751(a), which will create some ordinary income in nearly every case in which a partnership interest is sold. Section 751(a) applies whenever the selling partner receives payments attributable to that partner's share of the partnership's "unrealized receivables" or "inventory items." These are terms of art; the usual non-statutory term covering both these kinds of assets is "§ 751 property."

Whenever a partner sells an interest in a partnership that holds § 751 property, part of the seller's amount realized and outside basis are attributed to the seller's share of that § 751 property. The gain (or, conceivably, loss) from the § 751 portion of the sale is ordinary; whatever gain or loss results from subtracting the remainder of the seller's basis from the remainder of the amount realized is capital gain or loss under § 741. Here is a simple example.

---

2. Section 741, which characterizes gains and losses on "sales or exchanges" of partnership interests as capital (unless § 751 applies), does not cover dispositions that are not sales or exchanges.

Example 10–2: Edgar is a twenty-five percent partner in EFG. The partnership owns some unimproved land (a capital asset). It also owns an unrealized receivable—in this case, a right to payment for the performance of services. This unrealized receivable has a zero basis and a value of $20,000. The partnership has no other assets. Edgar sells his partnership interest to Faith for $35,000. Edgar's outside basis was $10,000.

On these numbers, $5,000 of Edgar's amount realized is pretty clearly attributable to his interest in the partnership's unrealized receivable, a § 751 asset. Section 751(a) makes this $5,000 "an amount realized from the sale or exchange of property other than a capital asset." The statute fails to say, however, how much of Edgar's basis to use in calculating the ordinary income from the sale. The regulations fill the gap by providing that the seller's ordinary income (or loss) attributable to the partnership's § 751 assets is the amount of ordinary income or loss the partner would have recognized if the partnership had sold all of its assets.[3] In this case, Edgar's share of the ordinary income from the sale of the receivable would have been $5,000 ($5,000 amount realized minus $0 tax basis), so that is the amount of ordinary income on which he is taxed by § 751(a) on the sale of his interest in the partnership.

We now turn to the calculation of Edgar's capital gain of loss under § 741. Edgar's basis in his partnership interest that was also not accounted for in the § 751 calculation is applied to the amount realized in the sale of his partnership interest also not accounted for in the § 751 calculation. Since the unrealized receivable has a 0 basis, none of Edgar's outside basis was accounted for in the § 751 calculation, leaving $10,000 basis for the § 741 calculation. With respect to the $35,000 amount realized, $5,000 was accounted for in the § 751 calculation, leaving $30,000 for the § 741 calculation. Thus, the remaining $10,000 outside basis is subtracted from the remaining amount realized on $30,000 to result in a $20,000 capital gain under § 741.

Section 751(a) may require a partner to report ordinary income on the sale of a partnership interest even though the partner's amount realized is less than the basis of the interest sold.

Example 10–3: The HIJK partnership has the following tax balance sheet (a record of the partnership's assets and liabilities showing both market values and tax bases):

---

3. Treas. Reg. § 1.751–1(a)(2).

ASSETS

	Basis	Value
Inventory	$ 4,000	$12,000
Capital Asset	28,000	4,000
Total:	$32,000	$16,000

CAPITAL

	Basis	Value
H	$ 8,000	$4,000
I	8,000	4,000
J	8,000	4,000
K	8,000	4,000
	$32,000	$16,000

Heloise, whose outside basis is $8,000, sells her one-fourth partnership interest to Leopold for $4,000. Under § 751(a), $3,000 of this amount is allocable to Heloise's interest in the partnership's inventory. If the partnership had sold all of its assets, Heloise would have recognized $2,000 of ordinary income because of her interest in the inventory, which is a § 751 asset. She therefore recognizes $2,000 of ordinary income under § 751(a) upon the sale of her partnership interest. These § 751(a) calculations have used $3,000 of Heloise's amount realized and $1,000 of her basis. This leaves $1,000 of amount realized and $7,000 of basis for use in calculating her capital gain or loss under § 741. She therefore recognizes a capital loss of $6,000.

Section 751(a) was designed to further the "aggregate" method of taxing partners. If the sellers in the examples above had been sole proprietors, who owned the assets themselves, they would have had some ordinary income and some capital gain or loss upon selling those assets. The thought behind § 751(a) is that the tax consequences should not differ dramatically if the seller is a partner. Section 751(a) falls considerably short of taxing those who sell interests in partnerships as if they had sold interests in their partnerships' assets, however. For example, if a partnership's only asset is § 1231 property having a basis higher than its value, a partner's sale of an interest in the partnership at a loss will produce a capital loss, even though a sale of the asset itself would have generated a § 1231 loss (often treated as ordinary).

"Unrealized receivables," and "inventory" are defined in §§ 751(c) and (d). The definitions are technical enough to justify a detailed discussion.

Ch. 10   TAXATION OF THE SELLER

"Unrealized Receivables." The first part of § 751(c)'s definition of "unrealized receivables" resembles the ordinary meaning of that term except that it is somewhat broader. Any right to payment for non-capital goods delivered (or to be delivered) or for services rendered (or to be rendered) is an unrealized receivable as defined in § 751(c), to the extent that the income in question has not yet been includable in income. This definition covers a cash-method taxpayer's accounts receivable, but it is broader than that. A right to payment for unbilled work in progress is an "unrealized receivable" under § 751, although it is not an account receivable in the usual sense.

Section 751(c) goes far beyond rights to payment. For purposes of most of the Code sections in which the term is used, "unrealized receivables" includes the variety of things listed in the "flush" language following § 751(c)(2). Most of the property on this list is property subject to some kind of recapture. For example, suppose a partnership buys § 1245 property for $10,000 and takes $6,000 in depreciation deductions, reducing the property's basis to $4,000. If this asset is now worth $5,000, the partnership has a $1,000 "unrealized receivable." For most (not all) purposes, § 751(c) includes in the list of unrealized receivables "section 1245 property ... to the extent of the amount which would be treated as [ordinary income under § 1245(a)] ... if ... such property had been sold by the partnership at its fair market value." Note that the unrealized receivable in this kind of case is not the whole property on which ordinary income will be recaptured. It is only a portion of the property, measured by the amount of recapture. The regulations describe the "unrealized receivable" that exists whenever a partnership has an asset that would generate income under § 1245(a) as "potential gain from section 1245 property."[4]

"Inventory Items." Section 751's definition of "inventory items" is also quite sweeping. According to § 751(d)(2), inventory items include not only property described in § 1221(a)(1) but also any other property that would not be a capital asset or a § 1231 asset if the partnership sold it. Therefore, many unrealized receivables (and, for that matter, receivables that are not "unrealized") are inventory items, too, because § 1221(a)(4) makes ordinary-income property of accounts receivable acquired in the ordinary course of a taxpayer's trade or business.[5]

---

4. Treas. Reg. § 1.751–1(c)(4)(iii).

5. Potential recapture income, however, is probably not "inventory" even though it may be an "unrealized receivable." Section 1245(a) characterizes gains as ordinary income, but it does not say that the property on which that gain is realized is something other than

A partner whose sale of a partnership interest triggers § 751(a) must notify the partnership of the sale. The partnership must file an information return identifying the transferor and transferee and furnishing information about the partnership's assets so that the ordinary income can be calculated.[6] One may reasonably doubt whether these requirements are widely observed, as many partners (like nearly all lawyers) have never heard of § 751.

3. Taxation of Look-through Gains Under Section 1(h)

Section 1(h) subjects some kinds of capital gains to a higher maximum tax rate than the usual fifteen percent rate. Among these are "collectibles gain," on which the maximum rate is twenty-eight percent, and "unrecaptured section 1250 gain," taxed at a maximum of twenty-five percent. Section 1(h)(5)(B) requires gain from the sale of a partnership interest "which is attributable to unrealized appreciation in the value of collectibles" to be treated as collectibles gain to the selling partner under rules similar to the rules of section 751. Section 1(h)(9) authorizes regulations applying § 1(h) to sales of interests in pass-thru entities, which include partnerships. The regulations call the share of collectibles gain and unrecaptured section 1250 gain allocable to a partnership interest "look-through capital gain."[7]

In simple cases, such as those in which a partnership has no assets on which a capital loss would be recognized, the application of § 1(h) to sales of partnership interests parallels § 751(a).

Example 10–4: The JKL equal partnership holds collectibles with a value of $90,000 and a basis of $30,000. It has no capital assets worth less than their bases. Partner Jill sells her one-third interest, which has a basis of $100,000, for $500,000. Jill recognizes a $400,000 long-term capital gain on the sale. Because Jill would have recognized $20,000 of collectibles gain if the partnership had sold all of its assets, she must recognize $20,000 of collectibles gain when she sells her partnership interest.[8] The $380,000 balance of her capital gain on the sale ("residual long-term capital gain") is taxable at a maximum rate of fifteen

---

a capital or § 1231 asset. Section 751(d)(2) turns upon the character of the asset, rather than the character of the gain that would be realized when the asset is sold. This is a delightfully fine distinction, though; perhaps too fine for the Service and for many courts.

Under § 751(a), it will not matter whether an asset that is an unrealized receivable is also an inventory item: either way, the selling partner will recognize ordinary income. Under § 751(b), however, the difference can be important, as we shall see in Chapter 12.

6. § 6050K.
7. Treas. Reg. § 1.1(h)–1(b)(1).
8. Treas. Reg. § 1.1(h)–1(f) (Example 1).

percent; the $20,000 of look-through gain is taxable at a maximum rate of twenty-eight percent.

If, instead of collectibles, the partnership had held a building, the sale of which would have triggered $60,000 of unrecaptured section 1250 gain, Jill would have recognized $20,000 of that kind of gain on the sale of her interest. That $20,000 of unrecaptured section 1250 gain would be taxed at a maximum rate of twenty-five percent

The calculation illustrated by Example 10–4 is identical to the calculation that would have been made under § 751(a) if the partnership had had § 751 property with a value of $90,000 and a basis of $30,000. Calculations under § 1(h) can differ from those under § 751(a), however. For example, if the JKL partnership's collectibles had been worth less than the total basis of those collectibles, Jill would not have had a collectibles loss on the sale of her partnership interest, even though she would have been allocated a collectibles loss if the partnership had sold all of its assets. Because § 1(h)(5)(B) deals only with gain attributable to unrealized appreciation in the value of partnership collectibles, the regulations say that any net collectibles loss is ignored when a partnership interest is sold.[9]

According to an example in the regulations, a selling partner may recognize a collectibles gain even if the partner would have recognized an overall capital loss on the sale of the partnership interest.[10] The partner in the example recognized $7,000 of ordinary income under § 751(a), $1,000 of collectibles gain under § 1(h)(5)(B), and a residual long-term capital loss of $2,000. Query whether a sale that produces an overall loss counting both capital and ordinary gains and losses can trigger § 1(h)(5)(B). That section makes collectibles gain of "any gain from the sale of an interest in a partnership ... attributable to unrealized appreciation in the value of collectibles...." If there is no overall gain from the sale of a partnership interest, § 1(h)(5)(B) would seem, on a literal reading, not to apply.

B. THE BUYER'S OUTSIDE AND INSIDE BASES

1. The Buyer's Outside Basis

Someone who buys a partnership interest will take that interest with a cost basis under § 1012. Like the seller's amount realized, the buyer's cost basis includes a share of the partnership's liabilities;

---

9. Treas. Reg. § 1.1–1(h)–1(f) (Example 3). Under § 751(a), the seller of a partnership interest will recognize an ordinary loss if the seller would have been allocated an ordinary loss on the sale by the partnership of all of its § 751 assets.

10. Treas. Reg. § 1.1–1(h)–1(f) (Example 3).

§ 752(d). The idea is to give the buyer the same cost basis as if a share of partnership assets, subject to liabilities, had been purchased.

Example 10–5: Oswald buys a twenty-five percent interest in the KLMN equal partnership from Nicole, paying her $60,000 in cash. The partnership has $40,000 of nonrecourse debt; Oswald's share of this becomes twenty-five percent, or $10,000. Oswald's cost basis for his partnership interest is $70,000.

2. Inside Basis Adjustments Under Section 743(b)

Just as § 751(a) taxes the seller of a partnership interest as being somewhat like a seller of a fraction of the partnership's assets, the buyer of a partnership interest can be treated in some respects like a buyer of assets. If the partnership has made an election under § 754, the basis of the partnership's assets will be adjusted under § 743(b) whenever a partnership interest changes hands "by sale or exchange or upon the death of a partner." Even if the partnership has not made a § 754 election, adjustments under § 743(b) are required if the partnership's total basis for its assets exceeds the assets' total value by more than $250,000.[11] The § 743(b) adjustment is made "with respect to the transferee partner only."[12]

Example 10–6: Paulette pays $100,000 to buy a twenty-five percent interest in QRST from Siegfried. The partnership's only asset is a machine worth $400,000. Because of depreciation deductions taken by the partnership, the machine's basis just before the sale was zero. If a § 754 election is in effect, the partnership will adjust the basis of the machine under § 743(b) "with respect to" Paulette only.

According to § 743(b)(1), the inside basis is adjusted upward. The amount of the adjustment is the difference between the buyer's outside basis and the buyer's proportionate share of the inside basis. In this case, since Paulette's outside basis is $100,000 and her share of the inside basis is zero, the adjustment is plus $100,000. During the useful life of the machine, the partnership will take $100,000 in depreciation deductions, and all of these deductions will be allocated to Paulette. If, shortly after Paulette bought her interest, the partnership had sold the machine for $400,000, the gain on the sale would have been $300,000—none of which would have been allocable to Paulette.

---

11. § 743(b) and (d).

12. § 743(b).

One way to look at the § 743(b) adjustment is to say that it puts the buyer of a partnership interest in much the same position as a buyer of partnership assets. In the example, if Paulette had bought a one-fourth interest in the machine itself for $100,000, she could have sold that interest for $100,000 without realizing any gain, or she could have taken $100,000 in depreciation on the machine. Allowing a step-up in the inside basis, with respect to her only, produces an equivalent outcome on these facts. Note that the § 743(b) formula for calculating basis adjustments makes the buyer's share of the inside basis (after the adjustment) equal to the buyer's outside basis.

a. Determining the Transferee's Share of Inside Basis

In very simple cases (those in which each partner has the same fractional interest in partnership capital, income, and losses and in which there are no assets subject to § 704(c)) the buyer's or heir's share of inside basis is simply the appropriate fractional share of the partnership's basis. Special allocations, allocations that must be made because of § 704(c), and differing interests in capital, profits, and losses require more complex calculations.

The regulations under § 743(b) provide that the transferee's share of inside basis is determined by examining a "hypothetical transaction" in which the partnership is deemed to sell all of its assets for their fair market values. If the partnership has no debt, the transferee's share of the inside basis is the amount of cash that would be received on a liquidation following the hypothetical transaction, plus any losses that would be allocated to the transferee, minus any gains that would be allocated to the transferee.[13] (The gains and losses are determined without regard to the § 743(b) adjustment.) This approach makes sense because the purpose of the § 743(b) adjustment is to make the transferee's share of inside basis equal to the transferee's outside basis. The gains and losses that the transferee would be allocated in the regulations' hypothetical transaction are a measure of the difference between what the inside basis is and what it should be.[14] Here is an example.

---

13. Treas. Reg. § 1.743–1(d).

14. This statement assumes that the transferee's outside basis equals the transferee's share of the value of all partnership assets. Cases in which a buyer pays too much or too little are dealt with by the regulations under § 755, which will be discussed below.

Example 10–7: The RST equal partnership holds these assets:

	Basis	Value
Asset A	$3,000	$12,000
Asset B	18,000	18,000
Asset C	6,000	9,000
Total:	$27,000	$39,000

Partner Ronald contributed Asset C to the partnership; its value and basis when contributed were the same as they are now. Under § 704(c), if the partnership should sell asset C for $9,000 or more, the first $3,000 of the gain would be allocated to Ronald.

Ronald sells his one-third interest in the partnership to Ursula for $13,000. In calculating Ursula's share of the inside basis, the regulations' hypothetical transaction consists of a sale by the partnership of all of its assets for $39,000 cash. If Ursula's interest were then liquidated, she would get $13,000 cash. Her share of the inside basis is this $13,000 minus her $3,000 share of the gain from the sale of asset A and also minus the entire $3,000 of gain that the partnership would recognize on selling Asset C (all of this gain would be allocated to Ursula, as Ronald's successor, by § 704(c)). Her share of the inside basis is therefore $7,000, and her § 743(b) adjustment is plus $6,000 (the difference between her outside basis of $13,000 and her share of inside basis of $7,000). Under § 755, the details of which will be examined below, $3,000 of this $6,000 adjustment will be allocated to Asset A, and the remaining $3,000 will be allocated to Asset C. Therefore, if the partnership should actually sell all of its assets for cash, Ursula's share of the partnership's gains would be zero, just as if she had bought a one-third interest in each asset for cash.[15]

If Ursula had bought her interest from a partner other than Ronald, her share of the inside basis would have been $10,000 and her § 743(b) adjustment would have been plus $3,000 (all allocated to Asset A). Again, if the partnership had then sold all of its assets for the values shown above, none of the gain would have been allocated to Ursula. She needs a larger positive

---

15. If Asset C had not been subject to a § 704(c) allocation, Ursula's share of the inside basis would have been $9,000 (one-third of the partnership's total inside basis). One can think of her $7,000 share of the inside basis as being this $9,000 reduced by the $2,000 extra gain she would have to recognize (but for § 743(b)) on the sale of Asset C.

If Ronald had contributed property with a basis exceeding its value, § 704(c)(1)(C) would have denied Ursula the use of that excess inside basis, even if no § 743(b) adjustments were made on the transfer. See Chapter 6. In effect, § 704(c)(1)(C) adjustments resemble mandatory negative adjustments under § 743(b).

adjustment when she buys Ronald's interest than when she buys one from another partner to offset the potential $3,000 of § 704(c) gain built into Asset C and allocable to Ronald, or his successor.

If a transferee partner has outside basis under § 752 because of partnership debt, the partner's share of the debt is added in calculating inside basis. Under this rule, if the RST partnership in Example 10–7 had had a $9,000 debt, and if Ursula had therefore paid $10,000 rather than $13,000 cash for her interest, her § 743(b) adjustment would have been the same as in the example. The amount of cash she would have received in the hypothetical transaction would have been $3,000 less, but this is offset by her $3,000 share of the debt.[16]

b. Allocating § 743(b) Adjustments to Particular Assets

Under prior law, a purchase or inheritance of an interest in a partnership that held more than one asset produced a very different result for the new partner than an equivalent transfer of assets.

Example 10–8: The VW equal partnership owns a capital asset with a basis of $200,000 and a value of $100,000. Its only other asset is inventory with a basis of zero and a value of $100,000. Victor dies, leaving his partnership interest to Junior.

If Junior had inherited a fifty percent interest in each asset, under § 1014 the basis of his fifty percent interest in each asset would have become that share's fair market value: $50,000. In other words, the basis of the capital asset would have been stepped down to $50,000 and the basis of the inventory would have increased to $50,000. When Junior inherits a partnership interest, however, the 743(b) formula produces an adjustment of zero, because Junior's $100,000 share of the inside basis equals his $100,000 outside basis. Under prior law, the usual outcome was therefore no adjustment to the basis of either asset.[17]

The current regulations under § 755, which controls the allocation of a § 743(b) adjustment among a partnership's assets, change the result

---

16. Treas. Reg. § 1.743–1(d)(1). The regulations define the transferee's share of inside basis as the transferee's share of previously taxed capital plus the transferee's share of partnership liabilities. They then say that the transferee's share of previously taxed capital is generally the sum of the cash that would be received in liquidation following the hypothetical transaction, plus any losses the transferee would recognize on the hypothetical sale, minus any gains that the transferee would recognize on that sale; id. Whatever exceptions may exist to this "general" approach are not mentioned.

17. Former Treas. Reg. § 1.755–1(a)(2) allowed adjustments that increased the basis of some assets and decreased the basis of others only with the District Director's permission.

of Example 10–8. As a rule, adjustments under § 743(b) can increase the bases of some assets and reduce the bases of others.[18] In Example 10–8, the total adjustment of zero would be made by reducing the basis of the capital asset by $50,000 and increasing the basis of the inventory by $50,000. (The approach of prior law is still used for cases in which the transferee's outside basis depends on the transferor's outside basis or on the basis of other property held by the transferee.[19])

The process of allocating basis adjustments consists of two steps. First, the adjustment is divided between two classes of partnership property: the "capital gain property class," consisting of all of the partnership's capital assets and § 1231 assets, and the class of "ordinary income property," consisting of everything else.[20] An amount equal to the net gain or loss from the sale of ordinary-income property that would have been allocated to the new partner (but for the § 743(b) adjustment) on a sale of that property by the partnership is allocated to the ordinary-income class. Any remaining adjustment goes to the capital-asset class. (There is one exception. If a negative adjustment to the capital-asset class would exceed the partnership's total basis for that property, the excess goes to the ordinary-income class.)

Example 10–9: The ABC partnership owns these assets:

	Basis	Value
Capital Asset A	$15,000	$30,000
Capital Asset B	12,000	30,000
§ 1231 Asset C	45,000	30,000
Inventory Item	15,000	18,000
Account Receivable	15,000	15,000
	$102,000	$123,000

Denise buys a one-third interest in the partnership, paying $41,000 (one-third of the value of the partnership's assets). Her

---

18. Treas. Reg. §§ 1.755–1(b)(1) through 1.755–1(b)(4).

19. For example, if someone transfers a partnership interest to a corporation in a transaction covered by § 351, the transferee corporation's basis is determined by reference to the transferee's basis for the partnership interest. In cases like this, if the total adjustment is zero, no adjustment is made to the basis of any asset; if the total adjustment is positive or negative, only positive or negative adjustments are made. Treas. Reg. § 1.755–1(b)(5).

20. Treas. Reg. § 1.755–1(b)(2). In dividing property between the capital-asset and ordinary-income-asset classes, property and potential gains treated as unrealized receivables under § 751(c) are considered ordinary-income assets; Treas. Reg. § 1.755–1(a)(1).

proportionate share of the inside basis, before any adjustment, is $34,000. Her § 743(b) adjustment is therefore plus $7,000 if a § 754 election is in effect.

The amount of the $7,000 adjustment allocated to the ordinary-income class is $1,000, the amount that would be allocated to Denise if the partnership were to sell its ordinary-income assets (the inventory and the account receivable) for their values. This leaves $6,000 to be allocated to the capital-gain class, which makes sense on these numbers because the net appreciation in the capital-gain class is $18,000, and Denise's one-third share of that appreciation is $6,000.

The allocation between classes in Example 10–9 resulted in an adjustment for each class equal to Denise's share of the appreciation of the property in that class. This will happen whenever the new partner's basis equals the value of that partner's share of partnership property. In cases of inherited partnership interests, this will always be the case. When a partnership interest is purchased, however, the buyer may over- or under-pay. In that kind of case, the total § 743(b) adjustment will be greater or less than the difference between the buyer's share of inside basis and the buyer's share of the value of the assets.[21] By starting with an allocation of the "right amount" to the ordinary-income class and allocating only what is left to the capital-gain class, the regulations assign any excess adjustment or any deficiency in the adjustment to the capital-gain class.

Example 10–10: The facts are the same as in Example 10–9 except that Denise paid only $40,000 for her partnership interest. Her § 743(b) adjustment is therefore plus $6,000. As in Example 10–9, $1,000 of the adjustment is allocated to the ordinary-income class. The $5,000 balance goes to the capital-gain class.

Once the adjustment has been divided between the two classes, the adjustment for each class must be allocated among the assets in that class. The basic idea (as with the allocation between classes) is to allocate the adjustment according to the amounts of gain or loss the transferee would be allocated if those assets were sold.[22] If the amount of

---

21. The fact that the purchase price of a partnership interest exceeds the value of an appropriate share of the partnership's tangible assets does not necessarily mean that the buyer has overpaid. The excess may be the cost of goodwill, or of some other intangible asset. If the partnership's assets consist of a trade or business, any excess in purchase price over the value of the partnership's tangible assets is first allocated to the partnership's section 197 intangibles and its goodwill (whether or not that goodwill is a section 197 intangible). Treas. Reg. § 1.755–1(a)(2) provides this general rule, the details of which are spelled out in Treas. Reg. § 1.755–1(a)(5). Under these rules, a buyer can never overpay for an interest in a partnership that conducts a business.

22. Treas. Reg. §§ 1.755–1(b)(3)(i)(A), 1.755–1(b)(3)(ii)(A).

the adjustment equals the net appreciation or depreciation for the class, this process will work perfectly.

Example 10–11: The facts are the same as in Example 10–9. The plus $1,000 adjustment for the ordinary-income class is allocated to the inventory. The plus $6,000 adjustment for the capital-gain class is allocated as follows:

        Capital Asset A: plus $5,000

        Capital Asset B: plus $6,000

        1231 Asset C: minus $5,000.

If the amount of the adjustment allocated to a class does not equal the buyer's share of the net appreciation or depreciation in that class, the intra-class allocation is more complex. In the case of ordinary-income assets, a buyer's total basis increase or decrease will differ from the buyer's share of the appreciation or depreciation for that class if an excess reduction to the capital-gain class was transferred to the ordinary-income class under the rules for the inter-class allocation.[23] When this occurs, the excess reduction is allocated among the ordinary-income assets in proportion to their values.[24] If the total adjustment for the buyer's share of assets in the capital-asset class differs from the amount of gain or loss the buyer would recognize if the partnership sold those assets,[25] the difference is also allocated among the assets according to their relative values.[26]

Example 10–12: The facts are the same as in Example 10–10. The ideal allocation of the adjustment (Example 10–11) cannot be accomplished because the total adjustment for the capital-gain class is only $5,000. The $1,000 deficiency is allocated among the assets in proportion to their relative values. As all are equal in value, the ideal allocation to each asset is reduced by $333. The adjustments are therefore:

        Capital Asset A: plus $4,667

        Capital Asset B: plus $5,667

        1231 Asset C: minus $5,333.

---

23. Treas. Reg. § 1.755–1(b)(2)(B), discussed in the text accompanying notes 19 to 20, above.

24. Treas. Reg. § 1.755–1(b)(3)(i).

25. This will happen whenever the buyer has over-or underpaid for the partnership interest.

26. Treas. Reg. § 1.755–1(b)(3)(ii) sets forth this simple rule in mathematical language that approaches the incomprehensible.

Basis adjustments allocated as described above sometimes shift to other property. For example, suppose that a $1,000 adjustment is made to the basis of a particular asset when a partner inherits an interest in the partnership. If this particular asset is later distributed to a partner other than the heir, the $1000 adjustment is reallocated to whatever property remains, so that the heir can still use the adjustment.[27]

c. Using the § 743(b) Adjustment

When a basis adjustment has been made, one describes the basis of the partnership property by saying that the property has a "common basis" (the inside basis before the adjustment) and a "special basis adjustment" with respect to the buyer or heir. Because this is an adjustment "with respect to the transferee partner only,"[28] it normally affects only the transferee's distributive share.[29] A partnership that recognizes gain or loss on selling property with respect to which there is a § 743(b) adjustment calculates partnership-level gain or loss using the property's common basis. The partnership allocates this gain or loss among the partners and then recalculates the transferee's distributive share to take the basis adjustment into account.[30]

> **Example 10–13:** The ABC partnership (Examples 10–9 through 10–12) sells its inventory item for $21,000. The partnership's income from this sale (calculated by using the partnership's common basis of $15,000) is $6,000, which is allocated $2,000 to each partner. Because Denise has a special basis adjustment of plus $1,000 for this item, her distributive share of the gain on the sale is $1,000.

Adjustments to the basis of depreciable property affect the transferee's share of depreciation. Positive adjustments are taken into account as if they were the purchase price of assets purchased by the partnership at the time of the transfer that triggered the adjustment.[31] So, if a partnership holds property with a recovery period of five years under § 168, and if the property gets a $1,000 positive § 743(b) adjustment when the partnership has two years of depreciation left, the $1,000 is recovered

---

27. Treas. Reg. § 1.743–1(g)(2).

28. § 743(b).

29. There are exceptions. For instance, if the partnership contributes its property to a corporation in a § 351 exchange, the corporation takes the property with a basis that includes any special basis adjustment; Treas. Reg. § 1.743–1(h)(2).

30. Treas. Reg. § 1.743–1(j)(2).

31. Treas. Reg. § 1.743–1(j)(4)(i)(B)(*1*). A special and somewhat complex rule applies when the asset in question is subject to § 704(c) and the partnership uses remedial allocations to correct ceiling-rule distortions; Treas. Reg. § 1.743–1(j)(4)(i)(B)(2).

over the five-year period beginning on the date of the adjustment. Negative adjustments to the basis of depreciable property reduce the transferee's distributive share of depreciation deductions over the partnership's remaining recovery period.[32]

d. The Section 754 Election and Adjustments Required Without a 754 Election for Substantial Built-in Loss

The adjustment to basis under § 743 occurs if the partnership makes an election under § 754 or if the partnership has a "substantial built-in loss" after the transfer. The partnership makes the § 754 election by filing a statement with its return for its taxable year for which the election first applies.[33] It is possible, therefore, to make the election after a transfer that triggers basis adjustments has taken place. Thus, if a member of a calendar-year partnership that has not made a § 754 election dies during year one, an election filed in year two with the partnership's return for year one will adjust the partnership's inside basis with respect to the decedent's successor. An election, once made, remains in effect until it is revoked, and revocation requires the District Director's permission.[34]

Making a § 754 election will often save taxes for transferee partners, especially when adjustments under § 743(b) increase the basis of depreciable property or of inventory, accounts receivable, and other assets which the partnership will dispose of in the course of its activities. Why, then, should not all partnerships file § 754 elections? There are three reasons. First, if the transferee partner's outside basis is lower than the proportionate share of the inside basis, the § 743(b) adjustment will reduce inside basis with respect to the transferee, and this will normally increase the transferee's taxes. Second, adjustments under § 743(b) can be cumbersome to calculate, especially if the partnership holds many assets. Third, if a § 754 election is in effect, inside basis must be adjusted not only upon transfers of partnership interests by sale or death, but also in many cases involving partnership distributions (§ 734(b)). Adjustments triggered by distributions may be unfavorable

---

32. Treas. Reg. § 1.743–1(j)(4)(ii)(A). If a partner's negative adjustment for a particular depreciable asset exceeds the partner's share of the basis of that asset, the excess first reduces the partner's share of other depreciation. If there isn't enough of that, the partner recognizes ordinary income; Treas. Reg. § 1.743–1(j)(4)(ii)(A).

33. Treas. Reg. § 1.754–1(b).

34. Treas. Reg. § 1.754–1(c). Treas. Reg. § 1.754–1(c)(2) gives partnerships with an election in effect for a taxable year that included December 15, 1999, the right to revoke that election without permission. December 15, 1999, was the effective date of the current regulations under §§ 743(b) and 755; these regulations differ from and are more complex than the earlier regulations.

for the partners; indeed, as we shall see, they sometimes produce remarkably strange outcomes, at least if the statute is read literally.[35]

Even if a § 754 election is not made, a partnership must adjust the inside basis of its assets if a partnership has a "substantial built-in loss" immediately after the transfer of a partnership interest. A built-in loss is "substantial" if the partnership's total basis for its assets exceeds the assets' total value by more than $250,000.[36]

Example 10–14: Austen and Barbara are equal partners in the AB partnership, which holds one asset with a basis of $500,000 and fair market value of $100,000. Alice purchases Austin's partnership interest for $50,000. Although the partnership has not and will not make a § 754 election, it must adjust the inside basis of its asset downward with respect to Alice because the partnership has a substantial built-in loss (the basis of AB's asset, $500,000, exceeds its fair market value of $100,000 by more than $250,000). As a result, Alice's share of the inside basis of the partnership's asset is $50,000.

3. Basis Adjustments Under Section 732(d)

Partnerships willing to distribute property to a new partner can get the equivalent of a one-shot election to adjust the basis of partnership property. Section 732(d) allows a partner who acquires an interest when a § 754 election was not in effect, and who receives a distribution of partnership property within two years of the transfer, to elect to determine the basis of the distributed property as if adjustments under § 743(b) had been made when the partner acquired the partnership interest.

Example 10–15: Igor buys a twenty-five percent interest in IJKL for $100,000. The partnership's assets at the time of the purchase consist of zero-basis inventory worth $200,000 and a capital asset with a basis and value of $200,000. No § 754 election is in effect. A year after the purchase, the partnership is contemplating selling its inventory for $200,000; this sale will result in Igor's having $50,000 of ordinary income. If the partnership had made § 743(b) adjustments when Igor bought his interest, the inventory's inside basis with respect to Igor would have become $50,000, and he would therefore have had no ordinary income when the partnership sold the inventory.

If the IJKL partnership distributes a one-fourth interest in its inventory to Igor,[37] and if Igor makes a § 732(d) election, the

---

35. See Chapter 14.
36. § 743(d).
37. On these facts, a distribution of one-fourth of the inventory would work, too, though that transaction is dealt with by very cumbersome calculations.

partnership's basis for the inventory it distributes to Igor will be $50,000, just as if a § 754 election had been in effect when Igor bought his interest. Under § 732,[38] Igor will take the inventory with this $50,000 basis. If he then sells the inventory for $50,000, he will recognize no gain or loss.[39]

C. COLLATERAL EFFECTS OF A SALE OF A PARTNERSHIP INTEREST

The sale of all of a partner's interest in a partnership closes the partnership's taxable year with respect to the seller (but not necessarily with respect to the other partners).[40] If the seller sells only a portion of a partnership interest, the sale does not close the partnership's taxable year even with respect to the seller.[41] Whether or not a sale closes the partnership's taxable year, the distributive shares of the seller and the buyer must be determined by taking into account "the varying interests of the partners in the partnership during such taxable year."[42] Under § 706(d)(2), several kinds of income and deductions must be prorated in order to measure the seller's and buyer's distributive shares accurately. As the regulations under § 706(d)(2) have not yet been written, there is a fair amount of uncertainty about how this proration is to be accomplished.

Some sales of partnership interests will cause the partnership to terminate under § 708(b). According to § 708(b)(1)(B), a partnership terminates if "within a 12–month period there is a sale or exchange of 50 percent or more of the total interest in partnership capital and profits." Thus, if a partner with a sixty percent interest in partnership capital and profits sells that interest, the partnership will terminate. A partnership will also terminate if a partner with a sixty percent interest in capital and profits sells half of that interest and, within a year of that sale, another partner with a thirty percent interest sells that entire interest.

---

38. Section 732 will be discussed in Chapter 11.

39. In some (rare) cases, adjustments under § 732(d) are mandatory. Mandatory adjustments will be made even if the partnership distributes the property more than two years after the transfer. For circumstances in which the adjustment would be mandatory, see Treas. Reg. § 1.732–1(d)(4). The mandatory basis adjustment keeps distributions from shifting basis from non-depreciable to depreciable property. This kind of shift once occurred fairly often because the former version of § 732(c) allocated the distributee's basis for distributed property to specific assets according to the bases of those assets in the partnership's hands. Section 732(c) has been amended to make it less distorting, and the mandatory adjustment may have outlived its usefulness. Not that it was ever all that useful: all of the reported cases involving mandatory adjustments were cases in which the taxpayer, rather than the Government, wanted the adjustment made.

40. § 706(c)(2)(A).

41. § 706(c)(1).

42. § 706(d)(1).

When a partnership terminates under § 708(b)(1), the partnership is treated as if it had contributed all of its assets and liabilities to a new partnership. (This new "partnership" has only one partner (the old partnership).) The old partnership is then deemed to liquidate, distributing its only asset (a 100–percent interest in the new partnership) to the members of the old partnership who did not sell their interests and to those whose purchases caused the partnership to terminate.[43] Because transfers of property to partnerships are normally tax-free, as are many liquidations, these events will seldom have adverse tax consequences to the remaining partners.[44] Furthermore, some of the consequences that would normally attach to an actual contribution of assets to a new partnership are called off by the regulations. For instance, property that was not subject to § 704(c) allocations when held by the old partnership is not treated as § 704(c) property in the hands of the new partnership, even if its value differs from its basis at the time of the constructive contribution.[45] The idea is to make the change from the old partnership to the new one as uneventful as possible.

D. COMPARISON WITH SUBCHAPTER S

1. Calculating Gain on the Sale of Stock

Because an S corporation's debt is not reflected in its shareholders' bases for their stock, there is no need to treat a portion of that debt as an "amount realized" when shareholders sell stock. Subchapter S therefore contains no provision comparable to § 752(d).

2. Character of Gain and Inside Basis Adjustments Upon Transfers of Interests

Neither § 751(a) nor § 743(b), the two provisions which make the taxation of transfers of partnership interests very complex in many cases, has a parallel in subchapter S. The gain recognized when the shareholder of an S corporation sells stock can be a capital gain, even if the corporation's assets consist entirely of accounts receivable, inventory, and depreciated machinery, all of which would produce ordinary income if sold by the corporation.[46] And no adjustment is made to the

---

43. Treas. Reg. § 1.708–1(b)(1)(iv).

44. The former version of the regulations treated the terminated partnership as distributing all of its assets to its partners, who were then treated as contributing them to the new partnership. Former Treas. Reg. § 1.708–1(b)(1)(iv). Some of these liquidating distributions were taxable (as when a partner's share of cash exceeded that partner's outside basis). In addition, this kind of liquidating distribution usually changed the basis of the distributed assets. The tax treatment of a constructive termination under the former regulations was complex and often harsh.

45. Treas. Reg. § 1.708–1(b)(1)(iv) (Example).

46. Section 1(h)(5)(B) does apply to S corporations, however, so the seller of stock of an S corporation that holds collectibles may be treated as recognizing collectibles gain. Section

inside basis when shares of an S corporation are sold. The taxation of those who hold shares of S corporations is in these respects cruder, and much more simple, than the taxation of partners.

Some inaccuracies created by subchapter S's failure to attribute ordinary income to the seller of stock and its refusal to allow inside basis adjustments with respect to the buyer of stock will cancel out. Consider a very simple case in which an entity holds no assets except zero-basis unrealized receivables, worth $75,000, and suppose that the owner of a one-third interest in that entity sells the interest for $25,000. If the entity is a partnership and if the seller's outside basis is zero, the seller will have $25,000 of ordinary income under § 751(a). If a § 754 election is in effect, the basis of the receivables will be stepped up, with respect to the buyer, to $25,000. This basis step-up will prevent the buyer's being taxed on $25,000 of ordinary income when the partnership collects or sells the receivables. If the entity is an S corporation, the seller will have no ordinary income on the sale and the buyer will get no step-up of inside basis. Therefore, the ordinary income will be taxed, but to those who are shareholders during the year in which the corporation sells the assets rather than to the seller.

The ability to adjust inside basis will sometimes be a reason for organizing an activity as a partnership rather than as an S corporation.

Example 10–16: Egmont and Felicia plan to buy and operate a hotel. Over the next thirty-odd years, depreciation deductions will reduce the hotel building's basis to zero. If one of the owners should die at that point, the owner's successor may be in a better tax position if the hotel is owned by a partnership which will make a § 754 election than if it is owned by an S corporation.

To make the matter concrete, suppose that the hotel building is the only asset, and that its value at Egmont's death is $2,000,000. The building's basis at that time is zero. If Egmont's heir, Gretel, inherits a 50–percent interest in a partnership which owns the hotel building and which has made a § 754 election, her outside basis will be $1,000,000 under § 1014. The basis of the hotel will increase, under § 743(b), to $1,000,000 with respect to Gretel. This increase will give Gretel $1,000,000 in depreciation deductions if she holds the partnership interest long enough. But if Gretel inherits half the stock of an S corporation, which owns the hotel, the hotel's basis will remain

---

1(h)(9) authorizes regulations applying all of § 1(h) to S corporations as well as to partnerships, but the regulations under § 1(h) distinguish between S corporations and partnerships by taxing selling partners, but not selling shareholders, on their shares of the entity's unrecaptured section 1250 gains. Taking into account an S corporation's potential collectibles gains while ignoring its potential ordinary income seems a curious policy decision.

zero. Gretel's basis for her stock will be $1,000,000, but that basis will seldom do her much good unless she disposes of the stock.

3. Termination by Sale

Unlike a partnership, an S corporation does not terminate when a large fraction of its stock is sold. The rule terminating a partnership on a sale of half its capital and profits interests in a twelve-month period is easy to avoid. For example, sales can be stretched out over a period of more than twelve months, or partners who are leaving can have their interests liquidated by the partnership instead of selling them. Whether the rule of § 708(b)(1)(B) is worth keeping is questionable.

Chapter Eleven

PARTNERSHIP DISTRIBUTIONS: AN INTRODUCTION

One might think that the tax treatment of a partnership's transferring money or property to one or more partners should be fairly simple; as simple, for instance, as the treatment of distributions by S corporations having no earnings and profits. Unfortunately, partnership distributions are subject to some of the most difficult Code provisions ever written. Section 736, for instance, attempts only the task of classifying payments to retiring partners (and to the successors of deceased partners). Judge Arnold Raum of the Tax Court has questioned whether this section is "reasonably comprehensible" even to "the average tax expert who has not given special attention and extended study to the tax problems of partners."[1] The statutory provisions in this area were drafted by people with a marvelous willingness to tolerate complexity.

This Chapter will present the fundamental rules for recognizing gain or loss and for determining basis when a partnership distributes money or property to a partner. Learning these rules by heart will not in itself put you in a position to advise anyone about even the simplest transaction. There are three complicating factors. First, not all payments by a partnership to a partner are distributions. For example, § 736 provides that many payments to a retiring partner or to a decedent's successor are guaranteed payments or distributive shares. Second, the usual rules for taxing distributions are often overridden by § 751(b), which treats some distributions as consisting of different, "constructive" distributions, followed by exchanges of the constructively distributed money or property between the partner and the partnership. Third, distributions can trigger inside basis adjustments if a § 754 election is in effect or if certain other circumstances discussed in Chapter 14 exist. Accurate advice about the tax treatment of distributions can be given only by one who has learned the workings of several complex Code provisions well enough to think about how they interact with each other in specific cases.

The cases in this Chapter have been kept unrealistically simple to avoid having to consider two or more sets of rules at the same time. Later Chapters will begin to approach real-life situations.

---

1. Foxman v. Commissioner, 41 T.C. 535, 551 n.9 (1964) (Acq.), affirmed, 352 F.2d 466 (3d Cir. 1965).

A. THE GENERAL PRINCIPLE OF NONRECOGNITION

As a rule, neither the partner nor the partnership recognizes gain or loss on a distribution of money or property in a current distribution (one that reduces the partner's interest in the partnership but does not eliminate it) or in a liquidating distribution.[2] Under § 731, a partner recognizes gain only when the partnership distributes cash in excess of the partner's outside basis and only recognizes losses in rare circumstances.[3] As usual with nonrecognition transactions, the basis rules preserve for future recognition whatever gains or losses went unrecognized when the distribution took place.

Example 11–1: Horatio, a twenty-percent partner in HIJ, receives a distribution of property from the partnership. The receipt of this distribution reduces Horatio's partnership interest to ten percent. The property is a capital asset worth $50,000, which had a basis in the partnership's hands of $40,000. Horatio's outside basis just before the distribution was $95,000.

Under §§ 731(a) and (b), neither Horatio nor the partnership recognizes gain or loss on the distribution. Section 732(a) provides that, as a general rule, the basis of the property in the partner's hands is the same as its basis in the partnership's hands; in this example, Horatio would take the property with a basis of $40,000. To make things work out right in the long run, the basis of Horatio's partnership interest is reduced by the basis (to *him*) of the distributed property; § 733. Horatio's new outside basis therefore becomes $55,000 ($95,000 minus $40,000). Horatio ends up with the same total basis for the property he owns (the partnership interest and the capital asset he received in the distribution) as before the distribution. This makes sense because Horatio has recognized no gain or loss. If Horatio sells the distributed property for $50,000, his gain on that sale will be $10,000 ($50,000 minus $40,000), the same as the gain the partnership would have recognized if it had sold the property for $50,000.

If Horatio's outside basis before the distribution had been less than the partnership's basis for the property, the rules applied in Example

---

2. § 731.

3. The circumstances in which partners recognize gains or losses under § 731 are discussed at page 151. A partner may also recognize gain or loss in certain other situations under sections 704(c) and 737, which are described at pages 84–86, and under § 751, which is described in Chapter 12.

11–1 would have given Horatio a negative basis for his partnership interest. To prevent this, § 732(a)(2) limits the distributee's basis for the property received to the distributee's outside basis before the distribution (less any money distributed in the same transaction).

Example 11–2: Assume the same facts as in Example 11–1 except that Horatio's outside basis is $33,000. Although the general rule under § 732(a)(1) is that a distributee takes property in a nonliquidating distribution with the same basis that the partnership had, § 732(a)(2) says that the distributee's basis in such property cannot exceed the distributee's outside basis. Thus, Horatio cannot take the distributed property with the partnership's inside basis of $40,000. Instead, his basis in the distributed property is limited to $33,000 and his new basis in his partnership interest is zero under § 733.[4]

Cash distributions reduce the recipient's outside basis dollar for dollar. If cash and other property are distributed together in a nonliquidating distribution, cash is applied first to reduce the distributee's basis before accounting for the other property.[5] This order is often beneficial because it allows the partner to apply the maximum amount of outside basis to the cash distribution and thereby minimize gain recognition. Any basis remaining after the cash distribution is then applied to determine the partner's basis in the other distributed property.

Example 11–3: Karen and Len are partners in the KL partnership. Karen's outside basis is $1,000.

In a nonliquidating distribution, the partnership distributes to Karen $400 cash and a partnership asset with an inside basis of $700. Karen's outside basis is reduced to $600 by the $400 cash distribution under § 733(1). Karen takes the distributed property with a basis of $600 under § 732(a)(2) and her outside basis becomes zero under § 733(2).

Because the cash distribution is accounted for first, Karen avoids recognizing gain. If the asset distribution had been accounted for first, Karen would take the distributed asset with a basis of $700 under § 732(a)(1) and would have had only $300 of outside basis left under § 733 to apply against the $400 cash distribution. This would have caused Karen to recognize $100 of gain under § 731 because the $400 cash distribution would have exceeded her outside basis of $300 by $100.

---

4. Section 733 provides that a distribution cannot reduce a partner's outside basis below zero. For property distributions, this limit is achieved automatically by § 732(a)(2), so the § 733 limit comes into effect only in cases involving distributions of cash.

5. Treas. Reg. § 1.732–1(a).

In a liquidating distribution (a distribution that terminates the partner's interest in the partnership), a partner takes a basis in the distributed property equal to her outside basis immediately before the distribution, less any money distributed; § 732(b). This rule preserves the recipient's unrecognized gain or loss. It also in effect requires that cash distributions be accounted for first in liquidating distributions, as is the case in nonliquidating distributions.

Example 11–4: Carla, Dave and Edna are equal partners in the CDE partnership. The CDE partnership has $900 cash and also holds three parcels of land, each of which has a tax basis of $1,000 and a fair market value of $3,000. Carla's outside basis in her partnership interest is $2,000.

The partnership distributes $300 cash and one parcel to Carla in liquidation of her partnership interest. The receipt of $300 cash reduces Carla's outside basis to $1,700 ($2,000 minus $300). Carla's basis in the parcel distributed to her is therefore $1,700 under § 732(b).

If the partnership distributes more than one asset, the total basis of those assets is calculated according to the rules described above. If the distribution does not change the basis of the distributed property, each asset has the same basis in the partner's hands as it had in the partnership's hands. But the total basis of the distributed property may change as a result of the distribution. This will generally happen in two cases: (1) the distribution is a current distribution and the partner's outside basis was less than the total bases of the distributed properties plus the cash distributed, or (2) the distribution is a liquidating distribution, in which case the partner's outside basis (less cash received) becomes the new total basis for the distributed property.[6] In these cases, the total basis of the distributed property is allocated according to rules set forth in § 732(c). These rules are designed to prevent the basis of unrealized receivables and inventory items (as defined in § 751)[7] from being stepped up, and to reduce basis-value differences for other assets, whenever possible.

The first step in allocating the total basis of distributed property among the assets the partner received is to allocate that basis to inventory items and unrealized receivables in an amount equal to the bases of those assets when they were held by the partnership.[8] If there is not enough total basis to allow this, unrealized receivables and inventory will have their bases reduced according to a formula provided by

---

6. Chapter 14 discusses other special situations in which § 734 will cause total basis of distributed property to change.

7. See the discussion in Chapter 8.

8. § 732(c)(1)(A).

§ 732(c)(3). If the distributee partner has received any unrealized receivables or inventory items with values less than basis, the decrease is allocated to those assets in proportion to their relative amounts of unrealized depreciation, but this allocation cannot reduce the basis of an item to less than its value.[9] Any further reduction is then allocated in proportion to the bases of all the unrealized receivables and inventory received by the distributee partner.[10] Any basis left over after unrealized receivables and inventory have received their shares is allocated to other assets.[11]

Example 11–5: John, a partner in JKL, receives a current distribution consisting of these assets:

Partnership's	Value	Basis
Inventory Item A:	$10,000	$6,000
Inventory Item B:	$10,000	$11,000
Capital Asset X:	$20,000	$15,000

John's outside basis before the distribution was $16,000, so the total basis for the distributed property in John's hands is $16,000. Under § 732(c)(1)(A), this $16,000 should be allocated to the two inventory items in the amounts of $6,000 and $11,000, respectively. As there is not enough total basis to do that, the $1,000 deficiency is allocated entirely to Inventory Item B (the only ordinary-income asset having unrealized depreciation). §§ 732(c)(1)(A); 732(c)(3)(A). The end result is that Inventory Item A has a basis of $6,000 in John's hands, Inventory Item B has a $10,000 basis, and Capital Asset X has a zero basis.

If John's outside basis before the distribution had been $22,000, the basis of Inventory Items A and B would have been $6,000 and $11,000, respectively (§ 732(c)(1)(A)), and the basis of the capital asset would have been $5,000 (§ 732(c)(1)(B)).

The rules described above guarantee that a distribution cannot increase the basis of an unrealized receivable or of inventory. This treatment keeps many distributions from reducing the amount of potential ordinary income in the tax base. Most ordinary-income assets are unrealized receivables or inventory (or both), and these assets cannot have their bases increased by distributing them to partners. However,

---

9. §§ 732(c)(1)(A) and 732(c)(3)(A).
10. §§ 732(c)(1)(A) and 732(c)(3)(B).
11. § 732(c)(1)(B).

there appears to be a major loophole. For purposes of the basis rules, potential recapture and various other items listed in § 751(c) are "unrealized receivables."[12] The portion of a depreciable asset that has a basis, however, is *not* an unrealized receivable. Thus, a nontaxable distribution can increase the basis of depreciable property. This increase will eventually reduce ordinary income.

Example 11–6: A partner with an outside basis of $30,000 receives a liquidating distribution of depreciable property having a basis of $20,000 in the partnership's hands and a value of $20,000. Under § 732, the basis of this asset in the partner's hands is $30,000, so the partner can take $10,000 more depreciation than the partnership could have taken.

What if the distributed asset had had a value of $25,000, with the $5,000 gain that would have been recognized on its sale being ordinary income under § 1245? In that case, the asset is viewed as being two assets: an unrealized receivable with a basis of zero and a value of $5,000 and an asset that is not an unrealized receivable with a basis of $20,000 and a value of $20,000. According to § 732(c), the "unrealized receivable" portion of this asset (the potential recapture) keeps its zero basis. The other portion of the asset gets a $10,000 basis increase, however, so the asset's total basis is still $30,000. Apparently, the partner will recognize no ordinary income on selling this property for its value, despite the Code's treatment of the potential recapture as an unrealized receivable.

After the total basis of distributed property is allocated to unrealized receivables and inventory items (up to the amount of basis those assets had in the partnership's hands) the remaining basis is allocated to other assets. The allocation of basis among assets other than unrealized receivables and inventory is also made according to their bases to the partnership. If there is not enough total basis to do this, the deficiency is allocated among the assets in the same way as deficiencies for inventory and unrealized receivables are allocated. If the basis of the assets (as a whole) is increased by the distribution, the basis increase is allocated first in proportion to unrealized appreciation, if there is any. Any further increase is allocated in proportion to the values of the assets.

Example 11–7: The KLM partnership holds the following assets:

---

12. See the reference to § 732 in § 751(c) (first sentence after § 751(c)(2)).

	Basis	Value
Cash	$60,000	$60,000
Inventory	30,000	36,000
Capital Asset A	10,000	20,000
Capital Asset B	10,000	30,000
Capital Asset C	25,000	40,000
Total	$135,000	$186,000

Partner Magda receives a liquidating distribution consisting of one-third of the inventory (basis $10,000, value $12,000) and all of Capital Assets A and B. Her outside basis immediately before the distribution was $45,000.

Magda recognizes no gain or loss on the distribution. Her total basis for the property she receives is $45,000: her outside basis less the amount of money (zero).[13] This $45,000 basis is allocated first to the inventory, in an amount equal to the partnership's basis for that inventory item, or $10,000.[14] The rest ($35,000) goes to Capital Assets A and B, in an amount equal to the bases of those assets, or $10,000 each.[15] This leaves $15,000, which is allocated to the capital assets in proportion to their unrealized appreciation.[16] As Capital Asset A has half as much unrealized appreciation as Capital Asset B, $5000 of the $15,000 excess goes to Asset A, and $10,000 goes to Asset B. In the end, Magda takes the inventory with a basis of $10,000, Capital Asset A with a basis of $15,000, and Capital Asset B with a basis of $20,000.

If Magda's outside basis had been $75,000, her basis for the inventory would still have been $10,000. Section 732(c)(1)(B) would then have allocated $10,000 each (the amount of their bases) to Capital Assets A and B. Then, § 732(c)(2)(A) would have allocated $10,000 of basis to Capital Asset A and $20,000 of basis to Capital Asset B (these are the amounts of unrealized appreciation for those assets). Finally, under § 732(c)(2)(B), the final $15,000 of basis would have been allocated $6000 to capital Asset A and $9000 to Capital Asset B, in proportion to the values of those assets. This would have left Magda with a

---

13. § 732(b).
14. § 732(c)(1)(A)(i).
15. § 732(c)(1)(B).
16. § 732(c)(1)(B); § 732(c)(2)(A).

$10,000 basis for the inventory, a $26,000 basis for Capital Asset A, and a $39,000 basis for Capital asset B.

B. CASES IN WHICH GAIN OR LOSS IS RECOGNIZED

1. Gain Recognition

If a partner with an outside basis of $12,000 gets a cash distribution of $15,000, either $3,000 of gain must be recognized or the partner's outside basis must be reduced to less than zero. The Code does not permit a negative basis in subchapters C, S or K. Indeed, negative basis would be particularly unappealing if the distribution has liquidated the partner's interest in the partnership, because the partner would own nothing that could have any basis, let alone a negative one. Section 731(a) provides for recognition of gain whenever the amount of cash distributed exceeds the partner's outside basis immediately before the distribution.

> **Example 11–8:** Lenny, whose outside basis is $50,000, receives a current distribution made up of $60,000 in cash and an asset worth $20,000. Because the amount of cash Lenny received exceeds his $50,000 outside basis by $10,000, Lenny recognizes a $10,000 gain.

Prior to 1994, partnerships could easily avoid gain recognition under § 731(a) by using cash to buy marketable securities and distributing those securities, rather than the cash. If the partner who would have received cash planned to invest that cash in securities anyway, this technique allowed nonrecognition at little or no non-tax cost. Section 731(c) currently provides that marketable securities (defined very broadly) are treated as "money" for purposes of § 731(a). When a partner recognizes gain on a distribution because marketable securities are treated as cash, the basis that those securities would otherwise have had under § 732 is increased by the amount of the gain.[17] Section 731(c) contains many exceptions. For example, investment partnerships are exempt, as are most distributions of marketable securities to the partner who contributed them to the partnership.

If a partnership buys securities, which then appreciate, a distribution of a partner's share of the appreciated securities should not trigger gain recognition, as the case is similar to one in which that partner simply bought that portion of the securities individually. For this reason, the gain that would otherwise have to be recognized under § 731(c) is

---

17. § 732(c)(1)(B).

reduced by the amount of the distribution that represents the distributee's share of partnership appreciation; § 731(c)(3)(B).

Example 11–9: The LMN equal partnership buys securities for $30,000 cash. The securities increase in value to $90,000. Partner Mike, whose outside basis is $40,000, receives a liquidating distribution consisting of $30,000 worth of these securities (basis to the partnership $10,000) and $20,000 in cash. Under the general rule of § 731(c), this would be treated as a distribution of $50,000 cash, and Mike would recognize a $10,000 gain. This would make little sense, as Mike would not have recognized any gain if he had bought this $30,000 worth of securities for $10,000 cash rather than making his investment through the partnership. Section 731(c)(3)(B) reduces the $10,000 gain that Mike would otherwise have to recognize by the $20,000 share of the gain that Mike would have recognized if the partnership had sold all of the securities just before the distribution.[18] This reduction cannot reduce the gain to less than zero,[19] so Mike recognizes no gain on the distribution. His basis for the distributed securities is $20,000 (his outside basis of $40,000 minus the $20,000 of cash distributed).

There are other situations where a partner may have to recognize gain upon a distribution. A partner who contributed property worth more than its basis may have to recognize gain if, within seven years of the contribution, (1) the contributed property is distributed to another partner (§ 704(c)(1)(B)), or (2) other property is distributed to the contributing partner (§ 737). These situations will be examined below at pages 155 to 156.

2. Liquidating Distributions on Which Loss Is Recognized

A partner can never recognize a loss on a current distribution. In contrast, if a liquidating distribution consists entirely of cash, and if the amount of the cash is less than the recipient's outside basis, the recipient will recognize a loss.

---

18. To account for cases in which the distributee gets a disproportionate share of the partnership's securities, the formula of § 731(c)(3)(B) is quite complex. The reduction in gain is the excess of the gain that the distributee would have recognized if the partnership had sold all its securities (of the same class and issuer as those distributed) over the distributee's share of the gain on a post-distribution sale by the partnership of securities of that class. In other words, one calculates the gain that the distributee would have recognized if the partnership had sold all of its securities before the distribution and the gain that the distributee would have recognized if the partnership had sold all the securities remaining after the distribution. The excess of the former over the latter then reduces the § 731(c) gain.

19. § 731(c)(3)(B).

A partner is also permitted to recognize a loss if the partner receives only certain other types of property in a liquidating distribution in addition to cash. A partner who receives a liquidating distribution consisting of nothing other than cash, unrealized receivables (§ 751(c)) and inventory (§ 751(d)) will recognize a loss if the amount of the cash plus the total *basis* (yes, basis!) of the unrealized receivables and inventory items is less than the partner's outside basis; § 731(a)(2).

Example 11–10: Norbert, whose basis for his interest in a partnership is $50,000, receives a liquidating distribution made up as follows:

	Basis	Value
Cash	$10,000	$10,000
Unrealized Receivable	0	40,000
Inventory	20,000	30,000
Total	$30,000	$80,000

Although the value of the cash and property distributed to Norbert ($80,000) exceeds the basis of his partnership interest ($50,000), Norbert recognizes a $20,000 loss on the distribution because: (1) no asset other than cash, unrealized receivables, and inventory was distributed, and (2) the total bases of those assets plus the amount of cash was $20,000 less than Norbert's outside basis.

The rationale for the rules applied in Example 11–10 is this: Treating the transaction as a nonrecognition event would require stepping up the basis of unrealized receivables and inventory, which would reduce the amount of ordinary income taxable to the partners. Taxing the distributee on a gain measured by the difference between the total value of the distribution and the distributee's basis would substitute capital gain for ordinary income because the distributee would get a higher basis for the assets at the cost of a capital gain under § 741. The statutory scheme preserves the ordinary-income potential of the distributed assets by keeping their bases in the partner's hands the same as their bases when they were held by the partnership.

Under § 735, unrealized receivables distributed to a partner keep their ordinary-income character after the distribution. Inventory does too, but only for five years. The § 735 "taint" applies also to substituted-basis property for which distributed unrealized receivables or inventory items are exchanged; § 735(c)(2). Were it not for these rules, the ordinary income that is preserved when § 732 limits the distributee's basis for these kinds of assets to the partnership's basis would change into capital gain whenever the assets became capital assets in the distributee's hands.

3. "De Minimis" Distributions of Property

Section 731(a)(2) says that recognition of loss on a liquidating distribution occurs only if nothing other than cash, unrealized receivables, and inventory is distributed. If this language is read literally, taxpayers will be able to create wholly unjustifiable tax benefits by including trivial amounts of capital or § 1231 assets in distributions that would otherwise trigger loss recognition. In particular, losses that would be capital if recognized under § 731 could easily be converted into § 1231 losses, which often end up being treated as ordinary losses.

> **Example 11–11:** The PQR partnership's assets consist mostly of stocks, bonds, and cash. Phil's interest is about to be liquidated by a distribution of $100,000 in cash. As Phil's outside basis is $300,000, this liquidation will lead to Phil recognizing a $200,000 capital loss, which he will be able to deduct only against capital gains plus $3,000 a year of ordinary income. Phil's accountant suggests that the partnership include a typewriter, worth about $200, in the distribution. Phil will use the typewriter in his business for more than a year and then sell it; the typewriter will, therefore, become a § 1231 asset in his hands.
>
> The accountant's reasoning is this: The typewriter is not the kind of property that can be received in a distribution on which loss is recognized under § 731(a)(2). Therefore, no loss will be recognized on the distribution and Phil's basis for the typewriter will be $200,000 (his outside basis less the amount of cash distributed). Therefore, his depreciation deductions while using the typewriter will be enormous, and he will have a large § 1231 loss when he sells it.

Although the issue has never been litigated, most courts would be reluctant to allow partners to convert undesirable capital losses into more-attractive ordinary losses so easily. In flagrant cases, at least, the distribution of a small amount of property for the purpose of taking the distribution out of § 731(a)(2) will be disregarded as being de minimis. This kind of transaction would also be vulnerable to attack under the anti-abuse regulations of § 701.[20]

---

20. See Treas. Reg. § 1.701–2(d) (Example 11). The example does not involve the problem discussed here, but a sentence from that example seems particularly apt: "Section 732 is not intended to serve as the basis for plans ... in which immaterial or inconsequen-

4. Distributions of Section 704(c) Property

Under § 704(c)(1)(B), a partner who contributed property to a partnership will sometimes recognize gain or loss if the partnership distributes that property to another partner within seven years of the contribution.[21] Technically, this gain or loss must be recognized by the contributing partner, not by the partnership. However, to prevent the distributee from recognizing the same gain or loss that the contributor recognized under § 704(c)(1)(B), the statute requires "appropriate adjustments" to the contributor's outside basis and to the distributee's basis for the distributed property.[22]

The details of the basis adjustments to be made when a contributor recognizes gain under § 704(c)(1)(B) are found in the regulations. The contributing partner's outside basis is increased by the gain or loss recognized because of § 704(c)(1)(B),[23] and the partnership's basis in the distributed property is increased by the same amount (this increase will in turn be taken into account in calculating the distributee's basis).[24] These adjustments lead to the results that would have been reached if the partnership had recognized gain or loss on the distribution. As a practical matter, therefore, you can think of partnership distributions of contributed property within seven years of the contribution as if those distributions caused the partnership to recognize some gain or loss on the distributed property. (The gain or loss will not necessarily be measured by the difference between the property's basis and value. Only gain or loss that would have been allocated to the contributing partner under § 704(c)(1)(A) if the partnership had sold the property must be recognized. See Chapter 6.)

5. Distributions Taxed Under Section 737

Suppose that a partner contributes a non-depreciable asset having a $10,000 basis and a $15,000 value to a partnership. If the partnership sells the asset at a gain or distributes it to another partner, the first $5,000 of that gain must be allocated to the contributing partner under § 704(c). If, while the partnership still holds the contributed asset, it distributes other property to the partner who contributed that asset, that partner must recognize the lesser of (1) the "net precontribution gain" the partner would have recognized under § 704(c)(1)(B) if the partnership had distributed (to another partner) all assets contributed

---

tial assets are included in the distribution with a principal purpose of obtaining substantially favorable tax results by virtue of the statute's simplifying rules."

21. See page 84, above.
22. § 704(c)(1)(B)(iii).
23. Treas. Reg. § 1.704–4(e)(1).
24. Treas. Reg. § 1.704–4(e)(2).

by the distributee partner during the seven-year period preceding the distribution, or (2) the excess of the value of the distributed property (other than cash) over the partner's outside basis (reduced by the amount of cash distributed).

Example 11–12: In 2010, Martha contributes Asset A, which has a basis of $10,000 and a value of $12,000, to the MNOP partnership. In 2011, she contributes Asset B, which has a $20,000 basis and a $19,000 value. In 2013, when Martha's outside basis is $50,000, the partnership makes a current distribution to her of $30,000 cash and property worth $25,000. At the time of the distribution, Asset A is worth $15,000 and Asset B is worth $19,500.

Under § 731, Martha would recognize no gain because the $30,000 cash she got was less than her outside basis. But § 737 requires her to recognize a gain of $1,500, calculated as follows:

The "net precontribution gain" is $1,500. If the partnership had distributed both of the assets contributed by Martha to another partner, Martha would have recognized a $2,000 gain because of Asset A and a $500 loss because of Asset B. Combining these figures yields a net gain of $1,500.

The value of the property distributed to Martha (not counting cash) is $25,000. Her outside basis before the distribution, reduced by the amount of cash distributed, is $20,000. Therefore, the value of the distributed property exceeds her outside basis, adjusted for the cash distribution, by $5,000.

Section 737(a) requires Martha to recognize the lesser of the $1,500 "net precontribution gain" or the $5,000 excess of the value of the distributed property over the outside basis.

Martha's outside basis will increase by the by $1,500 gain recognized under § 737, and the partnership will make "appropriate adjustments" to the basis of the property Martha contributed; § 737(c). These adjustments are needed so that the gain recognized under § 737 will not be recognized again when the partnership sells the property, distributes it, or makes another distribution to Martha. Section 737 does not apply to distributions of property to the partner who contributed that property.

C. TAX TREATMENT OF THE PARTNERSHIP

A partnership never recognizes gain[25] or loss on a distribution, whether current or liquidating. Of course, nothing in subchapter K is

---

25. This includes depreciation recapture; see §§ 1245(b)(3) and (b)(6); 1250(d)(3) and (d)(6).

ever quite that easy, because many distributions (probably most distributions) will be recharacterized by § 751(b) in a way that involves treating the partnership as selling or exchanging some of its property, and gains and losses on those sales will be recognized. Section 751(b) is the subject of Chapter 12.

D. COMPARISON WITH SUBCHAPTER S

In principle, partnership distributions and distributions by corporations, including S corporations, are very different, because the norm for partnership distributions is nontaxability to both the partnership and the partners. The practice is more complex. We have seen that partners can recognize gains and losses on some distributions, the all-cash liquidating distribution being one example. An all-cash liquidating distribution to a partner therefore receives much the same tax treatment as an all-cash liquidating distribution to the shareholder of an S corporation. Distributions of appreciated property by an S corporation will often be taxable events at the corporate level, with the gains taxed to the shareholder.

Chapter Twelve

DISTRIBUTIONS SUBJECT TO SECTION 751(b)

Section 751(b) seeks to prevent partners from shifting ordinary income and capital gains among themselves by selecting assets for distribution based on the assets' tax characteristics. Section 751, however, is not limited to cases in which the partners care about the character of their income. Section 751(b) works by recharacterizing distributions as transactions involving sales or exchanges. Even partners indifferent to whether their gains and losses are capital must pay careful attention to § 751(b), because § 751(b) will cause distributions that would have been tax free under § 731 to generate gains, losses, and basis adjustments at both the partner and partnership levels.

Section 751(b) is not easy to work with. Nevertheless, a thorough understanding of how that section functions is necessary for anyone who wants to be able to give accurate tax advice to partners and partnerships. Nearly all partnerships hold assets subject to § 751. When those partnerships make distributions (and remember that a distribution occurs whenever a partner's share of partnership liabilities decreases),[1] § 751(b) will come into play unless the distribution has been carefully structured. In real life, of course, most partners are advised by lawyers and accountants who have not mastered § 751(b); who often, one suspects, have never even heard of it. Keeping a provision in the Code when compliance with that provision is questionable for most taxpayers seems a dubious policy choice.

Before examining § 751(b), let us look at a simple example of the problem that section was intended to resolve.

Example 12–1: The RST equal partnership has these assets:

	Basis	Value
Cash	$1,200	$1,200
Inventory	600	1,200
Capital Asset	900	1,200
Total	$2,700	$3,600

Richard retires from the partnership, receiving a liquidating distribution of all the inventory (worth $1,200). Under the

---
1. § 752(b).

usual rules for distributions, this would lead to Richard's becoming the only partner to report ordinary income. Because the liquidation would result in Richard's having a basis of no more than $600 for the inventory,[2] he would report at least $600 of ordinary income upon selling that inventory for $1,200 within five years of the distribution. The other partners, Sophia and Tess, would report none of the ordinary income because their partnership (now the ST partnership) would hold only capital assets and cash.

If Richard's liquidating distribution consisted of the capital asset, only Sophia and Tess would report the ordinary income represented by the inventory's excess of value over basis because they would be the only partners when the partnership sold the inventory.

Section 751(b) was designed to prevent a distribution from shifting ordinary income among the partners in the ways shown in the example. As we shall see, it doesn't always work, but it will frustrate the simple attempts described in Example 12–1.

To determine whether § 751(b) applies to a distribution, one must view partners as owning their proportionate shares of partnership assets. Those assets are either "§ 751 property" or other property. "Section 751 property" consists of "unrealized receivables" and "substantially appreciated inventory items";[3] everything else is other property. Inventory is "substantially appreciated" if its value is more than 120 percent of its basis. § 751(b)(3)(A). The substantial-appreciation determination is made by looking to the partnership's total inventory. If one inventory item is worth less than its basis, that item is nevertheless part of the partnership's substantially appreciated inventory if the inventory as a whole meets the 120 percent test.[4] Inventory purchased to cause the partnership's inventory (as a whole) to fail the 120 percent test does not count in applying the test. § 751(b)(3)(B).[5]

---

2. Under the rules explained in the previous chapter, Richard would report a capital loss if his outside basis before the distribution was more than $600; see § 731(a)(2). If he had an outside basis of less than $600, that outside basis would become the basis of the inventory in his hands and no loss would be recognized on the distribution; §§ 732(a)(2), 731(a)(2).

3. "Unrealized receivables" and "inventory" are defined in §§ 751(c) and 751(d). See page 127, above.

4. Section 751(b)(1)(A)(ii)'s reference to "inventory items which have substantially appreciated in value" is misleading. If the partnership's inventory as a whole is substantially appreciated, a distribution of a disproportionate share of inventory triggers § 751(b) even if the particular items distributed are worth less than their basis. The statute should say, "inventory items, if the partnership's inventory has substantially appreciated in value."

5. Recall that § 751(d)'s definition of "inventory" is so broad as to include most unrealized receivables (and accounts receivable that are not "unrealized" as well); page

Section 751(b) applies when a distribution changes the distributee partner's proportionate interest in § 751 property. A distribution that reduces the distributee's interest in § 751 assets is one in which the distributee is seen as exchanging § 751 property for other property. § 751(b)(1)(A). A distribution that increases the distributee's interest in § 751 assets is an exchange of other property for § 751 property. § 751(b)(1)(B).

Example 12–2: The facts are the same as in Example 12–1. The partnership has no "unrealized receivables," so its only § 751 assets are its inventory items, which are substantially appreciated because their total value is more than 120 percent of their total basis.

If the partnership's liquidating distribution to Richard consists of $400 worth of inventory and $800 in cash, § 751(b) does not apply to the distribution. Both before and after the distribution, Richard's interest in § 751 property is one-third, so the distribution is not one in which Richard has exchanged § 751 property for other property, or vice versa. A liquidating distribution giving Richard more than $400 worth of inventory would be subject to § 751(b) because, under § 751(b)(1)(A), Richard would have received § 751 property in exchange for other property. A liquidating distribution giving Richard less than $400 worth of inventory would also be subject to § 751(b) because Richard would have exchanged some or all of his interest in § 751 property for other property.

In two cases, § 751(b) does not apply even though a distribution changes the distributee's interest in § 751 property. The first, and less important, is that in which the distribution consists of property contributed to the partnership by the distribute. § 751(b)(2)(A). The second involves payments to a retiring partner governed by § 736(a), which will be examined in Chapter 13. § 751(b)(2)(B). Generally speaking, payments to a retiring partner in exchange for that partner's share of "unrealized receivables" are payments described in § 736(a);[6] these payments are not subject to § 751(b). All of this Chapter's illustrations of § 751(b) will involve partnerships owning no unrealized receivables. Section 751(b)'s application to partnerships with unrealized receivables will be considered in Chapter 13, after we have looked at § 736(a).

127, above. Consider a partnership holding inventory (in the traditional sense) with a basis of $100,000 and a value of $105,000 and zero-basis accounts receivable worth $30,000. The partnership's inventory is substantially appreciated because its $135,000 value exceeds 120 percent of its $100,000 basis. If a partnership holds traditional inventory with a basis of $100,000 and a value of $121,000, its inventory will not be substantially appreciated if it also holds accounts receivable with a basis and value of $50,000.

6. However, a partner's interest in potential depreciation recapture is an "unrealized receivable" for purposes of § 751(b) but not for purposes of § 736.

A. LIQUIDATING DISTRIBUTIONS OF ASSETS OTHER THAN SECTION 751 ASSETS

Let us examine the way in which § 751(b) prevents a partnership from shifting the ordinary-income potential of substantially appreciated inventory away from a partner who will receive a liquidating distribution. For the sake of simplicity, we shall use a variation of the facts of Example 12–1 throughout this chapter.

Example 12–3: The RST equal partnership has these assets:

	Basis	Value
Cash	$1,200	$1,200
Inventory	600	1,200
Capital Asset	900	1,200
Total	$2,700	$3,600

Richard's basis for his partnership interest is $900. He retires from the partnership, receiving a liquidating distribution consisting of the capital asset. Were it not for § 751(b), Richard would recognize no gain on the liquidation and would take the capital asset with a basis of $900. All of the partnership's ordinary income would be taxed to Sophia and Tess when the partnership sold the inventory.

Section 751(b) applies to this case because the distribution is one in which Richard receives property other than § 751 property in exchange for his interest in § 751 property; § 751(b)(1)(B). Therefore, according to the statute, the transaction must be "considered as a sale or exchange of such property between the distributee and the partnership (as constituted after the distribution)". § 751(b). To put it more simply, § 751(b) says that Richard must be considered as exchanging inventory for some of what he actually received. This exchange will be a taxable event for both Richard and the other partners. (How do we know that Richard is to be treated as exchanging inventory, rather than something else? We know because only an exchange of § 751 property by Richard would give him the ordinary income that he otherwise would have shifted to Sophia and Tess.)

The statute tells us that there is a hypothetical exchange between Richard and the ST partnership, with Richard exchanging inventory for an interest in the capital asset. We must begin our set of hypothetical transactions earlier than that, however, because Richard has no inventory to give up in the exchange until we come up with a transaction to get inventory into his hands. According to the regulations, which cover § 751(b) very thoroughly, the first step is a constructive current distribution of inventory to Richard.[7]

To figure out how much inventory is deemed to be distributed to Richard in the first step of the series of constructive transactions under § 751(b), we must compare the amount of § 751 property he owns after the distribution (the real one) with his interest in that kind of property before the distribution. Because he has no § 751 property after the distribution, while he had a one-third interest as a partner, he will be viewed as receiving one-third of the inventory in the hypothetical current distribution. In this case, this distribution consists of $400 worth of inventory with a basis of $200.[8]

The constructive current distribution of $400 worth of inventory with a $200 basis is not a taxable event to either Richard or the partnership.[9] The distributed inventory has a basis in his hands of $200,[10] and the distribution reduces Richard's basis for his partnership interest to $700.[11]

The next step is to determine the tax consequences of the § 751(b) exchange. In that exchange, Richard gives up inventory worth $400 and having a basis of $200 to get $400 worth of capital asset. That $400 worth of capital asset had a basis, to the partnership, of $300 (one-third of the partnership's total basis for that property). The exchange therefore has these tax effects:

(1) Richard recognizes $200 of ordinary income ($400 amount realized less $200 basis of the inventory transferred in the exchange).

(2) The partnership (or, more precisely, the ST portion of the partnership) recognizes a $100 capital gain ($400 amount realized less $300 basis of the capital asset transferred in the exchange). This gain will be taxed to Sophia and Tess.

---

7. Treas. Reg. § 1.751–1(b)(3)(iii).
8. Treas. Reg. § 1.751–1(g) (Example(2)).
9. § 731.
10. §§ 732(a)(1); 732(c)(1).
11. § 733.

(3) The partnership's cost basis for the $400 worth of inventory it got from Richard in the exchange is $400.

(4) Richard's cost basis for the $400 worth of capital asset he acquired from the partnership in the exchange is $400.

We have now accounted for Richard possessing $400 worth of the capital asset. Recall, however, that Richard ended up holding $1,200 worth of the capital asset. The remaining $800 of that asset is treated as having been distributed to him in a liquidating distribution. That distribution is non-taxable, and Richard takes the asset (that is, the $800 portion that he is treated as having received in the liquidating distribution) with a basis equal to the basis of his partnership interest. Because the hypothetical current distribution of inventory (the first step) reduced the basis of Richard's partnership interest to $700, Richard takes $800 worth of the capital asset with a basis of $700. His total basis for that asset is therefore $1,100 ($700 for the portion received in the liquidating distribution plus $400 for the portion received in the § 751(b) exchange).

Here is the result of all this:

(1) Richard has $200 ordinary income and a basis of $1,100 in the capital asset, which is worth $1,200. He will therefore recognize a $100 capital gain if he sells the capital asset before its value changes.

(2) The ST partnership has recognized a $100 capital gain. The partnership's basis for its inventory is now $800 (its original $400 basis for the two-thirds of the inventory it is not treated as buying from Richard plus a $400 cost basis for the interest it purchased in the § 751 exchange). If the partnership sells its inventory for $1,200, it will recognize a $400 gain.

In this example, Richard was taxed on one-third of the inventory's ordinary-income potential. Sophia and Tess will recognize the rest of the ordinary income when the partnership sells the inventory. Section 751(b) has achieved its objective of taxing the ordinary income to the same partners who would have been taxed if the partnership had sold the inventory before liquidating Richard's interest. One odd thing has happened, though: $100 of capital gain has disappeared from the tax base.[12] This came about because the last step of the transaction, as reconstructed under § 751(b), was a distribution of a two-thirds interest in the

---

12. This disappearance may be temporary. The increase in the capital asset's basis was not matched by an increase in any partner's outside basis. In the long run (if no partner holds a partnership interest until death), partners' gains and losses depend ultimately on their outside bases.

capital asset. This distribution increased the basis of that two-thirds interest from $600 (its basis in the partnership's hands) to $700 (Richard's basis for his partnership interest), without anyone's having recognized gain. If the partnership has a § 754 election in effect, this basis change will be made up for by reducing the partnership's basis for capital assets it acquires in the future; see Chapter 16 for an explanation of this process.

Section 751(b) will not always work. Suppose that the RST partnership's inventory consists of three pieces of property. One of them has a basis of $400 and a value of $400; the other two are worth $400 each and their bases are $100 each. If the partnership makes a liquidating distribution to Richard of $800 worth of capital assets (or $800 cash) plus the inventory item with a basis and value of $400, the distribution will not trigger § 751(b). Richard has received his proportionate share of inventory, by value, so the distribution did not give him non-§ 751 property in exchange for § 751 property or vice versa. Richard will report no ordinary income upon selling the inventory item for $400; Sophia and Tess will report all $600 of the partnership's ordinary income when the partnership sells its retained inventory. The complications of § 751(b) would be less objectionable if that section actually solved the problem to which it is addressed.[13]

B. LIQUIDATING DISTRIBUTIONS OF SECTION 751 PROPERTY

Example 12–3 presented a case in which, but for § 751(b), the distributee would have been taxed on too little of the partnership's

---

13. It is even possible for § 751(b) to make things worse than they would have been without that section. Consider a partnership with inventory that is substantially appreciated, but which contains some inventory items that have appreciated only a little. The partnership makes a liquidating distribution to a one-third partner. The distribution includes more than one third of the partnership's inventory (by value) but gives the distributee inventory that has less than one third of the inventory's total appreciation. Without § 751(b), this distribution would shift ordinary income from the distributee to the remaining partners. Because § 751(b) looks at the values of distributed inventory, that section will treat the distributee as receiving property other than § 751 property and exchanging that property for some of the inventory. This § 751(b) exchange will require the remaining partners to recognize ordinary income. On these facts, § 751(b) responds to a distribution that shifts ordinary income to the remaining partners by shifting even more ordinary income to the remaining partners.

Another reason why § 751(b) will sometimes fail is that it does not apply to a distribution to a partner of property which that partner contributed to the partnership. This exception makes no sense. Suppose, for instance, that a distribution of capital assets would shift the ordinary-income potential of substantially appreciated inventory away from the distributee. Section 751(b)(1)(B) should apply. Whether the distribution consists of capital assets contributed by the distributee, capital assets purchased with partnership cash, or capital assets contributed by another partner is irrelevant to the purposes served by § 751(b).

ordinary income. If a distribution contains too high a percentage of the partnership's § 751 property, the concern is to prevent the distributee from being taxed on too much of the partnership's ordinary income. (Looking at things from the point of view of the continuing partners, § 751(b) tries to prevent those partners from having too small a share of the partnership's potential ordinary income.)

Example 12–4: As in the previous examples, the RST equal partnership has these assets:

	Basis	Value
Cash	$1,200	$1,200
Inventory	600	1,200
Capital Asset	900	1,200
Total:	$2,700	$3,600

Richard's basis for his partnership interest is $900. He receives all of the partnership's inventory in a liquidating distribution. Under § 731 (and ignoring § 751(b)) Richard would recognize a $300 capital loss on the distribution (the excess of his $900 outside basis over the $600 basis of the inventory).[14] Richard's basis for the inventory would be $600,[15] so he would have $600 of ordinary income if he sold the inventory for $1,200 within five years of getting it.[16] Sophia and Tess would have no ordinary income because their partnership would hold no ordinary-income property.

The § 751(b) exchange must be one that causes the partnership (really the Sophia and Tess portion of the partnership) to recognize ordinary income. The constructive current distribution to Richard must therefore be a distribution of property other than the § 751 property. Another way to think about this is that the constructive distribution must consist of non-§ 751 property because that is the property that Richard holds too little of.

Richard had a one-third interest in the inventory (worth $400) before his partnership interest was liquidated and ends up with inventory worth $1,200 after the liquidation. Richard also had a one-third interest in the non-§ 751 assets worth $800

---
14. § 731(a)(2).
15. §§ 732(b); 732(c)(1).
16. § 735(a)(2).

($400 cash and $400 capital asset) before the liquidation and has a $0 interest in those assets after the liquidation. The constructive distribution, therefore, must consist of $800 of the non-§ 751 assets. In this situation, the regulations allow the partners to specify which of the partnership's non-§ 751 assets are deemed to have been distributed.[17] If the partners fail to do that, the distribution will be treated as consisting of a portion of all of the partnership's non-§ 751 property.[18] Let us assume that the parties have agreed to treat Richard as receiving only cash in the constructive current distribution of non-§ 751 assets so that the distribution consists entirely of $800 cash.

Richard's $800 cash distribution causes him to recognize no gain or loss: no gain because the amount of cash is less than his outside basis immediately before the distribution;[19] no loss because loss can never be recognized on a current distribution.[20] The distribution reduces Richard's outside basis from $900 to $100.[21]

The next step is the § 751(b) exchange. In that exchange, Richard uses the $800 cash that he constructively received to buy $800 worth of inventory. In other words, we want Richard to buy two-thirds of the inventory, so that Sophia and Tess will report two-thirds of the ordinary income "built into" the partnership's § 751 property at the time of the distribution. Richard's constructive payment of $800 cash for $800 of the inventory generates ordinary income of $400 for the Sophia–Tess portion of the RST partnership ($800 amount realized less $400 basis). The payment also gives Richard an $800 cost basis for $800 worth of the inventory.

To complete the transaction, we view Richard as receiving a liquidating distribution of the remaining inventory with a value of $400 and a basis (in the partnership's hands) of $200. This distribution is non-taxable to both Richard and the partnership, and Richard takes the inventory with a basis of $100 (his outside basis just before the distribution).[22]

If Richard sells his inventory for $1,200 he will recognize ordinary income of $300, because his total basis for the inventory is $900 ($800 cost basis for inventory treated as received in

---

17. Treas. Reg. § 1.751–1(g) (Examples (3)(c) & (5)(c)).
18. Treas. Reg. § 1.751–1(g) (Example (4)).
19. § 731(a)(1).
20. § 731(a)(2).
21. § 733.
22. § 732(b).

the § 751(b) exchange plus $100 basis under § 732 for inventory treated as received in the liquidating distribution).

In this example, § 751(b) managed to tax Sophia and Tess on the right amount of ordinary income, but Richard was overtaxed. This happened because the constructive cash distribution reduced Richard's outside basis to a figure lower than the inventory's basis in the partnership's hands, and § 732 then gave this lower outside basis to the inventory. Careful planning would have avoided this result. The parties could have agreed to treat the constructive distribution as consisting of a two-thirds interest in the capital asset. Had they done that, the constructive distribution would have reduced Richard's outside basis by only $600, and he would have recognized a $100 capital loss on the liquidating distribution. (He would also have recognized a $200 capital gain on the § 751(b) exchange.)

C. SECTION 751(b) AND CURRENT DISTRIBUTIONS

The set of constructive transactions into which a current distribution containing too much or too little § 751 property is translated is much the same as with liquidating distributions: a current distribution, the § 751(b) exchange of the property treated as received in the current distribution for some of the property actually distributed, and a current distribution of the balance of the property actually distributed.

Example 12–5: The WAB equal partnership's assets consist of:

	Basis	Value
Cash	$30,000	$30,000
Inventory	15,000	30,000
Total:	$45,000	$60,000

Partner William, whose outside basis is $15,000, gets a current distribution of $10,000 in cash; this distribution reduces his interest in the partnership from one-third to one-fifth.[23]

---

23. Why one-fifth, rather than one-sixth (half of his former one-third interest)? Because the distribution reduces the value of the partnership's assets as well as William's proportionate interest in those assets. The distribution moves $10,000 in value from the partnership to William. Since the distribution should not change the total value of William's assets (including his partnership interest), William should continue to have an interest in $20,000 worth of property after the distribution. Because he owns $10,000 in cash outright, the value of his partnership interest should now be $10,000 also. The partnership's assets now have a total value of $50,000 ($60,000 less the $10,000 distributed

Because this distribution reduces William's interest in the partnership's § 751 property (the substantially appreciated inventory), § 751(b) will treat William as receiving a distribution of inventory and then selling that inventory to the partnership for cash.

According to the regulations, we calculate the amount of inventory William receives in the constructive current distribution by comparing the dollar value of his share of the inventory before the actual distribution, $10,000 (one third of $30,000), with the dollar value of his share after the distribution, $6,000 (one fifth of $30,000). This yields a constructive distribution of $4,000 worth of inventory ($10,000 less $6,000).[24] Then, on the § 751(b) exchange, William is seen as selling $4,000 of inventory to the AB portion of that partnership. (Note that this sale to the AB portion of the partnership means that only the partners other than William benefit from an increased basis for that portion of the inventory.[25])

The $4,000 of inventory received by William in the constructive current distribution has a basis of $2,000 and reduces his outside basis from $15,000 to $13,000.[26] On the § 751(b) exchange, William recognizes $2,000 of ordinary income from the sale of the inventory; the partnership takes a cost basis of $4,000 for $4,000 worth of the inventory. The partnership's basis for the inventory is now $17,000, and the additional $2,000 of basis can be used only in computing the gain of partners other than William when the partnership sells the inventory. The balance of the transaction is a current cash distribution to William of $6,000; this reduces his outside basis to $7,000.

D. THE SCOPE OF SECTION 751(b): AN EXAMPLE

A 1984 Revenue Ruling provides an instructive example of how § 751(b) can complicate the tax treatment of an apparently simple

---

to William). Therefore, William's share of the partnership's property should be worth $10,000, which it will be if he becomes a one-fifth partner in a partnership worth $50,000. The other two partners will have a combined interest of four-fifths of the partnership.

24. Treas. Reg. § 1.751–1(g) (Example (5)(c)).

25. Treas. Reg. §§ 1.751–1(b)(2)(ii) and 1.751–1(b)(3)(ii) provide that partnership-level gain or loss recognized on a § 751(b) exchange must "be allocated only to partners other than the distributee." (Note the way in which these regulations conflict with the statute, which describes the exchange as being with the partnership "as constituted after the distribution.") Consistency with allocating gains and losses to the non-distributee partners demands that partnership-level basis increases benefit only those partners. In the example, letting William use part of the partnership's additional basis for the inventory would eventually result in his being taxed on less than one-third of the partnership's ordinary income.

26. § 733.

transaction. Revenue Ruling 84–102[27] involved the admission of a new partner, D, to the ABC equal partnership. Like most partnerships, ABC had some debt ($100x in the ruling). Like virtually all partnerships, ABC held some unrealized receivables (recall that the definition of "unrealized receivables" in § 751(c) is very broad for most purposes). Before D was admitted, each of ABC's partners had a one-third share of the partnership's $100x debt, or $33.3x each. When the partnership admitted D as an equal partner, in exchange for D's contributing cash to the partnership, D's share of the partnership's debt became one-fourth, or $25x. The shares of A, B, and C in the debt dropped to $25x each.

Under § 752(b), any decrease in a partner's share of the partnership's liabilities creates a distribution of cash to that partner. A, B, and C therefore received constructive cash distributions when D became a partner. According to the Service, these constructive cash distributions to A, B, and C triggered § 751(b), causing A, B, and C to recognize ordinary income. The ruling asserted that D, upon becoming a partner, had a share of the partnership's unrealized receivables; the shares of A, B, and C in those receivables therefore declined. The constructive cash distribution under § 752(b) was therefore a distribution in which A, B, and C received property other than § 751 assets (cash) in exchange for part of their interests in the partnership's § 751 property (unrealized receivables). Therefore, said the Service, § 751(b) treats each of the partners (other than D) as having received a constructive current distribution of receivables and as then having sold those receivables to the partnership in a § 751(b) exchange, upon which they recognized ordinary income.

Revenue Ruling 84–102 may be wrong, at least if the partners allocate gains correctly after a new partner is admitted. Under some of the permissible ways of allocating a partnership's "built-in" gains when a new partner joins the partnership, those gains will be allocated to the old partners. (See pages 82–83, above.) The partnership can either write up the old partners' capital accounts to reflect the property's appreciation in value or it can allocate future gains from the disposition of those assets to the old partners, in an amount sufficient to tax the built-in gains to those partners, subject to the ceiling rule. Because the purpose of § 751 is to make sure that ordinary income is taxed to the right partners, § 751's reference to a partner's "interest" in partnership property should be read as referring to the partner's interest in the profits from that property.[28] If the ABCD partnership in the ruling

---

27. 1984–2 C.B. 119.
28. Alan J. B. Aronsohn, Partnership Income Taxes 176–77 (1978 ed.) (Given the purpose of § 751(b), the distributee's "interest" in § 751 assets should be the distributee's interest in profits, rather than in capital).

allocates its income so that only the old partners (A, B, and C) are taxed on the ordinary income built into the partnership's unrealized receivables at the time of D's admission, there is no need to tax the currently on that gain under § 751(b).

Whether or not Revenue Ruling 84–102 is right, however, the ruling shows that § 751(b) must be considered in advising partners about the tax consequences of transactions in which no partner would recognize income under the usual distribution rules[29] and in which no actual distribution occurs. Many events can change a partner's share of partnership liabilities: even a change in partners' distributive shares, for example (see Chapter 8). Only in the very uncommon case in which a partnership holds no § 751 assets can sound advice be given about any of these events without taking § 751(b) into account. (In practice, this means that most partners, most of the time, will not receive accurate advice. The idea that more than a handful of the lawyers and accountants who advise partnerships (especially small partnerships) can be expected to learn § 751(b) well enough to apply it in non-obvious situations is fantasy.)

E. COMPARISON WITH SUBCHAPTER S

Nothing like § 751(b) applies to S corporations. Those who advise S corporations and their shareholders should be grateful for this. This difference between subchapters K and S exists in part because of legislative inertia. There is some feeling among the tax bar that § 751(b) is too complex, and that the tax system should tolerate inaccuracies rather than subject small businesses to so unsatisfactory a set of rules, especially since the rules sometimes fail to prevent the abuse at which they were aimed.[30]

---

29. If a § 752(b) constructive distribution does not exceed any partner's outside basis, no partner will recognize gain under § 731.

30. The American Law Institute, in proposing a number of changes to subchapter K, has proposed that § 751(b) be repealed. See American Law Institute, Federal Income Tax Project, Subchapter K, 54 (1984). Most of the ALI's other proposed changes would complicate the Code considerably. The Institute has urged, for example, that § 743(b) basis adjustments be made mandatory; id. at 214. That an organization given to proposing changes that would make subchapter K much more complex than it is today finds § 751(b) to be too complex seems especially telling.

Recent proposals for repeal of § 751(b) have elicited from some practitioners the astonishing suggestion that repeal is unnecessary because most partnerships get their tax advice from people who ignore that section.

Chapter Thirteen

PAYMENTS TO RETIRING PARTNERS: SECTION 736 AND RELATED PROBLEMS

A. INTRODUCTION

Up to this point we have looked at how "distributions" to partners are taxed, but we have not considered carefully how to identify distributions. As a very rough guide, a payment by a partnership to a partner is a distribution unless the payment falls into some other category. Payments made to purchase property from partners, guaranteed payments, payments to partners for services other than in their "capacity" as partners (§ 707(a)), loans to partners, and a host of other kinds of payments are plainly not "distributions." These kinds of "non-distribution" transfers may be hard to identify in particular cases, but once they have been identified there is little danger that they will be mistaken for distributions. Nobody, for instance, would apply § 731 or § 751(b) to a payment of rent on property leased by a partner to a partnership. Sometimes, however, the Code classifies payments to partners as something other than "distributions" even though the payments are "distributions" in a non-technical sense. "Distribution" is a term of art.

Suppose a partnership makes a payment, or a series of payments, to a retiring partner.[1] For example, a partner withdraws from a partnership and receives $100,000 in cash from the partnership. In everyday speech, the $100,000 payment is a liquidating distribution. Technically, however, § 736 may characterize some or all of the payment as something other than a liquidating distribution: It may be taxed as a guaranteed payment, a payment of the partner's distributive share or as a liquidating distribution. Section 736 directs which characterization will apply to payments to a retiring partner.[2]

Before we examine the manner in which § 736 classifies payments, we will find it helpful to review briefly the implications of characterizing a payment to a retiring partner as a payment of a distributive share, a guaranteed payment or a distribution. If the payment to a retiring partner is treated as a payment of a distributive share, the retiring partner recognizes income that has the same character as the partner-

---

1. "Retiring" partners are not necessarily old-timers. Someone who has been expelled from a partnership or who has been persuaded to withdraw in exchange for a cash payment is as much a "retiring partner" as someone who gets a gold watch and a dinner.

2. Section 736 also classifies payments to the successors in interest of deceased partners. We discuss this aspect of § 736 in Chapter 15.

ship's income. In addition, the other partners do not include in their shares of partnership income the retiring partner's distributive share. If the payment is treated as a guaranteed payment, the retiring partner recognizes ordinary income and the partnership deducts the payment unless it is a capital expenditure.[3] If the payment is treated as a distribution, the retiring partner may recognize gain or loss under § 731 (unless § 751(b) applies), and the partnership will not deduct the payment.[4]

Example 13–1: Sharon is retiring from the STU partnership in which she is a one-third partner. The partnership has $300 of capital gain and pays $100 to Sharon.

If the payment is a payment of her distributive share of the partnership's capital gain, Sharon recognizes $100 of capital gain. The continuing partners include in their income the remaining $200 of capital gain.

If the payment is a guaranteed payment, Sharon recognizes $100 of ordinary income and the partnership deducts the payment unless it is a capital expenditure.

If the payment is a distribution, Sharon recognizes gain or loss under § 731. The partnership cannot deduct the payment because distributions are not deductible by a partnership.

It is important to remember that § 736 says nothing about how payments to retiring partners are taxed; all it does is classify payments. Once a payment has been classified, one looks to other sections to find the tax treatment of the payment. If, for example, § 736(b) says that part of a particular payment is a "distribution," the tax consequences of that part of the payment to the recipient and to the partnership depend upon §§ 731, 732, 733, and 751(b). If § 736(a) classifies the remainder of the payment as either a payment of a distributive share or a guaranteed payment, the tax consequences are determined by § 704(a) or § 707(c).

1. Interpreting Section 736—In General

Tax lawyers think of § 736 as dividing all payments to retiring partners into two classes: "§ 736(a) payments" and "§ 736(b) payments." A § 736(a) payment is a payment of a distributive share if the amount of the payment depends upon the partnership's income; it is a guaranteed payment if its amount is fixed. Section 736(b) payments are distributions.

Unfortunately, § 736 does not make it easy to determine whether the payment to the retiring partner is under § 736(a) or (b). Section

---

3. See pages 113 to 114, above and Treas. Reg. § 1.736–1(a)(4).
4. See pages 145 to 151, above.

736(a) says that all payments to a retiring partner are § 736(a) payments unless § 736(b) provides otherwise. Although § 736(a) precedes § 736(b), most distributions are governed by § 736(b). As a result, most tax lawyers treat § 736(b) as the rule and § 736(a) as a limited exception to that rule and start their analysis with § 736(b).

Looking to § 736(b), we see that (subject to some exceptions to be noted later), it applies to payments "made in exchange for the interest of [the retiring] partner in *partnership property*" (emphasis added). The critical determination, therefore, is whether the payment is for the retiring partner's interest in "partnership property." The portion of the payment that is for the partner's interest in "partnership property" is governed by § 736(b) and will be characterized as a distribution. The portion of a payment that is *not* for a partner's interest in "partnership property" is governed by § 736(a) and will be characterized as a distributive share or guaranteed payment.

Example 13–2: Donald is an equal partner in the DEF partnership, which has assets with a fair market value of $300. Donald's share of the partnership's property is $100 (one third of $300). Upon Donald's withdrawal from the partnership, the partnership pays him $175.

One hundred dollars of the payment to Donald is a § 736(b) payment because it represents a payment for Donald's share of "partnership property." As a § 736(b) payment, it is characterized as a distribution. The additional $75 payment is a § 736(a) payment because it is not a payment for Donald's share of "partnership property." Under § 736(a) it can be characterized as a guaranteed payment or distributive share. Since it is a fixed amount, it is treated as a guaranteed payment.

Note that the partnership might have paid Donald an extra $75 to induce him to retire or as a reward for his hard work. The motive is irrelevant. What matters is that the $75 payment was not for Donald's interest in "partnership property" and, therefore, § 736(a) applies.

Suppose that the partnership in Example 13–2 paid Donald an extra $75 because the partnership has an excellent reputation. In that situation, the $75 payment could be viewed as a payment for Donald's share of the partnership's goodwill. Payments for goodwill are treated as payments for "partnership property" and are classified as § 736(b) payments, subject to some exceptions discussed below.

2. Payments by Service Partnerships to Retiring General Partners

So far we have seen that § 736 divides payments to retiring partners into two categories by asking whether the payments are for the partners' interests in "partnership property." The inquiry becomes complex because § 736(b) further says that payments for certain types of property that are made to general partners in certain types of partnerships are not treated as payments for "partnership property."

Specifically, § 736(b)(2) and (3) state that if the retiring partner is a general partner in a partnership in which "capital is not a material income-producing factor" (i.e., a "service partnership"), the term "partnership property" does not include either "unrealized receivables" (as defined in § 751(c)) or good will (unless the partnership agreement provides for a payment for goodwill). Section 751(c) defines "unrealized receivables" for this purpose as including what we might call traditional unrealized receivables but excluding potential recapture income and other kinds of unrealized receivables listed in the flush language after § 751(c)(2). As to goodwill, § 736(b)(2) says that whether payments to a general partner for goodwill in a service partnership will be treated as a payment for "partnership property" depends upon the partnership agreement. If the partnership agreement provides for payments for goodwill to a retiring general partner in a service partnership, the payment is treated as a payment for "partnership property" and, therefore, as a § 736(b) payment. Tax lawyers refer to this type of goodwill as "stated goodwill," because it is "stated" in the partnership agreement. If the partnership agreement is silent, payments to a general partner in a service partnership for that partner's share of goodwill (that is, for "unstated goodwill") are governed by § 736(a).

Thus, if a service partnership makes a liquidating payment to a retiring general partner, the portions of the payment for the retiring partner's share of the partnership's "unrealized receivables" and the partnership's unstated goodwill are treated as not being payments for "partnership property" under § 736(b)(1) and will fall under § 736(a). In contrast, payments for a limited partner's share of property in any type of partnership (service or non-service) or for a general partner's share of property in a non-service partnership are § 736(b) payments regardless of the nature of the property.[5] The result of this complexity is that § 736 requires us to view payments by service partnerships as being

---

5. It is not clear how these rules apply to LLC's which do not have general or limited partners. Members of LLCs (and of other entities, such as some limited liability partnerships) resemble limited partners in not being personally liable for the entities' debts. However, they are like general partners in being able to participate in management. The special rules for general partners of service partnerships are intended to give favorable treatment to active participants in service partnerships. For this reason, an active member of an LLC conducting a service business such as the practice of law or medicine should be treated as a general partner under § 736. A passive member of an LLC conducting only investment activities should be treated as a limited partner. Where the line should be drawn in cases less clear than these is a matter on which authoritative guidance is badly needed.

for any of four different things. Here are the four different things and a detailed review of the applicable statutes:

(1) Some payments are not for the retiring partner's interest in "partnership property." As explained in Example 13–2, these payments are § 736(a) payments.

(2) Part of a payment to a retiring partner may be for that partner's interest in unrealized receivables. "Unrealized receivables" means unrealized receivables in the § 751(c) sense, except that potential recapture income and the other kinds of unrealized receivables listed in the flush language after § 751(c)(2) are not "unrealized receivables" for purposes of § 736. Section 736(b)(2) says that payments to general partners in a service partnership for "unrealized receivables" as defined in § 751(c) to are not to be treated as payments for an interest in "partnership property." Therefore, this type of payment is a § 736(a) payment in the service-partnership context.

(3) If a retiring general partner of a service partnership gets paid for a share of the partnership's goodwill, the payment's status depends on whether the partnership agreement (*not* just the agreement calling for the particular payment) provides for payments "with respect to good will." If the payment is for so-called "unstated goodwill" (that is, if it is for goodwill, but the partnership agreement does not provide for goodwill payments) the payment is a § 736(a) payment. (See § 736(b)(2)(B), which says in general that payments for goodwill are not payments "for partnership property" and then goes on to except from *that* exception payments for so-called "stated goodwill.") If the payment is for stated goodwill (that is, a payment for goodwill pursuant to a provision in the partnership agreement), it is a § 736(b) payment.

(4) Any payment for property other than unrealized receivables or unstated goodwill is a § 736(b) payment (i.e., a payment for the retiring partner's interest in "partnership property").

Here are some examples.

Example 13–3: Amy is an equal general partner in the ABC partnership. Her interest in the partnership is valued at $300 and consists of an interest in partnership land worth $200 and in unrealized receivables worth $100. Upon Amy's retirement from the partnership, the partnership pays her $300.

If the partnership is not a service partnership, the entire $300 payment is treated as a payment for Amy's interest in "partnership property" under § 736(b). It is, therefore, classified as a distribution.

If the partnership is a service partnership, the $200 payment for Amy's interest in the partnership's land is treated as a payment for "partnership property" and is a § 736(b) payment. However, the $100 payment for Amy's interest in the unrealized receivables is not treated as a payment for "partnership property" under § 736(b). Thus, the $100 payment is classified under § 736(a) as a guaranteed payment because it is a fixed amount.

Example 13–4: Guy is an equal general partner in the GHI partnership, which is a service partnership. The partnership's assets consist of capital assets worth $300 and goodwill worth $30. The partnership agreement does not provide for payments for goodwill to retiring partners. When Guy retires, the partnership distributes $110 to Guy.

$100 of the payment is for Guy's share of the partnership's capital assets and, therefore, is a § 736(b) payment. The other $10 payment is for goodwill. Since the partnership agreement does not provide for payments for goodwill, the payment is treated as though it was not for "partnership property" under § 736(b) and thus it is treated as a § 736(a) payment.

Example 13–5: Assume the same facts as in Example 13–4 except that the GHI partnership agreement does provide for payments to retiring partners for their share of partnership goodwill. All of the $110 payment to Guy will now be classified as a § 736(b) payment because Guy is receiving payment for his share of the partnership's capital assets and stated goodwill ("partnership property").

B. HOW SECTION 736 PAYMENTS ARE TAXED

After payments to a retiring partner have been divided into § 736(a) payments and § 736(b) payments, one determines the tax treatment of those payments as follows:

(1) The tax treatment of § 736(a) payments depends upon whether they are fixed in amount. If they are, § 736(a)(2) makes them guaranteed payments. This means that they are ordinary income to the recipient and deductible by the

partnership.[6] If the amount of the § 736(a) payments depends on the partnership's income, they are taxed as distributive shares. This means that the payments will be included in the recipient's income to the extent appropriate for the kind of income the partnership has. Suppose that a partnership has $10,000 of tax-exempt interest, $20,000 of capital gain, and $70,000 of ordinary income. A retiring partner gets a § 736(a) payment of 10 percent of the partnership's income. The retiree will report $1,000 of tax-exempt interest, $2,000 of capital gain, and $7,000 of ordinary income. (The remaining partners will report the balance as their distributive shares; functionally, therefore, they receive the equivalent of deductions for the portions allocated to A.)

(2) The § 736(b) payments are distributions. To the extent that they are payments for the distributee's interest in unrealized receivables (including recapture income) or substantially appreciated inventory, their tax consequences (to the partnership and to the distributee) depend on § 751(b), discussed in Chapter 12. Otherwise, their tax consequences depend on §§ 731, 732, and 733. (If a § 754 election is in effect, § 736(b) payments may also trigger adjustments to the basis of partnership assets under § 734(b); we examine this subject in Chapter 14.)

Note that § 736 serves a purpose similar to that served by § 751(b)—to assure that partners are taxed appropriately on their shares of (some kinds of) their partnerships' ordinary income. Consider, for instance, a § 736(a) payment made to a general partner of a service partnership (one in which capital is not a material income-producing factor) for his share of the partnership's unrealized receivables.

Example 13–6: Henry is a one-third partner in HIJ, the assets of which are:

	Basis	Value
Cash	$30,000	$30,000
Account Receivable	0	30,000
Capital Asset	15,000	30,000
Total:	$45,000	$90,000

Henry withdraws from the partnership, receiving a $30,000 cash payment. All of this payment is in exchange for Henry's

---

6. Treas. Reg. § 1.736–1(a)(4).

interest in some partnership property, but $10,000 of it is for his interest in unrealized receivables, so that $10,000 is a § 736(a) payment. Since this payment is fixed in amount, it is treated as a guaranteed payment and Henry has $10,000 of ordinary income. The other partners, Imogene and Jessie, get a $10,000 deduction. The $20,000 § 736(b) payment to Henry is a distribution, and because it is all cash, Henry will recognize a capital gain or loss measured by the difference between $20,000 and the basis of his partnership interest immediately before the distribution.[7]

The soundness of requiring Henry to recognize $10,000 of ordinary income is clear enough. As a one-third partner he would have recognized that amount of ordinary income when the partnership sold or collected the receivables, and his retirement should not shift this ordinary income to the other partners. But why should Imogene and Jessie get a $10,000 deduction? The answer is that, now that Henry is gone, Imogene and Jessie will have to report the entire $30,000 of ordinary income that the partnership will recognize when it sells or collects the receivables. $10,000 of this ordinary income has already been taxed to Henry, so Imogene and Jessie get a $10,000 ordinary deduction to make up for the extra ordinary income they will have to report.

Section 736 applies only to payments made in connection with the complete termination of a partner's interest. If Henry, in Example 13–6, had received $15,000 in cash, reducing his partnership interest to one-fifth, § 736 would not have applied because Henry would not have been a "retiring partner." However, § 751(b) would have taxed him on some of the ordinary income built into his share of the receivables and would have given the other partners an increase in the basis of those receivables to prevent double taxation. Section 751(b) and § 736 address the same kind of problem, but in different ways. The differences in the coverage of the two sections will be presented below.[8]

C. EXAMPLES

Once you have learned to work with § 736, you will find it fairly easy to apply. Its shortcomings are mostly shortcomings of drafting, rather than substance. It works quite well, at least for cash distributions, though it seems incomprehensible upon a first reading (or even a second

---

7. See § 731.
8. Page 181, below.

Ch. 13   EXAMPLES

or third).[9] You should therefore learn the rules of § 736 by heart. These examples may help.

Example 13–7: The KLMN equal general partnership has $20,000 in liabilities. Capital is not a material income-producing factor for the partnership. Its assets are as follows:

	Basis	Value
Cash	$26,000	$26,000
Account Receivable	0	8,000
Machine	4,000	36,000
Land (capital asset)	6,000	2,000
Goodwill	0	4,000
Total:	$36,000	$76,000

Kevin, a one-fourth partner, retires from the partnership, receiving a cash payment of $25,000. His outside basis was $9,000. The partnership agreement does not provide for payments to retiring partners for their shares of goodwill. The difference between the machine's value and its basis is attributable to depreciation deductions taken by the partnership.

Note that Kevin has received a payment of $30,000, consisting of $25,000 in actual cash plus $5,000 of constructive cash under § 752(b). Of this amount, $14,000 is a § 736(a) payment. (The payment exceeds Kevin's one-fourth share of the value of the partnership's assets by $11,000; that amount is a § 736(a) payment because it is not a payment "for property." Two-thousand dollars of the payment is for Kevin's share of the accounts receivable; this $2,000 is a § 736(a) payment because of § 736(b)(2)(A). Finally, $1,000 for unstated goodwill is a § 736(a) payment.) The $8,000 attributable to the value of Kevin's interest in the machine in excess of the machine's basis is not a payment for an unrealized receivable. Although potential recapture income is an unrealized receivable for most purposes, it is not an unrealized receivable for purposes of § 736. Therefore, the entire $9,000 payment for Kevin's interest in the machine is a § 736(b) payment. The $7,000 balance of the

---

9. Section 736 expresses its fairly simple rules in a shockingly indirect way. It creates a rule (§ 736(a)), an exception to that rule (§ 736(b)(1)), and then two exceptions to the exception (§ 736(b)(2) & (3)).

payment is also a § 736(b) payment, as it represents $6,500 for partnership cash and $500 for the capital asset.

Once we have broken down Kevin's $30,000 payment into a $14,000 § 736(a) payment and a $16,000 § 736(b) payment, we must determine whether the § 736(a) payment is a guaranteed payment or a distributive share. Because the amount of the payment does not depend on the partnership's income, it is a guaranteed payment. Kevin and the other partners are therefore taxed as if the partnership had made a deductible guaranteed payment of $14,000 to Kevin and had made a liquidating distribution to him of $16,000 cash.

As a result of all this, Kevin has $14,000 of ordinary income under § 736(a). That section also gives the partnership (now LMN) a $14,000 ordinary deduction. Kevin's § 736(b) cash liquidating distribution of $16,000 causes him to recognize $8,000 more of ordinary income. The machine, to the extent of the $32,000 potential recapture income, is an unrealized receivable for purposes of § 751(b) even though it was not an unrealized receivable for purposes of § 736. Kevin will also recognize a $1,000 capital loss.[10] The partnership, which is considered under § 751(b) to have bought a one-fourth interest in the machine's potential recapture income from Kevin, now has a basis of $12,000 for the machine.

Example 13–8: The facts are the same as in Example 13–7 except that capital is a material income-producing factor for the KLMN partnership. Because § 736(b)(2) does not apply, only $11,000 of Kevin's retirement payment (the payment in excess of the value of Kevin's interest in partnership property) is a § 736(a) payment. Therefore, § 736 gives Kevin $11,000 of ordinary income and the partnership has an $11,000 ordinary deduction.

Kevin's $19,000 § 736(b) payment is a distribution. The § 751(b) exchange will give Kevin $10,000 more ordinary income ($2,000 for the account receivable and $8,000 for the machine), and the LMN partnership will now have a basis of $2,000 for its unrealized receivables and $12,000 for the machine. Kevin will recognize no capital gain or loss.

Note that the only difference to Kevin between Example 13–7 and Example 13–8 has to do with the payment for his share of the partnership's goodwill. When § 736(b)(2) applies, a payment for unstated goodwill is a § 736(a) payment, which gives Kevin ordinary income and the

---

10. See 731(a)(2), which applies because Kevin's actual liquidating distribution was entirely in cash, despite the fictions engaged in by 751(b).

other partners ordinary deductions. Kevin's payment for the accounts receivable is a § 736(a) payment if § 736(b)(2) applies and a § 736(b) payment otherwise. Either way, the payment for the receivables generates ordinary income: § 751(b) makes the payment ordinary income if § 736 does not. The payment for Kevin's share of the receivables gives the remaining partners a deduction if § 736(b)(2) applies; if it does not, they get more basis for those receivables.

D. SOME COMPLICATIONS

1. The Relationship Between Section 736 and Section 751(b)

Why those who drafted the 1954 Code went about dividing the responsibility for assigning ordinary income to the right partners between § 736 and § 751(b) has always been a mystery. In cases involving non-liquidating distributions, § 751(b) is the only section dealing with the problem, because § 736 applies only to liquidations. In cases involving liquidations, § 751(b) handles situations involving substantially appreciated inventory and potential recapture income (which receive no special treatment under § 736), while § 736(a) deals with payments for services and (in service-partnership cases) for unrealized receivables and sometimes payments for the good will of the partnership. When the concern raised by a liquidating distribution is the distributee's reporting too much of the ordinary income from unrealized receivables, as when all of those assets are distributed to the retiring partner, § 751, rather than § 736, will control, even for service partnerships: § 736 applies only to payments "for" unrealized receivables, not to distributions "of" that kind of property.

Here is an example showing how §§ 736 and 751(b) interact in a case involving an all-cash liquidation of a partner's interest.

Example 13–9: The NOP equal general partnership has three assets: $9,000 in cash, a zero-basis unrealized receivable worth $9,000, and a zero-basis inventory item worth $9,000. Capital is not a material income-producing factor. Partner Nancy retires and gets $9,000 in cash from the partnership. The basis of her partnership interest was $2,000.

Section 736 is always applied before § 751(b), because it is § 736 that determines the extent to which a payment is a "distribution." Section 751(b) cannot come into play until we know whether a distribution has taken place. In this case, $3,000 of the payment (the payment for Nancy's one-third interest in the receivables) is a § 736(a) payment. Nancy therefore has $3,000 of ordinary income and the partnership gets a

$3,000 ordinary deduction. This leaves a § 736(b) $6,000 cash liquidating distribution to be analyzed.

Under § 751(b), Nancy has received $3,000 in cash for her one-third interest in the partnership's substantially appreciated inventory. (In applying § 751, we can ignore the fact that she got cash for her interest in unrealized receivables. That payment was not a "distribution"—only § 736(b) payments are distributions, and the payment for the receivables was a § 736(a) payment.) Section 751(b) treats Nancy as receiving $3,000 worth of zero-basis inventory in a current distribution and selling that inventory to the partnership for $3,000 cash; this step gives Nancy $3,000 in ordinary income and increases the partnership's basis in its inventory from zero to $3,000. Finally, Nancy is seen as receiving a $3,000 cash liquidating distribution. Because her outside basis just before the distribution was $2,000, she recognizes a $1,000 capital gain on the distribution.

What if the partnership in Example 13–9 had not been a service partnership or Nancy had been a limited partner? In those cases, none of the $9,000 payment would have been a $736(a) payment. Nancy would still have had $6,000 ordinary income, but now entirely because of § 751(b). The partnership would have had a $3,000 basis increase for its receivables instead of a $3,000 deduction.

2. A Refinement in the Definition of Section 736(a) Payments

Sometimes an "unrealized receivable" has a basis other than zero. For example, consider a partnership which has capitalized expenditures incurred in performing services. If this treatment increases the basis of the partnership's contract rights, the partnership's right to payment for those services is an "unrealized receivable" as defined in § 751(c), and that receivable has a non-zero basis. Goodwill may also have a basis, as when a partnership purchases a going business and pays a price in excess of the value of the business's assets other than its goodwill.

Although § 736, if read literally, says that the full amount of a payment by a service partnership for an unrealized receivable or for unstated goodwill is a § 736(a) payment, this treatment would make no sense when the receivable or goodwill has a basis. If a retiring partner gets $10,000 for an unrealized receivable, and if the partner's share of the basis of that receivable is $9,000, the partner should be taxed on $1,000 of ordinary income, not $10,000. The regulations correct the statute by classifying payments for unrealized receivables and unstated goodwill as § 736(b) payments to the extent of the distributee's share of the basis of those assets.[11]

3. Liquidation of an Entire Partnership

Section 736 was drafted on the assumption that the partnership would continue to exist after the distributee's interest had been liquidated. Suppose a partnership goes out of business, distributing all of its assets among the partners. Each partner has received a distribution, and § 736 does not apply.

There is one exception to the rule that § 736 does not govern payments to partners when the entire partnership, rather than one partner's interest in the partnership, is liquidated. Section 736 gives partners a great deal of flexibility in planning a partner's retirement so as to obtain favorable tax treatment. In particular, as we shall see, it often allows the parties to choose whether a partner's withdrawal is to be structured as a sale of the partner's interest to the other partners or as liquidation. To give the members of two-person partnerships this kind of flexibility, the regulations provide that a two-person partnership does not necessarily terminate when one partner withdraws, and that the partners may be subject to § 736.[12] Presumably, if one member of a two-partner firm receives cash and the other continues to operate the business, the partner who receives the cash is the retiring partner under § 736 and the other partner is "the partnership." How these rules are to apply if each partner receives some of the partnership's operating assets and carries on part of the former partnership's business is unclear. Indeed, even in cases in which the partnership continues after one partner's withdrawal, applying § 736 to distributions of property raises questions that have no obvious answers.

E. SALES AND RETIREMENT PAYMENTS DISTINGUISHED

The tax treatment of a partner who sells a partnership interest depends upon §§ 741 and 751(a), while retiring partners are taxed under §§ 736 and 751(b). There is often little if any non-tax difference between a liquidation of a partner's interest and a sale of that interest, yet the tax consequences may be very different.

Example 13–10: Stanley is a one-third partner in the RST equal partnership, which has $90,000 worth of assets and no liabilities.

---

11. Treas. Reg. §§ 1.736–1(b)(2) & (3). Treas. Reg. § 1.736–1(b)(3) also limits the amount of a payment for stated goodwill that can be treated as a § 736(b) payment to "a reasonable payment."

12. See Treas. Reg. §§ 1.708–1(b)(1)(i)(a) and 1.736–1(a)(6).

Stanley, who is contemplating retirement, expects to get $30,000 in cash for his interest. Apart from tax consequences, Stanley and the other partners, Robin and Tad, will seldom[13] care whether the transaction is structured as: (1) a liquidation of Stanley's interest by a $30,000 payment by the partnership to Stanley, or (2) a sale by Stanley of half of his partnership interest to Robin for $15,000 and of the other half-interest to Tad for $15,000.

Those who drafted subchapter K in 1954 understood the equivalence between a liquidation and a pro-rata sale of a partnership interest to the remaining partners. They intended to allow partners to structure these transactions in whichever way produces the more-favorable tax consequences to the parties.[14] The better-reasoned opinions recognize this flexibility and defer to the parties' choice of form. However, some courts have tried to decide whether a particular transaction amounted to a sale or a liquidation by looking for the "substance" of the transaction.[15] As the substance of a liquidation is the same as the substance of a pro-rata sale, the opinions are unpersuasive. In cases involving two-person partnerships, inquiries into substance tend to conclude that the transaction was a sale, probably because a "liquidation" finding would entail treating one of the partners, who has now become a sole proprietor, as "a partnership."[16]

How should the parties to a transaction that can plausibly be called either a sale or a liquidation go about exercising their choice? In a leading case, Foxman v. Commissioner, the Tax Court, in finding a sale, stressed the parties' intention to create a sale rather than a liquidation and the fact that the agreement placed the obligation to make the payments to the retiring partner primarily on the continuing partners rather than the partnership.[17] Careful tax planning, therefore, requires both of these things: The parties should use "sale" or "liquidation" terminology consistently and the obligation to make the payments should be upon the appropriate party (the partnership, if liquidation treatment is wanted; the remaining partners, if sale treatment is

---

13. We have said "seldom" rather than "never" only out of lawyerly caution. Non-tax consequences may attach to the parties' choice of form under some states' partnership laws or community property laws or under the laws of bankruptcy or products liability, or somewhere. We know of no such law, but in a society in which complex and obscure statutes govern most aspects of life, there are probably some.

14. See the discussion in Foxman v. Commissioner, 41 T.C. 535 (1964) (Acq.), affirmed, 352 F.2d 466 (3d Cir. 1965).

15. As part of the Health Care and Education Reconciliation Act of 2010, Pub. L. No. 111–152, § 1409(a), Congress added § 7701(o) (a so-called "clarification" of the economic substance doctrine) to the Internal Revenue Code. Although we believe that new § 7701(o) should not change the analysis in the text, the wording of § 7701(o) may leave some doubt.

16. The regulations, however, plainly allow one of two partners to be "the partnership" after the partnership is liquidated. See Treas. Reg. §§ 1.708–1(b)(1)(i)(a) and 1.736–1(a)(6).

17. 41 T.C. at 551–53.

sought).[18] In addition, payments should actually be made by the party or parties liable to make them.

Although the particular circumstances of every case must be considered, partners are more often likely to obtain favorable tax treatment if a partner's withdrawal is structured as a liquidation than if it is made a sale to the remaining partners. This is particularly true of partners who derive no great benefit from having their gains classified as capital gains. Consider a service partnership with unrealized receivables, inventory, unstated goodwill, and some other property, and assume that a withdrawing general partner will receive a fixed amount of cash and will recognize gain. Here are the principal ways in which payments attributable to the different kinds of partnership property will be taxed:

Payments for Unrealized Receivables. In a liquidation, these payments will give the distributee ordinary income under § 736(a) and the other partners will get ordinary deductions. If the transaction is set up as a sale, the departing partner will still have ordinary income (under § 751(a)), but the other partners will get no deduction. If a § 754 election is in effect, the remaining partners will get a basis step-up, which will reduce their taxes later. (When capital is a material income-producing factor, or when the retiree is a limited partner, the only difference between a sale and a liquidation will involve the basis of the receivables to the partnership.)

Payments for Inventory. If the partnership's inventory is "substantially appreciated," the partner who is cashing out will have ordinary income (under § 751(a) if the transaction is a sale; under § 751(b) if it is a liquidation). If the partnership's inventory is appreciated, but not substantially appreciated, that partner will have ordinary income on a sale but not on a liquidation. The other partners will get a cost basis for the departing partner's share of the inventory if the transaction is a liquidation; if it is a sale they will get an increase in the basis of inventory only if a § 754 election is in effect.

Payments for Unstated Goodwill. In a liquidation, these will generate ordinary income to the departing partner and ordinary deductions for the others. In a sale, payments for goodwill will generate capital gains for the seller and no benefit (except for more basis) for the remaining partners. It is a rare case in which one partner benefits more from having capital gains than the other partners lose by losing a deduction. (If § 736(b)(2) does not apply, the retiring partner will have capital gains and the re-

---

18. See R. Dale Swihart, *Tax Problems Raised by Liquidations of Partnership Interests*, 44 Texas L. Rev. 1209 (1966).

maining partners will get no benefit other than a basis increase, whether the transaction is a sale or a liquidation.)

Other Payments. Cash payments for the departing partner's interest in partnership capital assets other than unstated goodwill will generally not be taxed much differently upon a sale than upon a liquidation. If a § 754 election is in effect, the consequences for the partnership's inside basis may differ because of defects in the drafting of § 734 (see the next chapter for the details). If distributing assets other than cash is practical, the departing partner may avoid current gain recognition entirely in a liquidation (except for § 736(a) payments and the § 751 portion of the distribution); a sale of a partnership interest will always be a taxable event.

The collateral consequences of a liquidation may be more favorable than the collateral consequences of a sale. If the departing partner holds a 50–percent or greater interest in the partnership, a sale will terminate the partnership under § 708(b)(1)(B); a liquidation will not. The termination of a partnership may be undesirable: the partnership may lose a favorable taxable year, or the constructive transactions into which a termination is translated may have undesirable tax results.[19]

When a partner dies, the sale vs. liquidation question takes on some new aspects, which will be examined in Chapter 15.

F. PROBLEMS OF "FORM" AND "SUBSTANCE"

When a distribution is followed by a transfer of the bulk of the distributed assets back to the partnership, the transaction as a whole may be recast as a sale of a partnership interest. Suppose that partner Abby receives a liquidating distribution consisting of land used in the partnership's business (and in hers as well). The land is worth considerably less than Abby's outside basis. Because the liquidation is not a recognition event under § 731, Abby will take the land with a basis higher than its value.[20] If she sells the land to Bruno, her loss will be a § 1231 loss, which frequently results in an ordinary deduction. If Bruno then contributes the land to the partnership from which Abby withdrew, the transaction can plausibly be recharacterized as one in which Abby sold her partnership interest to Bruno.[21] Her loss on the sale should be a capital loss.[22] Indeed, the Service has argued (without success) for this

---

19. See pages 140–141, above.

20. § 732(b).

21. See Crenshaw v. Commissioner, 450 F.2d 472 (5th Cir. 1971), cert. denied, 408 U.S. 923 (1972).

22. § 741.

kind of recharacterization even when the buyer of the property did not contribute the property back to the partnership.[23]

The 1984 amendments to § 707(a)[24] support the Service's attempts to recharacterize purported liquidations as sales, at least if the distributed property finds its way back to the partnership pursuant to a plan agreed upon before the distribution. Under § 707(a), the key question is how the transfer should "properly" be characterized. This language cannot be reduced to a mechanical formula for identifying liquidations that should be recast, but it at least warns us that outcomes too good to be true probably won't come true. There may also be cases in which purported sales or exchanges are "properly" recharacterized as liquidations. Consider, for instance, a sale of a partnership interest to an outsider followed almost immediately by a liquidation of the new partner's interest.

The partnership anti-abuse regulations' insistence on the priority of substance over form[25] may help the Service's efforts to recharacterize some distributions or sales, but the regulations give no examples. The statutory "clarification" of the economic substance doctrine in 2010 may also assist the Service in such efforts.[26]

G. COMPARISON WITH SUBCHAPTER S

Just as subchapter S has no counterpart to § 751(b),[27] it contains nothing like § 736. This is one more example of the tendency of subchapter S to sacrifice refinement in the taxation of shareholders for the sake of (relative) simplicity.

---

23. Harris v. Commissioner, 61 T.C. 770 (1974)

24. See page 116, above.

25. Except, of course, for cases in which form controls because particular results were "contemplated."

26. Health Care and Education Reconciliation Act of 2010, Pub. L. No. 111–152, § 1409(a), codified as § 7701(*o*).

27. Chapter 12.

Chapter Fourteen

BASIS ADJUSTMENTS UNDER SECTION 734

We have seen that the basis of a partnership's assets can be adjusted under § 743(b) when an interest in the partnership changes hands by sale or exchange or upon the death of a partner.[1] Adjustments can also be made to the basis of partnership property when the partnership makes distributions to partners. The same election governs both kinds of inside-basis adjustments. If a § 754 election is in effect, partnerships will adjust inside basis under § 743(b) when partnership interests change hands and under § 734(b) when partnerships make distributions. In addition, even if a § 754 election is not in effect, § 734, like § 743, requires a partnership to reduce the inside basis of its assets for distributions that would have triggered a substantial downward reduction had a § 754 election been in effect.

Section 734(b) differs from § 743(b) in three important ways:

(1) Section 743(b) adjustments are made "with respect to the transferee partner only";[2] the benefits (or detriments) of adjustments required by § 734(b) are shared by *all* the partners.

(2) All sales, exchanges, or transfers at death will trigger § 743(b) adjustments if a § 754 election is in effect. However, as discussed below, many distributions will not lead to basis adjustments under § 734(b) even if the election has been made.

(3) Section 743(b) works well. As we shall see, § 734(b) sometimes produces absurd results, at least if it is read literally.

Here is a very important reminder. The "distributions" that trigger adjustments under § 734(b) are distributions *as determined by the law of partnership taxation*. A partnership's payment of $50,000 to a withdrawing partner will seldom be a distribution in full under § 734(b). One must first test the distribution against § 736, which will often categorize some of it as a guaranteed payment or distributive share. Next, one applies § 751(b), which will often treat part of the transaction as an exchange between the partner and the partnership. (The "constructive current distribution" first step in reconstructing a § 751(b) distribution may require § 734(b) calculations.) Only what is left after part of a

---
1. Chapter 10.
2. § 743(b).

"distribution" in the colloquial sense has been recharacterized as something else is a "distribution" for purposes of § 734(b).

A. ADJUSTMENTS UNDER SECTION 734

If a § 754 election is in effect,[3] 734(b) adjusts the basis of partnership assets whenever a distribution either:

(1) Changes the basis of a distributed asset,[4] or

(2) Causes the distributee to recognize gain or loss.[5]

Many distributions will do neither of these things. For example, a current distribution of $5,000 cash or of property with a basis of $5,000 to a partner having an outside basis of at least $5,000 will generate no gain, loss, or basis change.

Liquidating distributions usually cause the distributee to recognize gain or loss or change the basis of distributed assets, so § 734(b) almost always comes into play when liquidating distributions take place. Current distributions will result in § 734(b) adjustments only if the amount of cash or the basis of property distributed exceeds the distributee's outside basis.[6]

1. Distributions That Change the Basis of the Distributed Property

If a distribution changes the basis of the distributed property, that change will increase or decrease the amount of potential income in the world. To make up for this, § 734(b) will either (1) decrease the basis of property remaining inside the partnership to make up for an increase in the basis of distributed property, or (2) increase the basis of remaining partnership property to make up for a reduction in the basis of distributed property.

Example 14–1: Chester's basis for his interest in the CDE partnership is $10,000. The partnership holds a capital asset with an inside basis of $12,000 and distributes it to Chester. This distribution does not cause Chester to recognize gain (because no

---

3. As discussed at page 194, below, even if a § 754 election is not in effect, § 734, requires a partnership to reduce the inside basis of its assets with respect to distributions that would have triggered a substantial downward reduction had a § 754 election been in effect.

4. § 734(b)(1)(B) (distributions that reduce the basis of property) and § 734(b)(2)(B) (distributions that increase the basis of property).

5. § 734(b)(1)(A) (gain) and § 734(b)(2)(A) (loss).

6. If the cash distributed exceeds the distributee's outside basis, the distributee will recognize gain under § 731(a)(1). If a partnership distributes property to a partner whose outside basis is less than the basis of the property, the property's basis will be reduced by § 732(a)(2).

cash was distributed[7]) or loss (losses are never recognized upon a current distribution[8]). The distribution will, however, reduce the basis of the distributed asset by $2,000 to $10,000.[9] If no § 754 election is in effect, this reduced basis will result in an additional $2,000 gain being recognized upon the sale of all the partnership's assets and the asset distributed to Chester. This is not a satisfactory outcome because the distribution neither changed the value of any asset nor caused anyone to recognize gain or loss. Therefore, if a § 754 election is in effect, § 734(b)(1)(B) will increase the basis of partnership's remaining assets by $2,000.

The purpose behind § 734(b) adjustments in cases involving changes in the basis of distributed property is to keep the total amount of income in the world unchanged. Consistently with this objective, the regulations require that basis adjustments caused by changes in the bases of capital assets and § 1231 assets be allocated to the partnership's remaining capital and § 1231 assets; basis adjustments resulting from changes in the bases of ordinary-income assets must be allocated to ordinary-income property.[10] Were it not for this requirement, a reduction in the basis of inventory might be "made up for" by an increase in the basis of capital assets.

2. Distributions on Which Gain or Loss Is Recognized

A partner who recognizes gain or loss on a distribution (a partner who gets an all-cash liquidating distribution, for example) is often situated very similarly to a partner who has sold an interest in the partnership; the remaining partners resemble buyers of partnership interests. Just as sales of partnership interests are followed by basis adjustments under § 743(b), taxable distributions are followed by adjustments under § 734(b)(1)(A) (when the partner recognizes a gain) or § 734(b)(2)(A) (when the partner recognizes a loss). Basis adjustments caused by recognition of gain or loss are allocated to capital-gain property.[11] These adjustments are sometimes functionally equivalent to adjustments under § 743(b).

---

7. Under § 731(a)(1), a partner recognizes gain on a distribution only if cash distributed exceeds the partner's outside basis immediately before the distribution. Gain may be recognized under § 704(c)(1)(B) or § 737 when a distribution occurs. But those sections contain their own basis-adjustment provisions, so § 734(b) adjustments need not be made to reflect the recognized gains.

8. See § 731(a)(2).

9. § 732(a)(2).

10. Treas. Reg. § 1.755–1(c)(1)(i).

11. Treas. Reg. § 1.755–1(c)(1)(ii).

Ch. 14   ADJUSTMENTS UNDER SECTION 734

Example 14–2: Donna is a one-fourth partner in DEFG. The partnership has no unrealized receivables or inventory items. Its assets are as follows:

	Basis	Value
Cash	$40,000	$40,000
Capital Asset A	16,000	32,000
Capital Asset B	4,000	8,000
Total:	$60,000	$80,000

Donna's outside basis is $15,000. She receives a cash liquidating distribution of $20,000 from DEFG. All of this payment is in exchange for her interest in partnership property under § 736(b), and § 751(b) does not apply, so the payment is a liquidating distribution in full. Donna recognizes a $5,000 capital gain under § 731(a)(1).

If a § 754 election is in effect, the partnership (now EFG) will adjust the basis of its assets upward by $5,000, the amount of the gain Donna recognized on the distribution. (The basis of capital asset A increases by $4,000; the basis of capital asset B increases by $1,000.[12]) This makes excellent sense. The substance of this all-cash liquidation is that Donna received some of the cash in exchange for her interest in the partnership's appreciated capital assets. Section 731 taxes her as if she had sold those assets, and § 734(b) gives the other partners an increase in inside basis, as if they had bought those assets.

If a partner's share of the inside basis of partnership property differs from that partner's outside basis, § 734(b) can lead to absurdity.

Example 14–3: The facts are the same as in Example 14–2 except that Donna, who bought her partnership interest several years ago, has an outside basis of $40,000. No § 754 election was in effect when she bought her interest, but one has since been made. Donna recognizes a loss of $20,000 on the liquidating distribution. Under § 734(b)(2)(A), the partnership must reduce the basis of its assets by the amount of the $20,000 loss. This is hard on E, F, and G, as from their point of view they have bought Donna's share of appreciated capital assets for cash; the bases of those assets should increase, not decline. If Donna had

---

12.   Treas. Reg. § 1.755–1(c)(2)(ii).

sold her partnership interest to the other partners, pro rata, § 743(b) would have increased the basis of the capital assets.

If the partners in Example 14–3 had been well advised, they would have structured the transaction as a sale of Donna's interest to the other three partners. Donna would have been taxed in exactly the same way, and the other three partners would have had inside-basis increases under § 743(b).

The reason why § 734(b) breaks down in Example 14–3, although § 743(b) would have worked well if the interest had been sold, is that § 734(b) makes the amount of the adjustment equal to the distributee's gain or loss. Section 743(b) works very differently: It compares the buyer's basis for the interest (which in the case of a sale will be the seller's amount realized) with the buyer's share of the *inside* basis. Whether the seller recognized a gain or loss is irrelevant under § 743(b); it should also be irrelevant under § 734(b). The House and Senate versions of § 743(b) contained the same defect as § 734(b), but the mistake was corrected by the Conference Committee.[13]

3. Allocating the Adjustment to Particular Assets

As noted earlier, § 734(b) adjustments triggered by changes in the basis of distributed property are allocated to property of a character similar to that of the property distributed, while allocations resulting from recognition of gain or loss are allocated to capital-asset property. Allocation of the adjustment for a class among the assets in that class begins by allocating increases among appreciated assets in proportion to those assets' relative basis/value differences. Decreases are allocated similarly among depreciated assets.[14] This portion of the allocation uses only that amount of the allocation equal to the total unrealized appreciation or depreciation in the class, so it may not allocate all of the adjustment. For example, if a partnership has a $1,000 positive adjustment for capital-gain assets, and if it has only two appreciated capital-gain assets, with a total appreciation of $600, the allocation in proportion to basis/value differences will take care of only $600 of the $1,000 adjustment. Any excess positive adjustment is allocated among all the assets in the class in proportion to their relative values.[15] Excess negative

---

13. Under the House and Senate versions of § 743(b), the adjustment was the difference between the transferor's outside basis and the transferee's outside basis. The Conference Committee described its version as a "simplification" of the Senate's formula; H.R.Rept. No. 2543, 83d Cong., 2d Sess. at 61–64 (Conference Committee Report, 1954). Apparently, the error in the earlier versions of § 743(b) was corrected by accident, not because someone had noticed it.

14. Treas. Reg. §§ 1.755–1(c)(2)(i) & (ii).

15. Treas. Reg. § 1.755–1(c)(2)(i).

adjustments are allocated in proportion to the bases of all the assets in the class.[16] Negative adjustments cannot reduce an asset's basis to less than zero; if this limit prevents using all of a negative adjustment, the unused portion becomes a carryover, which will reduce the basis of property the partnership acquires in the future.[17]

Example 14–4: The FGH partnership has a positive $30,000 adjustment to be allocated to assets in the capital-gain class. It has three capital assets, with these bases and values:

	Basis	Value
Capital Asset A	$20,000	$10,000
Capital Asset B	5,000	10,000
Capital Asset C	10,000	20,000

The first step in allocating the $30,000 positive adjustment is to allocate it between Capital Assets B and C (the only appreciated assets) in proportion to the amount of appreciation for each asset. This step increases the basis of Capital Asset B to $10,000 and the basis of Capital Asset C to $20,000 (the allocation in proportion to basis/value differences cannot increase an asset's basis to more than its value). This portion of the allocation uses $15,000 of the adjustment, leaving another $15,000 to be allocated among all three assets in proportion to their values. Capital Asset A's value is one-fourth of the total, so one-fourth of this $15,000 ($3,750) is allocated to Capital Asset A, increasing its basis to $13,750. Similarly Capital Asset B's basis increases to $13,750. The remaining half of the $15,000 adjustment goes to Capital Asset C, the basis of which becomes $27,500.

As noted earlier,[18] adjustments under § 734(b) are shared by all of those who are partners after the distribution. In some cases, this approach makes sense. In Example 14–3, for instance, the liquidation of Donna's interest by the partnership was in substance no different from a purchase of that interest by the remaining partners. Partners who buy a partnership interest when a § 754 election is in effect, get the benefit of inside-basis adjustments (under § 743(b)), to treat them much as if they had purchased shares of assets. Similarly, when a partnership interest is

---

16. Treas. Reg. § 1.755–1(c)(2)(ii).

17. Treas. Reg. §§ 1.755–1(c)(3) & (4). The carryover approach also comes into play for both increases and decreases if an adjustment cannot be made because the partnership has no property in the class to which an adjustment is to be made; Treas. Reg. § 1.755–1(c)(4).

18. Page 188, above.

liquidated, all the remaining partners are, in effect, purchasers, and all of them should and do share in any increase or decrease in inside basis under § 734(b). Adjustments triggered by current distributions are a different matter, however. For instance, if a distribution of property reduces that property's basis, as in Example 14–1, the distributee partner bears the burden of that decrease.[19] Because the purpose of the § 743(b) adjustment is to make up for that increased burden, one might think that the adjustment should benefit only the distributee. The regulations, however, allocate the adjustment among all of the partnership's assets. Similarly, adjustments triggered by recognition of gain on current distributions benefit all of the partners, not just the partner who had to recognize the gain.[20]

4. Adjustments Required Without a § 754 Election: Substantial Basis Reductions

Even if no § 754 election is in effect, § 734 mandates that the partnership reduce the basis of its assets in situations where a "substantial basis reduction" would have occurred had a § 754 election been in effect. A "substantial basis reduction" is one that would have reduced the partnership's basis in its assets by more than $250,000. § 734(d).

Example 14–5: Cesar is a one third partner in the CNW partnership, which has not made a § 754 election and has the following assets:

	Basis	Value
Capital Asset A	$50,000	$400,000
Capital Asset B	400,000	400,000
Capital Asset C	150,000	400,000

Cesar's outside basis is $400,000. The partnership distributes Capital Asset A to Cesar in liquidation of his partnership interest. As a result of § 732(b), Cesar takes Capital Asset A with a basis of $400,000. Had the partnership made a § 754 election, § 734(b) would have required the partnership to reduce the basis of its remaining assets by $350,000 (the difference between the

---

[19] For example, by recognizing more gain when the asset is sold than the partnership would have recognized if it had sold the asset.

[20] For a detailed criticism of the regulations' approach in the case of non-liquidating distributions, see Howard E. Abrams, The Section 734(b) Basis Adjustment Needs Repair, 57 Tax Law. 343 (2004). Professor Abrams shows that the problems created by distributions that change the basis of property require legislative changes (analogous to § 704(c)) in addition to a revision of the allocation regulations under § 755.

partnership's basis in Capital Asset A of $50,000 and Cesar's new basis of $400,000). Because the amount of this downward adjustment exceeds $250,000, the partnership must reduce the inside basis of its remaining assets by $350,000, even though no § 754 election has been made. § 734(b) and (d).

Note that the partnership could have avoided the mandatory basis reduction by distributing Capital Asset C to Cesar because the basis reduction in that situation would have been only $250,000 (the difference between the partnership's basis in Capital Asset A of $50,000 and Cesar's new basis of $400,000). A "substantial basis reduction" occurs only if the adjustment *exceeds* $250,000.

B. SECTION 734 AND THE ANTI-ABUSE REGULATIONS

The anti-abuse regulations stress the importance of taxing transactions according to their substance, except for cases in which a provision clearly contemplates that form will control. Section 734(b) adjustments are elective (except in the case of substantial basis reductions), and an election is the strongest possible example of a decision to let form control: the existence of an election necessarily means that identical transactions will be taxed differently, depending on the formality of whether an election is made. It is therefore not surprising that the anti-abuse regulations treat a partnership's failure to make a § 754 election as not abusive. This is the case, as a general rule, even if § 734(b) adjustments would have prevented a pro-taxpayer distortion if the election had been made, and even if the partners' selection of the asset to be distributed is made to reduce taxes.

Example 14–6: Krissa is a one-fourth partner in HIJK, which holds only these assets:

	Basis	Value
Capital Asset A	$45,000	$25,000
Capital Asset B	5,000	25,000
Capital Asset C	25,000	25,000
Capital Asset D	25,000	25,000
Total	$100,000	$100,00

Krissa's outside basis is $25,000. The partnership and Krissa have agreed that her interest is to be liquidated. In selecting property to distribute to her, the partnership picks Capital Asset B, because that asset's basis will be increased to $25,000 if it goes to Krissa in a liquidating distribution.[21] (Distribution of an interest in Capital Asset A would have reduced the basis of the distributed property; distributing Capital Asset C or D would have left basis unchanged.) If a § 754 election had been in effect, the $20,000 increase in the basis of the distributed asset would have reduced the basis of Capital Asset A by $20,000.

Holding that the distortions attributable to failure to make a § 754 election were "clearly contemplated" by Congress, an example in the anti-abuse regulations holds that the distortion illustrated by Example 14–6 is not necessarily an abuse.[22]

Some distortions, however, so offended the drafters that they declared them abusive. Another example in the anti-abuse regulations says that if a partnership is formed and high-basis, low-value property is contributed to that partnership just so that later distributions without making a § 754 election can be made, the transactions may be recast.[23] In this example, one partner contributes land with a tax basis greater than its fair market value to a new partnership, while two other partners (both related to the partner who contributed the land) contribute cash. The partnership uses the cash to buy an investment asset. The land is leased to an outsider, who plans to buy it after a few years. The partnership distributes the investment asset to the partner who contributed the land. That partner takes the asset with the land's high basis and sells it at a loss. The partnership also recognizes a loss on the subsequent sale of the land. The example concludes that using a partnership to duplicate losses in this way is inconsistent with the intent of subchapter K. In any event, as the example notes, the transaction is vulnerable to attack under the disguised-sale provisions of § 707.

The anti-abuse regulations were adopted prior to the amendment to § 734(b) that mandates basis reductions in excess of $250,000 regardless of whether a § 754 election has been made. The mandatory adjustment should address abusive situations involving § 734(b) that are important enough to worry about.

C. COMPARISON WITH SUBCHAPTER S

An S corporation's distribution of property other than cash will usually cause the corporation to recognize gain or loss. There is, there-

---

21. § 732(b).
22. Treas. Reg. § 1.701–2(d) (Example 9).
23. Cf. Treas. Reg. § 1.701–2(d) (Example 8).

fore, no need to adjust the basis of remaining assets to make up for changes in the bases of distributed assets. In principle, the same considerations that make inside-basis adjustments appropriate when a distributee partner recognizes gain or loss could apply to S corporations. In fact, the Code does not provide for inside-basis adjustments following corporate distributions.

Chapter Fifteen

THE DEATH OF A PARTNER

This Chapter reviews the concept of "income in respect of a decedent" ("IRD") and shows how classification of an inherited partnership interest as a right to receive IRD affects the successor's basis in the partnership interest under § 1014. It then shows how the method selected for transferring a deceased partner's interest in the partnership affects the income tax liabilities of the successor and the surviving partners.

A. INCOME IN RESPECT OF A DECEASED PARTNER

1. Introduction

As a rule, a decedent's estate (or other successor) takes the decedent's property with a fair-market-value basis under § 1014(a).[1] If the decedent's accounting method resulted in the deferral of income, however, § 1014(a) would cause income to disappear for some taxpayers while other taxpayers, who used different methods of accounting, would recognize income. For example, consider two lawyers, Elise and Felix, who each engage in separate law practices. Each performs work for her or his client, sends the client a bill for $50,000, and then dies. Elise, who reports on an accrual method of accounting, recognizes income of $50,000 when she bills her client. Felix, who uses the cash method, reports no income upon billing his client. For the sake of simplicity, assume that each lawyer's account receivable is worth $50,000 at the date of death and that each client pays the estate $50,000 soon after the lawyer's death. If each lawyer's account receivable took a $50,000 basis under § 1014(a), neither estate would have any income when the client

---

[1]. Congress temporarily repealed the estate tax for the 2010 calendar year and changed the tax basis rules applicable to decedents dying during that period. If a decedent dies on or after January 1, 2010 and before January 1, 2011, the amount by which an estate may step-up the basis of its assets to reflect increases in value is limited. Under § 1022(b), an estate can increase the basis of its assets by no more than $1,300,000. The limitation for the increase of the basis of property transferred to a surviving spouse is more generous. That property's basis may be increased by up to $3 million, if certain requirements are satisfied. § 1022(c).

As this book goes to press at the end of 2010, the fate of § 1022 is uncertain. Unless Congress acts to change the result, the estate tax will be revived after December 31, 2010, and § 1022 will not apply after that date. Instead, § 1014 will be effective for decedents dying on or after January 1, 2011. For that reason, the text discusses § 1014 and not § 1022.

paid. As a result, Elise's income would be taxed in full (to her), while Felix's income would escape taxation entirely.

Section 1014(c) prevents income from the performance of services (and some other kinds of income as well) from disappearing from the tax base when the taxpayer dies after earning income but before recognizing it under the taxpayer's accounting method. It does so by classifying the right to the income as "property which constitutes a right to receive an item of income in respect of a decedent,"[2] and by making § 1014 inapplicable to that kind of property. (Section 691 provides that the estate or heir who eventually receives the money in question must include the IRD in income, but the key section is § 1014(c), which prevents the right to that income from taking a fair-market-value basis.) In the example used in the previous paragraph, the income Felix would have had to report upon collecting his receivable is IRD. Section 1014(c) denies a stepped-up basis to the right to collect the payment. Felix's estate will therefore take the receivable with a zero basis, and the estate will have $50,000 income when the client pays.

The Code does not define IRD,[3] but the two most common examples are clear enough. IRD includes (1) rights to payment for services performed by the decedent, to the extent that the income in question was not reportable because of the decedent's accounting method, and (2) gains from the decedent's sale of property which were not includable in the decedent's income.[4] The idea is that a taxpayer's accounting method should affect the timing of income, but not whether the income is taxable at all. By denying a stepped-up basis to the estate or heir, § 1014(c) preserves income that the decedent died too early to recognize.

2. The Basis of an Inherited Partnership Interest

Like other property, a partnership interest that changes hands when its owner dies receives a basis determined by § 1014. This basis will be the fair market value of the interest unless part of the interest is an IRD item, so that § 1014(c) applies.[5]

---

2. § 1014(c).

3. Treas. Reg. § 1.691(a)–1(b) says that "income in respect of a decedent" refers to:"those amounts to which a decedent was entitled as gross income but which were not properly includable in computing his taxable income for the taxable year ending with the date of his death or for a previous taxable year under the method of accounting employed by the decedent."

4. Under § 443(a)(2) and Treas. Reg. § 1.451–1(b)(1), a taxpayer's taxable year closes when the taxpayer dies. Income not includable in the decedent's income for that last, short year or some earlier year cannot be taxed to the decedent.

5. See note 1, supra, for circumstances in which basis increases occurring at death will be limited in years in which there is no estate tax.

The application of § 1014(c) upon the death of a partner depends upon the kind of interest the decedent's successor receives. There are two fundamentally different ways of disposing of a partnership interest when a partner dies:

(1) The partnership agreement may provide that the partner's interest will be liquidated after the partner's death. When this happens, the estate or other successor receives not a partnership interest as such, but the right to a payment or a series of payments in liquidation of the decedent's interest. Section 736 covers this kind of case. Recall that § 736 classifies payments as either "§ 736(a) payments" or "§ 736(b) payments."[6] Section 736(a) payments are guaranteed payments or distributive shares; they are includable in the recipients' incomes and deductible or excludable by the other partners.

(2) The partnership interest may pass to the decedent's estate, and then to the heirs, just like any other kind of property. Some partnership agreements require the surviving partners to buy this partnership interest from the estate (or other successor) at a price determined by a formula set out in the partnership agreement.

When the decedent's successor receives a right to liquidating distributions from the partnership, the statute provides expressly for treatment of part of the payments as IRD. Section 753 says that the successor's § 736(a) payments are IRD. Therefore, the successor will take a zero basis for the right to receive § 736(a) payments and a fair-market-value basis for its right to § 736(b) payments.

Example 15–1: Gloria, a one-third general partner in GHI, dies. Capital is not a material income-producing factor for the partnership. According to the partnership agreement, Gloria's estate is to receive a $90,000 payment from the partnership in liquidation of Gloria's interest. At the date of death, the partnership's assets were:

	Basis	Value
Cash	$100,000	$100,000
Accounts Receivable	0	90,000
Capital Asset	60,000	80,000
Total:	$160,000	$270,000

---

6. See Chapter 13.

If, as seems likely on these facts, $30,000 of the payment to the estate is for Gloria's interest in the accounts receivable ("unrealized receivables" as defined in § 751(c)), the estate will get a $30,000 § 736(a) payment and a $60,000 § 736(b) payment. Section 753 makes the § 736(a) payment IRD. Therefore, the estate's right to that $30,000 gets a zero basis under § 1014(c).

The estate will have $30,000 ordinary income when it receives the $30,000 § 736(a) payment, and the partnership will get a $30,000 ordinary deduction. The estate will have a $60,000 basis for the right to its § 736(b) payment (if that right is worth $60,000); it will therefore recognize no gain or loss upon receiving that payment.

A common arrangement gives a deceased partner's successor a right to receive payments equal to the decedent's distributive share of partnership income for some period. For instance, a partnership agreement may provide that a partner's spouse will receive payments equal to the deceased partner's distributive share of income received by the partnership for two years after the partner dies. This is an example of a successor's receiving partnership payments in liquidation of a deceased partner's interest. Whatever portion of each payment is classified as a § 736(a) payment will be taxed as IRD.

Whether a portion of an inherited right to payments under § 736(b) can be an IRD item is unclear. The Code's expressly providing that § 736(a) payments are IRD items while saying nothing about § 736(b) payments seems to say, by implication, that § 736(b) payments are not IRD items. That conclusion makes little sense, however. Suppose that Gloria, in Example 15–1, had been a limited partner. Under today's version of § 736, her right to $30,000 for her share of the accounts receivable would be part of her § 736(b) payment, because of § 736(b)(3). Giving her a stepped-up basis for her entire right to the § 736(b) payment conflicts with the principle that zero-basis receivables do not have their bases stepped up under § 1014(a). A similar problem arises when a portion of a right to a § 736(b) payments is attributable to a partnership's holding installment obligations arising from the sale of low-basis assets. Alan Gunn has argued that the portion of a § 736(b) payment attributable to partnership assets that would have been IRD items if left directly to the heir should be an IRD item.[7]

What if the successor receives a partnership interest (either outright or subject to a buy-sell agreement), rather than a right to liquidating distributions? Subchapter K says nothing about IRD in this situation:

---

7. Alan Gunn, Federal Tax Problems of Income in Respect of a Deceased Partner, 3 J. P'ship Tax. 23, 44–45 (1986).

§ 753 does not apply because the successor gets no § 736(a) payments. Many commentators once thought that the successor in this kind of case should get a fair-market-value basis for the entire partnership interest under § 1014(a). The partnership interest, they reasoned, was "property," and nothing in subchapter K made any part of that property an IRD item.[8] The courts, however, have held that an inherited partnership interest is an IRD item to the extent that its value is attributable to property rights that would have been IRD items if held by a soleproprietor.[9] Therefore, if a service partnership's assets consist entirely of zero-basis accounts receivable (which would have been IRD items if left by an individual decedent), the estate of a partner who dies will take the partnership interest with a zero basis under § 1014(c).

Example 15–2: The JKL partnership holds the following assets:

	Basis	Value
Cash	$ 60,000	$ 60,000
Accounts Receivable	0	30,000
Machine	15,000	45,000
Land	50,000	90,000
Total:	$125,000	$225,000

Jennifer, a one-third partner in JKL, dies, and her estate succeeds to her partnership interest, which is worth $75,000. The estate's basis under § 1014(c) is $65,000. If § 1014(a) applied to the entire partnership interest, that interest would take a basis of $75,000. But the courts treat the interest as an IRD item to the extent that its value arises from partnership assets that would have been IRD items if left by an individual decedent.

If Jennifer had been a sole proprietor who had died owning one-third of each of the assets held by JKL, the accounts

---

8. E.g., M. Carr Ferguson, James J. Freeland & Richard B. Stephens, Federal Income Taxation of Estates and Beneficiaries 238–241 (1970). Another argument, advanced by the taxpayer in Woodhall v. Commissioner, 454 F.2d 226 (9th Cir. 1972), rested on the cross-reference in § 691(e), which says, "For application of this section to income in respect of a deceased partner, see section 753." The argument seems to have been that because § 691(e) refers only to § 753 in connection with deceased partners, the only kind of IRD a deceased partner can leave is that described in § 753. Section 7806(a), however, says that cross-references using the word "see" are to have "no legal effect."

9. Woodhall v. Commissioner, 454 F.2d 226 (9th Cir. 1972); George Edward Quick Trust v. Commissioner, 54 T.C. 1336 (1970) (Acq.), affirmed, 444 F.2d 90 (8th Cir. 1971).

receivable would have represented a right to IRD and so would have kept their zero basis when she died. Therefore, § 1014(c) prevents the estate from taking a stepped-up basis in the partnership interest to the extent that the interest has value because of the cash-method partnership's receivables. (Note that the machine is not an IRD item to any extent, even though it may be, in part, an "unrealized receivable" under § 751(c) because of potential depreciation recapture. If an individual decedent leaves property subject to depreciation recapture the property gets a § 1014 basis. There is no reason to treat a deceased partner's successors less favorably than those who succeed deceased sole proprietors.)

Although the principles illustrated in Example 15–2 are not spelled out in the statute, they make sense because they tax partners as if they were sole proprietors to the extent feasible. The regulations,[10] the legislative history of subchapter K,[11] and the two cases in point[12] support that treatment. While no tax issue can ever be definitively resolved without action by the Supreme Court or Congress, this one comes close.

B. CLOSING THE PARTNERSHIP'S TAXABLE YEAR UPON THE DEATH OF A PARTNER

An individual taxpayer's taxable year ends when the taxpayer dies.[13] Until 1998, a partnership's taxable year did not close, even with respect to the decedent, when a partner died.[14] These rules meant that a deceased partner's distributive share for the partnership taxable year that was in progress when the decedent died was reported by the decedent's successor (either the estate or someone who succeeded to the interest under the partnership agreement) rather than on the decedent's final return. This rule sometimes caused hardship. For example, income reportable on the decedent's final return might have been taxed at a lower rate than if reportable by the estate.[15] The problem could be dealt

---

10. Treas. Reg. § 1.742–1. Note also the portion of the anti-abuse regulations allowing the Commissioner to treat a partnership as an aggregate of its partners when necessary to further the purposes of a Code section; Treas. Reg. § 1.701–2(e).

11. The House version of § 753 spelled out the *Quick Trust* and *Woodhall* result. The Senate Finance Committee Report said that the change in the language enacted was made to broaden the scope of IRD, not to narrow it; S.Rept.No. 1622, 83d Cong., 2d Sess. 405–406 (1954).

12. *Quick Trust* and *Woodhall*.

13. § 443; Treas. Reg. § 1.451–1(b)(1).

14. § 706(c)(1). If a partner's death terminated the partnership under § 708(b)(1)(A), the partnership's taxable year closed because of the termination.

15. The income-tax rates for estates and trusts are quite compressed. Furthermore, if the deceased partner was married, income reportable on the final return could have been

with by careful planning: if the partnership agreement required the surviving partners to buy the decedent's interest at death, that sale would close the partnership's taxable year with respect to the decedent.

In 1997, Congress amended § 706(c) to make a partnership's taxable year close with respect to any partner whose entire interest terminates.

Example 15–3: Mark, a calendar-year taxpayer, is a partner in MNOP, a calendar-year partnership. Mark dies on November 28, year one. The partnership's taxable year closes (with respect to Mark) when he dies. Mark's distributive share for this short partnership taxable year is includable in his income for his final taxable year because of § 706(a).

C. SALE OR LIQUIDATION OF A DECEASED PARTNER'S INTEREST

The principal choice facing successors who want to dispose of a decedent's partnership interest will often be whether the interest is to be liquidated or sold to the surviving partners. The choice may depend upon whether the partnership has made a § 754 election. If it has not, a sale may lead to "double taxation" of ordinary income, as the estate will have ordinary income under § 751(a) without the buyers' (the surviving partners) getting any step-up in inside basis. A liquidation will typically cause the estate to have ordinary income under § 736(a) and § 751(b), but the surviving partners will get deductions (or the equivalent) under § 736(a) and an inside cost basis for property deemed purchased by the partnership in the § 751(b) exchange.

If the partnership does have a § 754 election in effect, the inside basis of the decedent's share of the assets (other than IRD items) will be stepped up at death to market value. A sale of the decedent's interest to the surviving partners will give inside basis adjustments for those partners under § 743(b); these adjustments will eliminate double taxation of ordinary income. Nevertheless, a liquidation may be better for the surviving partners, especially in cases involving service partnerships.[16]

D. COMPARISON WITH SUBCHAPTER S

An important difference between subchapters S and K is that inside-basis adjustments cannot be made when stock of an S corporation changes hands upon the death of a shareholder. This is particularly

---

taxed at joint-return rates; income taxed to the estate or other successor could not unless the successor was the decedent's spouse.

16. See the discussion of the relative advantages of sales and liquidations in the case of retiring partners, pages 183–186, above.

important if the successor plans to hold the interest rather than to dispose of it. The basis of a zero-basis building held by a partnership will increase, with respect to a deceased partner's successor, if a § 754 election is in effect; the basis of an identical building held by an S corporation will not. The successor's share of depreciation deductions and other tax benefits that depend on the basis of property held by an entity will therefore tend to be greater if the entity is a partnership than if it is an S corporation.

Section 1367(b)(4) extends IRD rules to S corporations similar to those that apply to partnerships. It requires a person acquiring S corporation stock from a decedent to treat as IRD his share of the S corporation's income that would have been IRD had such income been acquired directly from the decedent. § 1367(b)(4)(A). The basis of S corporation stock cannot include the value of any items of the S corporation that constitute IRD. § 1367(b)(4)(B). Thus, like a partnership interest, the basis of inherited stock in an S corporation may be less than its value at the time of decedent's death.

Example 15–4: The stock of Smallco, an S corporation that conducts a cash-method service business, is owned equally by Roger and Sally. Roger dies, leaving his half of the stock to Trent. Smallco's assets consist entirely of zero-basis accounts receivable worth $400,000. Because the accounts receivable constitute IRD, Trent's basis in the stock is zero.

Chapter Sixteen

WHAT IS A PARTNERSHIP?

The question whether two or more persons conducting a business or investment activity together have formed a partnership seldom presents serious difficulties. Most partnerships, small and large, plainly are partnerships unless they elect to be taxed as corporations. Organizations that are formally incorporated are not taxed as partnerships. Limited liability companies, limited liability partnerships, and other similar entities can choose whether to be taxed as partnerships or as corporations. Inevitably, though, borderline cases arise. For instance, ownership of unimproved land as joint tenants or tenants in common does not itself create a partnership, but two or more persons who own and operate a hotel will surely have created an "entity," taxable as a partnership unless it elects to be taxed as a corporation.

Sections 761(a) and 7701(a)(2) define "partnership" in almost identical terms:

> [T]he term "partnership" includes a syndicate, group, pool, joint venture, or other unincorporated organization through or by means of which any business, financial operation, or venture is carried on, and which is not ... a corporation or a trust or estate.[1]

Although this definition falls short of providing a specific set of rules, or even of standards, it conveys some useful information. For instance, the reference to a "business, financial operation, or venture" suggests (correctly) that co-owners of property do not become partners simply because of that co-ownership; some amount of business or investment activity is necessary before co-owners become partners.

The check-the-box regulations, which are promulgated under § 7701[2], provide more detail about when an undertaking will give rise to a partnership. The regulations first ask whether the taxpayers' activities have created an "entity" separate from the taxpayers.[3] If such activities create an "entity" for federal tax purposes, the entity is then classified as a corporation, partnership or trust pursuant to rules that we will examine in Section C of this chapter. Whether an undertaking by taxpayers creates an entity separate from the taxpayers for federal tax

---

1. The language quoted is that of § 761(a); § 7701(a)(2) uses almost the same words.
2. Reg. §§ 301.7701–1, –2, and –3. The regulations under § 761(a) refer to regulations under § 7701 for the definition of a partnership.
3. Reg. § 301.7701–1(a)

purposes does not depend on whether the taxpayers have actually formed an organization that is recognized under local law.[4] Rather, the regulations say that a joint venture or other contractual arrangement may "create a separate entity for federal tax purposes if the participants carry on a trade, business, financial operation, or venture and divide the profits therefrom."[5]

A. CO–OWNERSHIP OF PROPERTY

The check-the box regulations provide guidance about activities that will create a separate entity. One issue that frequently arises is the circumstances in which co-ownership of property will give rise to a separate entity. The regulations state:

> [M]ere co-ownership of property that is maintained, kept in repair, and rented or leased does not constitute a separate entity for federal tax purposes. For example, if an individual owner, or tenants in common, of farm property lease it to a farmer for a cash rental or a share of the crops, they do not necessarily create a separate entity for federal tax purposes.[6]

This makes sense—no purpose would be served by subjecting all cotenants or other co-owners to the intricacies of subchapter K. Co-owners whose roles consist largely of collecting rents or royalties and paying expenses can calculate their incomes well enough without having to worry about basis-adjustment elections, § 736 payments, and hypothetical distributions under § 751(b).

In contrast, if co-owners of property use that property in an active business, it becomes difficult or impossible to calculate each co-owner's separate taxable income without first determining the income for the business. At that point, the co-owners should be treated as having created a separate entity. Consider, as an illustration, the feasibility of co-owners' using different accounting methods. If the co-owners are passive investors, their use of different methods creates no serious tax problems. If they are carrying on an active business and dividing the profits therefrom, separate accounting would be impractical.

> **Example 16–1:** Cheryl and Doug own Blackacre, an undeveloped tract of land, as joint tenants. They lease Blackacre to Flora, who raises tulips on the land. Each month, Flora sends a check for $5,000 each to Cheryl and Doug. No serious tax difficulties arise if Cheryl uses an accrual method of accounting and Doug uses the cash method; Cheryl will simply report her

---

4. Reg. 301.7701–1(a)(2).
5. Id.
6. Id.

income for each month when Flora's liability accrues; Doug will report his income when he gets his rent check. No reason exists for calculating an overall "income from Blackacre" figure.

If Cheryl and Doug build a hotel on Blackacre, their continued use of different accounting methods for calculating their own incomes without first calculating total income from the venture would be awkward. Everyday business considerations require that an income figure for the business itself be calculated. The two owners of the business may perform different services, and the difference must be reflected in their compensation, which in turn may depend on how well the business does. And they must have some agreement, explicit or otherwise, for sharing losses. These considerations make entity-level calculations desirable, and perhaps even necessary. As a result, Cheryl and Doug will be deemed to have created a separate entity.

Cheryl and Doug in Example 16–1 cannot avoid this result by hiring an agent to manage the hotel. The regulations state that co-owners who lease space and provide services to tenants have created a separate entity, even if an agent performs the services.[7] Again, this makes sense because it is the act of dividing profits from a trade or business that creates the need to determine profits at an entity-level. That need exists regardless of whether Cheryl and Doug conduct the business themselves or through agents.

B. COST–SHARING AND EMPLOYMENT ARRANGEMENTS

Suppose that when you visit your dentist you find a receptionist who takes your name, asks you whether your appointment is with Dr. Payne or Dr. Suffrin, and guides you to the appropriate chair upon hearing your answer. Should you conclude that Payne and Suffrin have created a separate entity that may be taxable as a partnership (if they have not, as discussed in Section C, incorporated their practice or elected to be taxed as a corporation)? No: They may be sole proprietors, who share the rent and the receptionist's salary. Perhaps each dentist sees only that dentist's own patients, collects fees from those patients, and pays the costs of treating those patients. If so, each dentist can easily make an independent calculation of income and deductions, and there is no good reason for treating them as separate entities and requiring them to file tax returns as partners. Because of the complexity of partnership income taxation, partnership treatment should never be required if the persons in question can feasibly be treated as sole proprietors.

---

7. Id.

The regulations recognize that a cost-sharing arrangement that does not divide profits should not create a separate entity:

> [A] joint undertaking merely to share expenses does not create a separate entity for federal tax purposes. For example, if two or more persons jointly construct a ditch merely to drain surface water from their properties, they have not created a separate entity for federal tax purposes.[8]

Whether two (or more) persons sharing some business costs have created a separate entity depends upon whether they are carrying on one business or two. If the two dentists in the previous paragraph have really pooled their activities (if they treat the same patients, if they take steps that affect both of them (like launching an advertising campaign or regularly choosing equipment together), and if they send patients bills and calculate an income figure for "the practice," and divide that income between themselves) they have created a separate entity. Referring back to the standard articulated in the regulations, the dentists in that situation "carry on a trade, business, financial operation, or venture and divide the profits therefrom."

It is not necessary that the division of profits be in cash. In Madison Gas & Electric Co. v. Commissioner,[9] three utility companies jointly constructed a nuclear power plant, jointly operated it and shared the electricity generated by it. Each sold its share of the generated electricity to its customers. The court held that dividing the electricity produced by their joint operation was the same as dividing profits. Consequently, the court determined that the utilities had created an entity separate from themselves that was taxable as a partnership.

Persons dividing profits (either in kind or in cash) may not always be deemed to have created a separate entity if the alternative characterization is an employer-employee or independent-contractor relationship. If sole proprietor Anne employs Ben, compensating him in part by paying him a fraction of her profits, their relationship will be that of employer and employee. How does this case differ from one in which Anne and Ben form a partnership in which Anne, as the senior partner, can make decisions about matters on which they disagree? The check-the box regulations do not provide useful guidance. Cases decided prior to the issuance of the regulations suggest that the difference is one of intent.[10] If the parties speak and act consistently as if they intended to be in one kind of relationship rather than the other, they can usually expect to be taken at their word. Another important consideration is whether

---

8. Id.

9. 633 F.2d 512 (7th Cir. 1980)

10. See e.g. Commissioner v. Culbertson, 337 U.S. 733 (1949); In re Leroy A. Boyd, 208 B.R. 230, 97–1 USTC ¶ 50,324 (Bankr. W.D. Okla.1997).

they will share losses. If both Anne and Ben have put up money to get their business underway, and if both stand to lose that money if they fail, they have probably created a separate entity that may be taxed as a partnership.[11] The converse does not follow, however. A separate entity can exist even though all the participants do not bear the risk of losses (other than the loss of the time and effort one has put into the business). A common arrangement, the "expert/moneybags" partnership, involves one or more investors who put up cash and another person whose special skills are expected to turn that cash into profits.[12]

The borderline between employment relationships and partnerships will always be fuzzy. Employees compensated with a share of profits do not differ in any fundamental way from junior partners who have put no capital into the business. Whenever the law turns on the "capacity" in which someone works, the outcome depends upon the fact finder's reaction to the many features of a particular case.[13]

C. PARTNERSHIP vs. CORPORATION

State laws allow businesses a variety of organizational forms: it is not uncommon today for a new business to be able to choose from a menu of nine or more categories. For most of our tax history, most state-law partnerships were taxed as partnerships and state-law corporations were taxed as corporations. Questions about the status of other entities, such as LLCs, were approached by asking whether the entity more closely "resembled" a partnership or a corporation. Former regulations distinguished partnerships from "associations" (taxed as corporations) by asking how many of four key "corporate characteristics" (continuity of life, centralization of management, limited liability, and free transferability of interests) the organization had.[14] If it had three or more, it was an association; otherwise, it was a partnership.[15]

The former regulations classified organizations according to attributes those organizations possessed in theory, rather than according to any practical differences between incorporated and unincorporated busi-

---

11. See e.g. Richards v. Commissioner, 13 T.C.M. 1191 (1954).

12. E.g., United States v. Frazell, 335 F.2d 487 (5th Cir. 1964) (geologist and investors).

13. See e.g. Luna v. Commissioner, 42 T.C. 1067 (1964). Compare the issue of whether payments for services are made to someone acting in a partner "capacity" under § 707; Chapter 7, above.

14. Former Treas. Reg. § 301.7701–2(a)(1). Two other corporate characteristics, "associates" and "an objective to carry on business and divide the gains," were common to corporations and partnerships and so were not used to distinguish partnerships from associations; Former Treas. Reg. § 301.7701–2(a)(2).

15. Former Treas. Reg. § 301.7701–2(a)(3) required an unincorporated organization to have more corporate than non-corporate characteristics to be classified as an association.

nesses.[16] In practice, small partnerships and closely held corporations are almost indistinguishable with respect to the four key "corporate characteristics."[17] Because classification of entities turned upon attributes having almost no practical meaning for the parties, taxpayers had considerable freedom to select whatever form of organization promised favorable tax treatment. Doctors and other professionals incorporated their practices under state "professional corporation" statutes, allowing them to become employees of their corporations.[18] Tax-shelter limited partnerships, though providing limited liability for their investors, achieved partnership status in nearly all cases, allowing losses to be passed through to the investors. In 1997, the Treasury threw in the towel and adopted the "check-the-box" regulations allowing most entities to elect whether to be taxed as corporations or partnerships.

As discussed above, the first inquiry of the check-the-box regulations is whether an "entity" has been created. Any entity that has more than one owner and that is not a trust[19] or otherwise treated specially by the Code is then classified as a corporation or a partnership.[20]

Some business entities (commonly called "*per se* corporations") must be taxed as corporations. Examples include entities organized under state or Federal laws that refer to them as "corporations" or "incorporated," insurance companies, state-chartered banks that have

[16]. See generally Boris I. Bittker, Professional Service Organizations: A Critique of the Literature, 23 Tax L.Rev. 429, 434–438 (1968).

[17]. Consider, for example, "continuity of life." Under the original version of the Uniform Partnership Act, a partnership is dissolved when one of its members dies, while the death of a shareholder does not affect a corporation's legal existence. This is why continuity of life was thought to be relevant in distinguishing partnerships from corporations. But partnership agreements often provide that when a partner dies or retires the remaining partners may form a new partnership to carry on the business of the old one. When this is done, only the theoretical legal existence of the partnership terminates when a partner dies or withdraws; the partnership business continues. Similarly, the "limited liability" thought to distinguish corporations from partnerships is more theoretical than real; limited partners have limited liability and corporate shareholders may not, because they are liable for whatever torts they commit as corporate employees and because lenders often require them to guarantee their corporations' debts. As for "transferability," almost all closely held corporations restrict their shareholders' ability to transfer their interests freely, in order to limit ownership of stock to those active in the business or to members of a particular family. And management of small businesses may in practice be no more "centralized" for closely held corporations than for partnerships. In theory, all general partners "manage" the business, while ownership of stock entitles the owner to no role in managing a corporation. In practice, those who put up the capital for a small business direct its operations or delegate that power to others, whatever the business's form.

[18]. This enabled them to establish qualified pension and profit-sharing plans, which provided much-more-generous tax benefits than the plans then available to sole proprietors and partners at that time.

[19]. Trusts are defined in Treas. Reg. § 301.7701–4.

[20]. A one-owner entity that is not a corporation, such as a one-member LLC that has not elected to be taxed as a corporation, is disregarded: in the jargon, it is a "tax nothing." Treas. Reg. § 301.7701–2(a).

deposits insured under the Federal Deposit Insurance Act, and any of a long list of specified foreign entities.[21] Business entities that are not *per se* corporations may choose whether to be taxed as corporations or (if they have more than one owner) as partnerships.[22] As a rule, domestic business entities that fail to make an election will be taxed as partnerships (or ignored, if they have only one owner)[23]; most foreign entities that fail to elect are taxed as corporations if all of their members have limited liability.[24]

Example 16–2: Eddie and Fiona form an LLC to carry on a business (not banking or insurance). The LLC may elect to be taxed as a corporation. If it makes no election, it will be taxed as a partnership.

The check-the-box regulations differ so much (at least in form) from prior law that their validity was subject to some doubt.[25] The Court of Appeals for the Second Circuit has determined, however, that they represent a reasonable exercise of the Treasury's regulatory power.[26] There seems to be universal agreement in the profession that the new regulations are a substantive improvement over the old approach; legislation expressly authorizing the new approach would therefore be desirable.

D. ELECTION OUT OF SUBCHAPTER K

Regulations authorized by § 761(a) allow some partnerships to elect out of subchapter K if the partners' incomes can be "adequately determined without the computation of partnership taxable income."[27] All partners must consent to the election and the partnership must be engaged in one of the following activities:

(1) Investment;[28]

(2) The "production, extraction, or use of property" (but not the sale of the property produced or extracted);[29] or

(3) Short-term underwriting, sale, or distribution of securities by securities dealers.[30]

---

21. Treas. Reg. §§ 301.7701–2(b); 301.7701–3(a).
22. Treas. Reg. § 301.7701–3.
23. Treas. Reg. § 301.7701–3(b)(1).
24. Treas. Reg. § 301.7701–3(b)(2).
25. For discussion, see Hugh M. Dougan, Lori S. Hoberman & John W. Harper, Check the Box: Looking under the Lid, 75 Tax Notes 1141 (1997).
26. McNamee v. Department of Treas., 488 F.3d 100 (2d Cir. 2007); Medical Practice Solutions, LLC v. Commissioner, 132 T.C. 125 (2009).
27. § 761(a).
28. § 761(a)(1).
29. § 761(a)(2).

If a qualifying partnership fails to make the election, the regulations allow the partnership to be "deemed" to have elected out of subchapter K, "if it can be shown from all the surrounding facts and circumstances" that the partners intended "to secure exclusion" from subchapter K.[31] In practice, persons who intend to elect out of subchapter K will do so unless their tax advisers foul up badly. The real use of the "deemed" election is to shield taxpayers who never realized that they were partners, and who reported their incomes consistently with non-partnership status, from the unhappy consequences of being partners without knowing it. If taxpayers who are partners for tax purposes without knowing it were held strictly to the standards of subchapter K, they would, among other things, lose the benefits of most elections they had made, as most elections involving partnership income must be made by the partnership; § 703(b).

Small partnerships can be excused from some of subchapter K's formalities even though they fail to meet the requirements for electing out of partnership treatment. Revenue Procedure 84–35[32] provides that some partnerships having ten or fewer partners will not be penalized for failing to file partnership returns if all the partners accurately report their shares of partnership income, deductions, and credits. The partnerships in question must have no partners who are non-resident aliens, trusts, or corporations, and all partnership items must be allocated in the same way. Many small family-owned businesses should meet these requirements. As a matter of sound tax planning, however, even these small partnerships should file partnership returns. For one thing, Revenue Procedure 84–35 does not expressly dispense with the requirement that most elections be made by the partnership, rather than by the partners. Furthermore, serious errors in reporting a partner's income will disqualify the partnership from the exemption, and will therefore lead to the imposition of a penalty for failure to file a partnership return in addition to whatever penalties apply to the specific omission.

E. PUBLICLY TRADED PARTNERSHIPS

The Tax Reform Act of 1986 made C corporations unattractive for many businesses. The Act extended the "double taxation" of corporate income by preventing corporations from distributing appreciated property without a corporate-level tax, and it made the tax rates of many

---

30. § 761(a)(3).

31. Treas. Reg. § 1.761–2(b)(2)(ii).

32. 1984–1 C.B. 509.

corporations higher than the rates for high-income individuals.[33] C corporations had never been a good choice for ventures expected to report losses, and the 1986 changes made them unappealing for some profitable enterprises as well.

By increasing the tax burden on C corporations, the 1986 legislation encouraged the establishment of large limited partnerships. So-called "master limited partnerships" had already been used as a vehicle for widespread ownership of businesses that would generate tax losses, particularly in the oil and gas industry. (The curious term "master limited partnership" came into use because the earliest widely held partnerships in the oil and gas industry were formed by combining many small partnerships.) The 1986 provisions encouraged businesses that would report income to disincorporate as well.

Concern for the revenue loss that would occur if large businesses adopted the partnership form led Congress to enact § 7704 in 1987. That section provides that most publicly traded partnerships are to be taxed as corporations. Section 7704(c) creates an exception for publicly traded partnerships carrying on investment, rather than business, activities. If 90 percent or more of the income of a publicly traded partnership consists of interest, dividends, rents from real property, and specified other kinds of income, the entity will be taxed as a partnership. (Publicly traded partnerships that are not taxed as corporations are subject to a stringent version of the passive-loss rules; see § 469(k).) Section 7704 also exempts partnerships in the mineral and timber industries from its coverage;[34] these industries have long been effective lobbyists.

Partnerships are "publicly traded" if interests in those partnerships are either (1) "traded on an established securities market" or (2) "readily tradable on a secondary market (or the substantial equivalent thereof)."[35] "Established securities markets" include not only the New York Stock Exchange and other national exchanges but also over-the-counter markets. If price quotations for interests in a particular partnership are regularly available from securities brokers or dealers, or if the interests can otherwise be easily bought and sold, the partnership is publicly traded under the "readily tradable" provision.[36] The possibility

---

33. Under current law, the highest rates for individuals are once again higher than the top corporate rates.

34. Section 7704(d)(1)(E) defines income from these activities as "qualifying income." A partnership is excluded from § 7704 if 90 percent or more of its income is "qualifying income."

35. § 7704(b).

36. Treas. Reg. § 1.7704–1(c)(2). Some involvement by the partnership in trading is, however, required for the interests to be considered publicly traded; Treas. Reg. § 1.7704–1(d). Examples of the kind of involvement needed include recognizing transfers by admitting the transferee as a partner (or at least recognizing the transferee's rights to distributions) and participating in the inclusion of the interests in the market in question.

that a partnership interest can be sold with the help of a securities broker does not by itself make that interest "readily tradable"; the sales have to be reasonably easy to make.

F. ELECTING LARGE PARTNERSHIPS

The Taxpayer Relief Act of 1997 enacted sections 771 through 777 to simplify the tax treatment of large (but not publicly traded) investment partnerships. These provisions, which are elective, attempt to simplify compliance for investors in these "electing large partnerships."[37]

An electing large partnership ("ELP") is a partnership which has 100 or more partners and which has elected ELP treatment. In counting the number of partners, service partners are not included.[38]

The income, deductions, and credits of an ELP can be reported to partners more simply than is the case with other partnerships. Only the kinds of income, deductions and credits listed in § 772(a) need to be separately stated. To illustrate, an ELP calculates its own net capital gain or loss (separately for passive activities and other activities) and reports the net amount to its partners. Similarly, partners are told their shares of the partnership's alternative minimum tax adjustment, rather than having to know their shares of each item that could affect a partner's AMT. (As with capital gains and losses, separate statement of AMT adjustments for passive activities and other activities is required.) The charitable contribution deduction is calculated at the partnership level.[39] Similarly, most limits on credits and deductions are calculated at the partnership rather than the partner level.[40] Recaptured tax credits are also taxed at the partnership level, rather than to the partners.[41]

The idea here is to keep small investors from having to wrestle with a long list of special kinds of income and deduction items in preparing their returns.

In order to allow large investment partnerships to have interests that are freely tradable, § 708(b)(1)(B), which terminates a partnership's

---

[37]. § 775. Elsewhere, however, the Code refers to them as "electing partnerships"; e.g., §§ 771, 772.

[38]. § 775(b)(1). Furthermore, if substantially all the members of a partnership are service partners, retired service partners, and spouses of service partners or retired service partners the partnership cannot be an ELP. In addition, partnerships engaged in trading commodities or commodities options, futures or forward contracts cannot be ELPs; § 775(c).

[39]. § 773(a)(1).

[40]. § 773(a)(3).

[41]. § 774(b).

existence if fifty percent or more of the interests in the partnership are sold during a twelve-month period, does not apply to ELPs.[42]

---

42. § 774(c).

TABLE OF CASES

References are to Pages.

Armstrong v. Phinney, 394 F.2d 661 (5th Cir.1968), 10

Boyd, In re, 208 B.R. 230 (Bkrtcy.W.D.Okla. 1997), 209

Campbell v. Commissioner, 59 T.C.M. 236 (U.S.Tax Ct.1990), 35
Crenshaw v. United States, 450 F.2d 472 (5th Cir.1971), 186
Culbertson, Commissioner v., 337 U.S. 733, 69 S.Ct. 1210, 93 L.Ed. 1659 (1949), 88, 89, 209

Diamond v. Commissioner, 56 T.C. 530 (U.S.Tax Ct.1971), 32

Foxman v. Commissioner, 41 T.C. 535 (Tax Ct.1964), 144, 184
Frazell, United States v., 335 F.2d 487 (5th Cir.1964), 210

Hale v. Commissioner, 24 T.C.M. 1497 (Tax Ct.1965), 32
Harris v. Commissioner, 61 T.C. 770 (U.S.Tax Ct.1974), 187

In re (see name of party)

Kenroy, Inc. v. Commissioner, 47 T.C.M. 1749 (U.S.Tax Ct.1984), 35

Lucas v. Earl, 281 U.S. 111, 50 S.Ct. 241, 74 L.Ed. 731 (1929), 87

Luna v. Commissioner, 42 T.C. 1067 (Tax Ct.1964), 210

Madison Gas and Elec. Co. v. Commissioner, 633 F.2d 512 (7th Cir.1980), 209
McDougal v. Commissioner, 62 T.C. 720 (U.S.Tax Ct.1974), 31
McNamee v. Department of the Treasury, 488 F.3d 100 (2nd Cir.2007), 212
Medical Practice Solutions, LLC v. Commissioner, 132 T.C. 125 (U.S.Tax Ct.2009), 212

Orrisch v. Commissioner, 55 T.C. 395 (U.S.Tax Ct.1970), 49

Philadelphia Park Amusement Co. v. United States, 126 F.Supp. 184 (Ct.Cl.1954), 29
Pratt v. Commissioner, 550 F.2d 1023 (5th Cir.1977), 116
Pratt v. Commissioner, 64 T.C. 203 (U.S.Tax Ct.1975), 121

Quick's Trust v. Commissioner, 54 T.C. 1336 (U.S.Tax Ct.1970), 202

Richards v. Commissioner, 13 T.C.M. 1191 (Tax Ct.1954), 210

St. John v. United States, 1983 WL 1715, 53 A.F.T.R.2d 84-718, 84-1 USTC ¶ 9158 (C.D.Ill.1983), 35

United States v. ___ (see opposing party)

Woodhall v. Commissioner, 454 F.2d 226 (9th Cir.1972), 202

TABLE OF INTERNAL REVENUE CODE SECTIONS

Section	Pages
1(h)	128–129, 142
1(h)(5)(B)	128–129, 141
1(h)(9)	128, 141
1(h)(11)	3
62(a)(1)	10
67	8, 10
67(a)	11
79	11
83	29, 33, 35, 37
119	10
132(a)(5)	11
151(d)	11
162(a)	113
162(c)	29
162(L)	11
163(e)(5)	13
168	76, 79, 137
197	135
212	7, 8
213(a)	11
267(a)(2)	114, 116
267(b)	114
267(e)	114
301—385	2
351	42, 86, 134, 137
351(a)	24, 42
356	42
357	112
357(b)	42
357(c)	42, 43
358	112
358(d)	42–43, 111–112
411	37
443	203
443(a)(2)	199
444	9
465	19–21
465(a)(6)	22
469	19–20, 22
469(a)(1)	22
469(a)(2)(B)	23
469(c)(7)	23
469(d)(1)	22
469(h)(2)	22
469(i)	23
469(j)(1)	23
469(k)	22, 214
691	199
691(e)	202
701	6, 12, 79, 82, 87, 9
702	6, 8
702(a)	6
702(a)(1)	8
702(a)(1)—(a)(6)	6
702(a)(2)	8
702(a)(4)	8
702(a)(7)	6, 8
702(a)(8)	6, 116
702(b)	6, 28
703(a)	7, 8
703(a)(1)	8
703(a)(2)(E)	8
703(b)	2, 213
703(b)(3)	69
704	44–45, 48, 53, 57,
704(a)	172
704(b)	44
704(b)	45–46, 53, 56, 71–72
704(c)	41, 44, 64, 68, 72, 145
704(c)(1)(A)	71–72, 75–76, 82–84
704(c)(1)(B)	41, 84–85, 152, 155
704(c)(1)(B)(iii)	84, 155
704(c)(1)(C)	84, 86, 131
704(d)	19, 21, 21, 96
704(e)	87–88
704(e)(1)	89
704(e)(2)	88, 90
704(e)(3)	89–90
705	17, 110
705(a)(1)(A)	16
705(a)(1)(B)	17
705(a)(2)	17, 104
705(a)(2)(B)	17, 48
706	9
706(a)	9, 113–114, 204
706(b)	9
706(b)(1)(C)	9
706(c)	204
706(c)(1)	140, 203
706(c)(2)(A)	140
706(d)	90–91
706(d)(1)	140
706(d)(2)	91, 95, 140
707	39–41, 85, 196, 210
707(a)	113–121, 171, 187
707(a)(1)	35
707(a)(2)	38–39
707(a)(2)(A)	116
707(a)(2)(B)	41
707(b)(1)	122
707(b)(2)	122
707(c)	12, 113–114, 117–118
708(a)	10

219

TABLE OF INTERNAL REVENUE CODE SECTIONS

708(b)	10, 140
708(b)(1)	141
708(b)(1)(A)	10, 203
708(b)(1)(B)	140, 143, 186, 215
708(b)(2)	10
721	16, 24, 27, 30–32, 4
721(a)	24
721(b)	24–25
722	16–18, 24–26, 71, 10
723	16, 24–26, 71, 123
724	28
724(a)	28
724(b)	28
724(c)	28
731	24, 26–27, 41, 85, 1
731(a)	18, 145, 151
731(a)(1)	17, 27, 104, 166, 18
731(a)(2)	153–154, 159, 165–16
731(b)	145
731(c)	151–152
732	140, 149, 151, 154,
732(a)	145
732(a)(1)	146, 162
732(a)(2)	146, 159, 189–190
732(b)	147, 150, 165–166, 1
732(c)	140, 147, 149
732(c)(1)	162, 165
732(c)(1)(A)	147, 148
732(c)(1)(A)(i)	150
732(c)(1)(B)	148, 150–151
732(c)(2)(A)	150
732(c)(2)(B)	150
732(c)(3)	148
732(c)(3)(A)	148
732(c)(3)(B)	148, 152
732(d)	139–140
733	17–18, 24–25, 145–14
733 (1)	146
733 (2)	146
734	147, 186, 188–189, 1
734(b)	177, 188–196
734(b)(1)(A)	189–190
734(b)(1)(B)	189–190
734(b)(2)(A)	189–191
734(b)(2)(B)	189
734(d)	194
735	153
735(a)(2)	165
735(c)(2)	153
736	144, 160, 171–175, 1
736(a)	160, 172–181, 185–18
736(a)(2)	176
736(b)	172–183, 191, 200–20
736(b)(1)	174, 179
736(b)(2)	174–175, 179–181, 18
736(b)(2)(A)	179
736(b)(2)(B)	175
736(b)(3)	174, 179, 201
737	41, 85, 145, 152, 15
737(a)	85
737(c)	156
741	124–126, 153, 183, 1
743	138, 188
743(a)	25
743(b)	130–131, 133–135, 13
743(b)(1)	130
743(d)	130, 139
751	124–125, 127–129, 14
751(a)	124–126, 128–130, 14
751(b)	128, 144, 157–172, 1
751(b)(1)(A)	160
751(b)(1)(A)(ii)	159
751(b)(1)(B)	160–161, 164
751(b)(2)(A)	160
751(b)(2)(B)	160
751(b)(3)(A)	159
751(b)(3)(B)	159
751(c)	28, 126–127, 134, 14
751(c)(2)	149, 174–175
751(d)	28, 126, 153, 159
751(d)(2)	127–128
752	18, 21, 40–42, 96–10
752(a)	18, 19, 96, 108
752(b)	18–19, 26–27, 43, 10
752(d)	123, 130, 141
753	200–203
754	25, 130, 135, 138–14
755	131, 133, 138, 194
761(a)	206, 212
761(a)(1)	212
761(a)(2)	212
761(a)(3)	213
771—777	215
771	215
772	215
772(a)	215
773(a)(1)	215
773(a)(3)	215
774(b)	215
774(c)	216
775	215
775(b)(1)	215
775(c)	215
901	69
957	13
1012	29, 129
1014	133, 142, 198, 203
1014(a)	198, 201–202
1014(c)	199–203
1016	75
1022	198
1022(b)	198
1022(c)	198
1032	30
1033	1
1033(a)(2)(A)	2
1221	2
1221(a)(1)	127
1221(a)(4)	127
1223 (1)	16, 25
1223 (2)	16, 25–26
1231	7, 16, 28, 126–128
1231(b)	25–26
1239	122

TABLE OF INTERNAL REVENUE CODE SECTIONS

1245	27, 127, 149
1245(a)	127
1245(a)(1)	27
1245(a)(2)	27
1245(b)(3)	27, 156
1245(b)(6)	156
1245(d)	27
1250	128–129, 142
1250(d)(3)	156
1250(d)(6)	156
1361—1379	4
1366	6, 70
1366(a)	6, 14
1366(e)	95
1367(b)(4)	205
1367(b)(4)(A)	205
1367(b)(4)(B)	205
1372	14, 122
1377(a)	70
1377(a)(1)	95
1377(a)(2)	95
1402	12
1402(a)	12
6050K	128
7519	9
7701	206
7701(a)(2)	206
7701(a)(14)	6
7701(a)(30)	13
7704	214
7704(b)	214
7704(c)	214
7704(d)(1)(E)	214
7806(a)	202

TABLE OF TREASURY REGULATIONS AND RULINGS

RULINGS

69–180	119
81–300	121
84–102	169–170
88–77	96

REGULATIONS

1.1(h)—1(b)(1)	128
1.1(h)—1(f)	128
1.1–1(h)—1(f)	129
1.83–3(L) (proposed)	37
1.132–9 (b)	11
1.451–1(b)(1)	199, 203
1.469–5T(e)	22
1.691(a)–1(b)	199
1.701–2(a)(3)	13, 92
1.701–2(b)	12, 91
1.701–2(c)	92
1.701–2(c)(1)	13, 82, 93
1.701–2(c)(2)	93
1.701–2(c)(3)	93
1.701–2(c)(5)	93
1.701–2(d)	79, 93, 154, 196
1.701–2(e)	12, 203
1.701–2 (f)	13
1.702–1(a)(8)(ii)	6
1.704–(b)(2)(iv)(c)	48
1.704–1(b)(1)(i)	54
1.704–1(b)(1)(iii)	91
1.704–1(b)(2) (former)	44–45
1.704–1(b)(2)(ii)(d)	54, 56
1.704–1(b)(2)(ii)(d)(3)	68–69
1.704–1(b)(2)(ii)(d)(4)	56
1.704–1(b)(2)(ii)(d)(5)	56
1.704–1(b)(2)(ii)(d)(6)	56
1.704–1(b)(2)(iii)(a)	58
1.704–1(b)(2)(iii)(b)	59
1.704–1(b)(2)(iii)(c)	59, 62
1.704–1(b)(2)(iii)(c)(2)	61
1.704–1(b)(2)(iv)(d)	46
1.704–1(b)(2)(iv)(F)(5)	48
1.704–1(b)(2)(iv)(g)	46
1.704–1(b)(2)(iv)(g)(3)	75
1.704–1(b)(3)	63
1.704–1(b)(3)(iii)	55
1.704–1(b)(4)(ii)	69
1.704–1(b)(4)(viii)(a) (temporary)	70
1.704–1(b)(5)	55, 61–62, 83, 92, 9

REGULATIONS

1.704–1(c)(2)(i) (former)	72
1.704–1(d)(1)	20
1.704–2(b)(1)	63
1.704–2(b)(4)	67
1.704–2(d)(1)	64
1.704–2(d)(3)	64
1.704–2(e)(1)	67
1.704–2(e)(2)	67
1.704–2(e)(3)	65
1.704–2(e)(4)	67
1.704–2(f)	65–66
1.704–2(f)(1)	65
1.704–2(f)(3)	66
1.704–2(f)(6)	65
1.704–2(g)(1)	68–69
1.704–2(g)(1)(i)	65, 105
1.704–2(i)	64
1.704–2(i)(1)	67
1.704–2(j)(2)(i)	66
1.704–3(a)(1)	74, 82
1.704–3(a)(3)	75
1.704–3(a)(10)	81–82
1.704–3(b)(1)	72
1.704–3(b)(2)	76–78
1.704–3(c)	73
1.704–3(c)(4)	78
1.704–3(d)	73, 79
1.704–3(d)(2)	80
1.704–3(d)(3)	74
1.704–3(d)(7)	74, 80
1.704–3(e)(1)	74
1.704–3(e)(2)	74
1.704–4(e)(1)	155
1.704–4(e)(2)	155
1.706–1(c)(2)	91
1.707–1(a)	118
1.707–1(c)	10, 119
1.707–3(b)(1)	39
1.707–3(b)(2)	39
1.707–3(c)(1)	39
1.707–3(d)	39
1.707–4(a)	40
1.707–4 (a)(4)	40
1.707–4(d)	40
1.707–5(a)(2)(ii)	41
1.707–5(a)(7)	41
1.707–5 (f)	41
1.708–1(b)(1)(i)(a)	183–184
1.708–1(b)(1)(iv)	141

REGULATIONS

Regulation	Page
1.708–1(b)(1)(iv) (former)	141
1.721–1(a)	38
1.721–1(b)(1)	29, 32
1.721–1(b)(2) (proposed)	31
1.732–1(a)	146
1.732–1(d)(4)	140
1.736–1(a)(4)	172, 177
1.736–1(a)(6)	183–184
1.736–1(b)(2)	183
1.736–1(b)(3)	183
1.742–1	203
1.743–1(d)	131
1.743–1(d)(1)	133
1.743–1(g)(2)	137
1.743–1(h)(2)	137
1.743–1(j)(2)	137
1.743–1(j)(4)(i)(B)(1)	137
1.743–1(j)(4)(i)(B)(2)	137
1.743–1(j)(4)(ii)(A)	138
1.751–1(a)(2)	125
1.751–1(b)(2)(ii)	168
1.751–1(b)(3)(ii)	168
1.751–1(b)(3)(iii)	162
1.751–1(c)(4)(iii)	127
1.751–1(g)	162, 166, 168
1.752–1(a)(1)	98–99
1.752–1(a)(4)	96
1.752–1(a)(4)(i)	96
1.752–1(f)	19
1.752–2(a)	100
1.752–2(b)(1)(i)—(v)	99
1.752–2(b)(3)	100
1.752–2(b)(6)	100
1.752–2(e)(4)	109
1.752–2(f)	103, 109
1.752–3(a)	104
1.752–3(a)(3)	106
1.752–3(b)	68
1.752–6	96
1.752–7	96, 112
1.754–1(b)	138

REGULATIONS

Regulation	Page
1.754–1(c)	138
1.754–1(c)(2)	138
1.755–1(a)(1)	134
1.755–1(a)(2)	135
1.755–1(a)(2) (former)	133
1.755–1(a)(5)	135
1.755–1(b)(1)	134
1.755–1(b)(2)	134
1.755–1(b)(2)(B)	136
1.755–1(b)(3)(i)	136
1.755–1(b)(3)(i)(A)	135
1.755–1(b)(3)(ii)	136
1.755–1(b)(3)(ii)(A)	135
1.755–1(b)(5)	134
1.755–1(c)(1)(i)	190
1.755–1(c)(1)(ii)	190
1.755–1(c)(2)(i)	192
1.755–1(c)(2)(ii)	191–193
1.755–1(c)(3)	193
1.755–1(c)(4)	193
1.761–2(b)(2)(ii)	213
1.1032–1(a)	30
1.1223–3(a)	26
1.1245–4(c)(1)	27
1.1245–4(c)(4)	27
1.1402(a)–1(a)(2)	12
1.1402(a)–(2) (proposed)	12
1.7704–1(c)(2)	214
1.7704–1(d)	214
301.7701–2(a)	211
301.7701–2(a)(1) (former)	210
301.7701–2(a)(2) (former)	210
301.7701–2(a)(3) (former)	210
301.7701–2(b)	212
301.7701–3	212
301.7701–3(a)	212
301.7701–3(b)(1)	212
301.7701–3(b)(2)	212
301.7701–4	211

INDEX

References are to Pages

ACCOUNTING METHODS
Book depreciation and tax depreciation distinguished, 74
Capital Accounts, this index
Drawing accounts, 47
Income accounts, 47
Income in respect of a deceased partner, accrual vs cash accounting, 198
Timing of partnership income, 9
Timing of service partner payments, 113

AGGREGATE APPROACH TO TAXATION
See also Check-the-Box Regulations, this index; What is a Partnership, this index
Anti-abuse rules, 12, 203
Entity approach distinguished, 1

ALLOCATIONS OF TAX ITEMS
Generally, 44 et seq.
See also Assignments of Income, this index
Anti-abuse regulations, 82, 91
Avoidance motives for special allocations, 44
Basis of partnership assets, adjustment allocations, 192
Buyer basis in partnership interests, allocating Section 743(b) adjustments, 133
Capital Accounts, this index
Ceiling rule, contributed property, 72
Character, allocations affecting, 87
Character allocations, 58
Contributed property
    Generally, 44, 71 et seq.
    Ceiling rule, 72
    Depreciation allocations, 74
    Distribution allocations, 83
    Distributions to contributing partners, 85
    Encumbered property, 103
    Gain allocations, 71
    Loss allocations, 72

ALLOCATIONS OF TAX ITEMS—Cont'd
Contributed property—Cont'd
    S corporation taxation compared, 86
    Contributing partners, distributions to, 85
Credits, this index
Curative allocations
    Generally, 73
    Depreciation, 77
    Remedial allocations distinguished, 79
Deductions, this index
Depreciation deductions
    Generally, 60
    Contributed property, 74
    Substantial economic effect test, 49
Distributions
    Contributed property, 83
    Contributing partners, distributions to, 85
    Partnership assets, basis adjustment allocations, 192
Family partnership income allocations, 87
Gain allocations, contributed property, 71
Guaranteed nonrecourse debt, 108
Guaranteed recourse debt, 102
Income
    Assignments of Income, this index
    Income, this index
Indemnified recourse debt, 102
Last-minute partners, assignments of income to, 90
Loss allocations, contributed property, 72
Motives for special allocations, 44
Nonrecourse deductions, 68
Nonrecourse financing, 60, 63
Nonrecourse liabilities, 104 et seq.
Notional allocations, 73
Obligations that are not liabilities, 109
Partnership assets, basis adjustment allocations, 192
Partnership debt
    Generally, 96 et seq.
    Contributions of property encumbered by recourse debt, 103

INDEX
References are to Pages

ALLOCATIONS OF TAX ITEMS—Cont'd
Partnership debt—Cont'd
  Guarantees of nonrecourse debt, 108
  Guarantees of recourse debt, 102
  Indemnification of recourse debt, 102
  Nonrecourse liability allocations, 104 et seq.
  Obligations that are not liabilities, 109
  Recourse liability allocations, 100
  Risk of loss and constructive liquidation, 98
  S corporation liabilities allocations compared, 112
  Tiers of nonrecourse debt allocations, 104
Partnership interests, allocating Section 743(b) adjustments, 133
Recourse liability allocations, 100
Remedial allocations
  Generally, 73
  Curative allocations distinguished, 79
  Depreciation, 79
Retroactive allocations, service partnerships, 59
Reverse allocations, 82
S corporation taxation compared
  Generally, 70
  Contributed property allocations, 86
  Liabilities allocations, 112
Service partnerships, retroactive allocations, 59
Shifting tax consequences, allocations having effect of, 59
Substantial economic effect test
  Generally, 45 et seq.
  Creation, 44
  Credits allocations, 69
  Depreciation deductions, 49
  Family partnership income allocations, 87
  Regulations, 53
Substantiality rules, 56, 58
Tiers of nonrecourse debt allocations, 104
Transitory allocations rule, 59

ANTI-ABUSE RULES
Allocations of tax items, 82, 91
Assignments of income, 91
Basis adjustments of partnership asset, 195
Discretionary applications, 14
Economic effect, 45, 58
Entity and aggregate approaches to taxation, 12, 203
Family partnerships, 91
Intent of Subchapter K, 13
Partnership asset basis adjustments, 195
Pass-through principle, 12
S corporation taxation, 15
Subchapter K intent, 13

ASSIGNMENTS OF INCOME
Generally, 87 et seq.

ASSIGNMENTS OF INCOME—Cont'd
Anti-abuse regulations, 91
Culbertson test, 88
Last-minute partners, 90
Overcompensated partners in family partnerships, 89
S corporation taxation compared, 95

AT-RISK RULES
See also Shelters, this index
Allocations of recourse liability, 100
Qualified nonrecourse financing exemption, 21
Section 465, 20

BASIS
Generally, 16 et seq.
Adjustments of partnership assets without a Section 754 election, 194
Allocation of contributed property gain, 71
Anti-abuse regulations, partnership asset basis adjustments, 195
At-risk rules of Section 465, 20
Buyer basis in partnership interests
  Generally, 129 et seq.
  Allocating Section 743(b) adjustments, 133
  Inside basis, 129
  Section 754 elections, 138
  Section 732(d) adjustments, 139
  Transferee's share of inside basis, 131
Contributed property, gain allocations, 71
Contributions to partnership, 16
Death of a partner, basis adjustments, 204
Debt transactions affecting, 18
Distributions affecting basis of partnership assets, 188
Distributions that change basis of distributed property, 189
Distributions triggering inside basis adjustments, 144
Gain or loss recognition distributions, 190
Goodwill, 182
Inherited partnership interests, 199
Inside and outside basis distinguished, 16
Inside basis adjustments after distributions, 144
Inside basis of buyer of partnership interests, 129
Loss deduction limitations, 19
Outside basis limitations on loss deductions, 19
Partnership assets
  Generally, 188
  Adjustments required without a Section 754 election, 194
  Allocating the adjustment to particular assets, 192
  Anti-abuse regulations, 195
  Death of a partner, basis adjustments, 204
  Distributions affecting, 188

INDEX
References are to Pages

BASIS—Cont'd
Partnership assets—Cont'd
  Distributions that change basis of distributed property, 189
  Gain or loss recognition distributions, 190
  Inside and outside basis distinguished, 16
  S corporation basis adjustments compared, 196
  Section 734 adjustment rules, below
  Section 754 elections, below
  Substantial basis reductions, 194
Partnership debt inclusion limitations, 20
S Corporation rules compared, 23
Sales of partnership interests, taxation of seller, 123
Section 734 adjustment rules
  Generally, 189
  Anti-abuse regulations, 195
  Sections 734(b) and 743(b) distinguished, 188
Section 754 elections
  Adjustments required without, 194
  Buyer basis in partnership interests, 138
  Section 732(d) adjustments to buyer basis in partnership interests, 139
Service partners, 29
Substantial basis reductions in partnership assets, 194
Unrealized receivables, 182

BOOT
Contributions to partnerships
  Generally, 24
  S corporation contributions compared, 42
Distributions distinguished, 24

C CORPORATIONS
S corporations distinguished, 2

CAPITAL ACCOUNTS
Generally, 46
Charge backs, 50
Deficits
  Generally, 47
  Nonrecourse deductions, 68
  Restoration obligations, 54
Definition, 48
Negative balances, 47, 54, 68
Nonrecourse deductions, capital account deficits, 68
Restoration of deficits, 54
Simple test, 49
Substantial economic effect test, 53

CAPITAL GAINS AND LOSSES
See also Gain, this index; Loss, this index
Holding periods, asset contributions to partnerships, 25

CAPITAL GAINS AND LOSSES—Cont'd
Liquidating distributions
  Non-Section 751 assets, 161
  Section 751 assets, 164
Sales of partnership interests, taxation of seller, 124

CAPITAL INVESTMENT PARTNERSHIPS
Services partnerships distinguished, 88

CAPITAL PARTNERS
Guaranteed payments for use of capital, 113
Passive Activity Rules

CHARACTER OF TAX ITEMS
See also Shelters, this index
Allocations affecting character, 87
Allocations of character, 58
Contributions to partnerships, character issues, 28
Credits, character determinations, 6
Distributions, Section 751(b) limitations, 158

CHECK-THE-BOX REGULATIONS
Generally, 206
Adoption, 211
LLC elections, 7, 206
Validity, 212

CONSTRUCTION
Section 736, retiring partner payments, 172

CONTINUITY OF LIFE TEST
Generally, 211

CONTRIBUTIONS TO PARTNERSHIPS
  Generally, 24 et seq.
  See also Transactions With Partners, this index
Allocations
  Generally, 44, 71 et seq.
  See also Allocations of Tax Items, this index
Basis, 16
Boot adjustments
  Generally, 24
  S corporation contributions compared, 42
Capital asset contributions, holding periods, 25
Ceiling rule, property contributions, 72
Character issues, 28
Debt allocations
  Generally, 96 et seq.
  See also Allocations of Tax Items, this index
Depreciation recapture, 27
Distributions of Section 704(c) property, 155
Encumbered property contributions, 26
Family partnerships, contributions tests, 89

CONTRIBUTIONS TO PARTNERSHIPS —Cont'd
Gain or loss resulting from service contributions, 30
Gain recognition, 24
Inventory items, 28
Loss recognition, 24
Mortgaged property contributions, 26
Property contributions
    Generally, 24
    Allocations
        Ceiling rule, 72
        S corporation taxation compared, 86
    Ceiling rule, 72
    Depreciation allocations, 74
    Distribution allocations, 83
    Distributions of Section 704(c) property, 155
    Encumbered property, 26
    Gain allocations, 71
    Loss allocations, 72
Recapture of depreciation, 27
Recourse debt encumbered contributions, 103
Reverse allocations, 82
S corporation contributions compared, 42
Sales and exchanges between partners distinguished, 41
Sales and exchanges to partnership distinguished, 38
Sales of partnership interests distinguished, 123
Service contributions
    Generally, 28
    See also Service Partners, this index
    Profits interests of service partners, 32
Tainted contributions, 28
Unrealized receivables, 28

CORPORATIONS
C and S corporations distinguished, 2
Limited Liability Companies, this index
Partnerships distinguished, 210
Per se corporations, 211
Professional corporation statutes, 211
S Corporation Taxation, this index

CREDITS
Allocations
    Generally, 44
    See also Capital Accounts, this index
    Economic effect test, 69
    Foreign tax credits, 69
    S corporation taxation compared, 70
    Substantial economic effect test, 45 et seq.
    Substantiality rules, 56, 58
Character determinations, 6
Passive loss rule limitations, 22

CULBERTSON TEST
Assignments of income, 88

DEATH OF A PARTNER
Generally, 198 et seq.
Accrual vs cash accounting, 198
Basis adjustments, 204
Basis of inherited partnership interests, 199
Closing of partnerships' taxable year, 203
Distributions and decedent's successor payments distinguished, 144
Estate taxes, 198
Income in respect of a decedent (IRD)
    Generally, 198
    S corporation taxation compared, 205
Liquidation of a deceased partner's interest, 204
Liquidation provisions in partnership agreements, 200
S corporation member deaths compared, 204
Sale of a deceased partner's interest to survivors, 204
Taxable year closings, 203

DEBT
Allocations of Tax Items, this index
Nonrecourse Debt, this index
Recourse Debt, this index

DEDUCTIONS
Allocations
    Generally, 44
    See also Capital Accounts, this index
    Anti-abuse regulations, 82, 91
    Ceiling rule, 72
    Curative allocations, below
    Nonrecourse deductions, 68
    Nonrecourse liability allocations, 104 et seq.
    Notional, 73
    Recourse liability allocations, 100
    Remedial allocations, below
    S corporation taxation compared, 70
    Substantial economic effect test, 45 et seq.
    Substantiality rules, 56, 58
Allocations of depreciation deductions, 60
Curative allocations
    Generally, 73
    Depreciation, 77
    Remedial allocations distinguished, 79
Depreciation
    Allocations, 60
    Substantial economic effect test, 49
Last-minute partner allocations, 90
Losses, limitations on deductibility of, 19
Nonrecourse deduction allocations, 68
Notional allocations, 73
Passive activity loss rules, 22
Pass-through principle, separate statement requirements, 8
Real estate losses, deductibility, 23
Remedial allocations
    Generally, 73

INDEX
References are to Pages

DEDUCTIONS—Cont'd
Remedial allocations—Cont'd
  Curative allocations distinguished, 79
  Depreciation, 79
Section 704(d) limitations on loss deductions, 20
Substantiality rules, allocations, 56, 58

DEFINITIONS
Abusive allocation, 93
Basis, 16
Bottom line income or loss, 6
Capital account, 48
Charge back, 50
Constructive distribution, 144
Curative allocation, 73
Distribution, 144, 171
Distributive share, 116
Drawing account, 47
Economic effect, 45, 58
Goodwill, 174
Income account, 47
Inside basis, 16
Inventory, 126
Liability, partnership, 96
Liquidating distribution, 147
Losses, 19
Nonrecourse debt, 97
Notional allocation, 73
Outside basis, 16
Partner capacity payment, 118
Partnership, statutory, 206
Partnership liability, 96
Partnership property, 174
Per se corporation, 211
Profits interest, 36
Recourse debt, 97
Remedial allocation, 73
Retiring partner, 171
Safe harbor partnership interest, 37
Section 751 assets, 158
Service partner, 29
Service partnership, 174
Stated goodwill, 174
Substantial economic effect, 45, 58
Tax item, 44
Unrealized receivable, 126, 174

DEPRECIATION
Allocations of contributed property depreciation, 74
Allocations of deductions, 60
Book and tax depreciation distinctions, 74
Contributed property
  Depreciation allocations, 74
  Recapture, 27
Deductions
  Allocations, 60
  Substantial economic effect test, 49
Recapture, contributions of depreciable property to partnerships, 27

DEPRECIATION—Cont'd
Substantial economic effect test, depreciation deductions, 49

DISTRIBUTIONS
Allocations, contributed property distributions, 83
Basis adjustments
  Generally, 188 et seq.
  See also Basis, this index
  Allocations, 192
  Distributions affecting basis of partnership assets, 188
  Distributions that change basis of distributed property, 189
  Distributions triggering inside basis adjustments, 144
Boot distinguished, 24
Character of distributions, Section 751(b) limitations, 158
Constructive, 144
Contributed property, distribution allocations, 83
Contributing partner distribution allocations, 85
Current distributions, Section 751(b) limitations, 167
De minimis distributions, 154
Death of partner
  Decedent's successor payments distinguished, 144
  Liquidation provisions in partnership agreements, 200
Decedent's successor payments distinguished, 144
Definition, 144, 171
Gain or loss recognition, 151, 190
Guaranteed payments distinguished, 171
Inside basis adjustments, 144
Liquidating
  Death of partner liquidation provisions, 200
  Definition, 147
  Loss recognition, 152
  Nonrecognition principle, 145
  Non-Section 751 assets, 161
  Retiring partner payments, liquidation of partnership through, 183
  Retiring partner payments distinguished, 171
  S corporation distributions compared, 157
  Section 751 assets, 164
Loans to partners distinguished, 171
Loss recognition, liquidating distributions, 152
Nonrecognition principle, 145
Partnership tax treatment, 156
Payments to partners for services distinguished, 171
Retiring partner payments distinguished

INDEX
References are to Pages

DISTRIBUTIONS—Cont'd
Retiring partner payments distinguished
—Cont'd
  Generally, 144, 171 et seq., 181
  See also Retiring Partner Payments, this index
S corporation distributions compared
  Generally, 157
  Section 751(b) limitations on partnership distributions, 170
Section 737 taxation, 155
Section 707(a) payments to partners, 115
Section 751(b) limitations
  Generally, 158 et seq.
  Current distributions, 167
  Definition of Section 751 assets, 158
  Liquidating distributions, 164
  Retiring partner payments distinguished, 181
  Retiring partner Section 736 payments distinguished, 181
  S corporation, 170
  Scope of section, 168
  Taxation of seller of Section 751 property, 123
Section 704(c) property, 155
Shares, distributive
  Generally, 116
  See also Transactions With Partners, this index
  Section 707(a) payments to partners distinguished, 115
Tax treatment of partnership, 156

DONEE PARTNERS
Family partnerships, 89

DRAWING ACCOUNTS
Generally, 47

DURATION OF PARTNERSHIP
Continuity of life test, 211
Pass-through principle, 10

ELECTING LARGE PARTNERSHIPS (ELP)
Generally, 215

EMPLOYEE PARTNERS
  See also Service Partners, this index
Pass-through principle, 10
Profit sharing, 31
Service contributions to partnerships, 28 et seq.

EMPLOYMENT ARRANGEMENTS
Partnership distinguished, 208

ENCUMBERED PROPERTY
Contributions to partnerships, 26

ENTITY APPROACH TO TAXATION
Aggregate approach distinguished, 1
Anti-abuse rules, 12

EXPULSION OF PARTNER
Generally, 171, 183
  See also Retiring Partner Payments, this index
Liquidation of partnership distinguished, 183

FAMILY PARTNERSHIPS
Anti-abuse regulations, 91
Contributions tests, 89
Donee partners, 89
Income allocations
  Generally, 87
  Substantial economic effect test, 87
Overcompensated partners, 89
S corporation taxation provisions compared, 95
Services vs capital investment partnerships, 88

FRINGE BENEFITS
S corporation stockholder employees, 14, 122
Service partners, 11

GAIN
Allocation of contributed property gain, 71
Contributed property, gain allocations, 71
Contributions to partnerships, gain recognition, 24
Distributions, this index
Look-through gains, taxation of seller of partnership interest, 128
Nonrecognition principle, distributions, 145
Partnership interests sales, unrecaptured Section 1250 gain, 123
Sales of partnership interests
  Generally, 124
  Look-through gains, 128
Service contributions to partnerships, gain or loss resulting from, 30

GOODWILL
Basis, 182
Definitions, 174
Retiring partner payments, 174, 182

GUARANTEED PAYMENTS
Capital partners, guaranteed payments for use of capital, 113
Distributions distinguished, 171
Retiring partner payments, 172, 176
Service partners
  Generally, 117
  Timing, 113
Transactions With Partners, this index

GUARANTEES
Nonrecourse debt allocations, 108
Recourse debt allocations, 102

INDEX

References are to Pages

HOLDING PERIODS
Capital asset contributions to partnerships, 25

INCOME
Allocations
    Generally, 44
    See also Capital Accounts, this index
Anti-abuse regulations, 82, 91
Assignments of Income, this index
Ceiling rule, 72
Curative, 73, 79
Last-minute partners, 90
Notional, 73
Remedial, 73, 79
S corporation taxation compared, 70
Substantial economic effect test, 45 et seq.
Substantiality rules, 56, 58
Assignments of Income, this index
Bottom line income or loss, 6
Culbertson test, assignments of income, 88
Curative allocations
    Generally, 73
    Remedial allocations distinguished, 79
Family partnership income allocations
    Generally, 87
    Substantial economic effect test, 87
Last-minute partners, assignments of income, 90
Notional allocations, 73
Pass-through principle, separate statement requirements, 8
Payments to partners measured by partnership gross income, 121
Remedial allocations
    Generally, 73
    Curative allocations distinguished, 79
Substantiality rules
    Allocations, 56, 58
Timing
    Generally, 9
    Service partner payments, 113

INCOME ACCOUNTS
Generally, 47

INCOME IN RESPECT OF A DECEDENT (IRD)
Generally, 198
See also Death of a Partner, this index

INDEMNIFICATION
Recourse debt allocations, 102

INVENTORY
Contributions of inventory items to partnerships, 28
Definition, 126

LIABILITIES, PARTNERSHIP
See also Debt, this index
Definition, 96

LIABILITIES, PARTNERSHIP—Cont'd
Obligations that are not liabilities, 109

LIMITED LIABILITY COMPANIES (LLC)
Capital accounts deficits, restoration obligations, 54
Check-the-box regulations, 7, 206
Limited partnerships and LLCs compared, 7
Medicare taxation of members, 12
One-member LLCs, 211
Partnership taxation elections, 7
Partnerships distinguished, 210
Retiring member payments, 174
Social Security taxation of members, 12

LIMITED PARTNERSHIPS
Liabilities of limited partners, 54, 98
Limited partner losses, 22
LLCs compared, 7
Master limited partnerships, 214
Passive-activity rules, 23
Social Security and Medicare taxes, 12

LIQUIDATING DISTRIBUTIONS
See Distributions, this index

LIQUIDATIONS OF PARTNER INTERESTS
Death of a Partner, this index
Retiring Partner Payments, this index
Sales of partnership interests distinguished, 123

LIQUIDATIONS OF PARTNERSHIPS
Death of partner liquidation provisions, 200
Distributions, this index
Form vs substance of the transaction, 186
Substance doctrine, 183
Withdrawal or expulsion of partner distinguished, 183

LOANS TO PARTNERS
    See also Transactions With Partners, this index
Distributions distinguished, 171

LOANS TO PARTNERSHIPS
    Generally, 18
Allocations of Tax Items, this index
Nonrecourse Debt, this index
Recourse Debt, this index

LOSS
    Generally, 19
Allocation of contributed property losses, 72
At-risk rules of Section 465, 20
Bottom line income or loss, 6
Contributed property, loss allocations, 72
Contributions to partnerships, loss recognition, 24
Distributions, this index
Limitations on deductibility of, 19
Liquidating distributions, loss recognition, 152

INDEX

LOSS—Cont'd
Nonrecognition principle, distributions, 145
Outside basis limitations on loss deductions, 19
Passive activity loss rules, 22
Real estate losses, deductibility, 23
S Corporation rules compared, 23
Sales of partnership interests, taxation of seller, 124
Section 465 at-risk rules, 20
Section 704(d) limitations on loss deductions, 20
Service contributions to partnerships, gain or loss resulting from, 30

MASTER LIMITED PARTNERSHIPS
Generally, 214

MEDICARE TAXES
Limited liability company members, 12
Pass-through principle, 12
S corporations compared, 12

NONRECOGNITION PRINCIPLE
Generally, 16
Contributions to partnerships
    Generally, 24 et seq.
    Service contributions, 28, 32
Distributions, 145
Elections, nonrecognition, 1

NONRECOURSE DEBT
See also Recourse Debt, this index
Allocations of nonrecourse liabilities, 104 et seq.
Allocations of tax items, 60, 63
At-risk rules, 21
Capital accounts deficits, nonrecourse deductions, 68
Definition, 97
Guarantees, partnership debt allocations, 108
Risk of loss and constructive liquidation, 98
Tiers of nonrecourse debt allocations, 104

OVERCOMPENSATED PARTNERS
Family partnerships, 89

PARTNER CAPACITY PAYMENTS
Definition, 118

PARTNERSHIP ASSETS BASIS
See Basis, this index

PARTNERSHIP DEBT
See Debt, this index

PARTNERSHIP LIABILITIES
See Liabilities, Partnership, this index

PARTNERSHIP LIQUIDATION
See Liquidations of Partnerships, this index

PARTNERSHIP PROPERTY
See Property, Partnership, this index

PARTNERSHIP STATUS
See What is a Partnership, this index

PASSIVE ACTIVITY RULES
Generally, 19, 22
See also Shelters, this index
Electing large partnerships, 215
Publicly traded partnerships, 214

PASS-THROUGH PRINCIPLE
Generally, 6 et seq.
Anti-abuse rules, 12
Deductions, separate statements of, 8
Duration of partnership, 10
Employee partners, 10
Income
    Separate statements of, 8
    Timing, 9
Medicare taxes, 12
S corporations compared, 14
Separate statement of income and deduction, 8
Social Security taxes, 12
Timing of partnership income, 9

PAYMENTS TO PARTNERS
Distributions, this index
Service Partners, this index
Transactions With Partners, this index

PROFITS INTERESTS
Definition, 36
Service partners, 32, 34

PROPERTY, PARTNERSHIP
Basis of partnership assets. See Basis, this index
Contributions to Partnerships, this index
Definition, 174
Distributions, this index

PUBLICLY TRADED PARTNERSHIPS
Generally, 213

RECEIVABLES
See Unrealized Receivables, this index

RECOURSE DEBT
See also Nonrecourse Debt, this index
Allocations of recourse liabilities, 100
Contributions of property encumbered by recourse debt, 103
Definition, 97
Guarantees, partnership debt allocations, 102
Indemnification, partnership debt allocations, 102
Revised Uniform Partnership Act, 99
Risk of loss and constructive liquidation, 98

RETIRING PARTNER PAYMENTS
Distributions distinguished, 144, 171, 181
Form vs substance of the transaction, 186
Goodwill, 174, 182

INDEX
References are to Pages

RETIRING PARTNER PAYMENTS—Cont'd
Guaranteed payments, 172, 176
Interpretation of Section 736, 172
Liquidating distribution distinguished, 171
Liquidation of partnership through, 183
Retirement defined, 171
S corporation taxation compared, 187
Sales of partnership interests, distinguished, 183
Section 736 payments
    Interpreting the section, 172
    S corporation taxation compared, 187
    Section 751(b) payments distinguished, 181
    Tax calculations, 176
    Unrealized receivables, 182
Service partnership payments to retiring general partners, 173
Substance doctrine, 183
Unrealized receivables, 174, 182

RETURNS
Reporting, minimum requirements, 8
Small partnerships, Subchapter K requirement exceptions, 213

REVISED UNIFORM PARTNERSHIP ACT
Aggregate and entity approaches to partnership status, 1
Recourse debt, 99

RISK OF LOSS
See also At-Risk Rules, this index
Recourse and nonrecourse debt, 98

S CORPORATION TAXATION
Generally, 2
Allocations of tax items, 70
Allocations relating to contributed property, 86
Anti-abuse rules, 15
Assignments of income, 95
Basis
    Generally, 23
    Adjustments following distributions, 196
Bottom line income or loss, 6
Contributed property
    Generally, 42
    Allocations, 86
Death of a member, 204
Distributions
    Generally, 157
    Basis adjustments, 196
Employee-shareholders, transactions with, 122
Family partnership provisions compared, 95
Fringe benefits, stockholder employees, 14, 122
Liabilities allocations to shareholders, 112
Liquidating distributions, 157
Losses, 23
Medicare taxes, 12

S CORPORATION TAXATION—Cont'd
Partnerships and S corporations distinguished, 210
Pass-through principle, 14
Section 736 payments to retiring partners compared, 187
Section 751(b) limitations on partnership distributions compared, 170
Social Security taxes, 12
Stock sales and sales of partnership interests compared, 141
Tax shelters, 23
Transactions with shareholder-employees, 122

SAFE HARBOR PARTNERSHIP INTERESTS
Definition, 37

SALES OF PARTNERSHIP INTERESTS
Generally, 123 et seq.
Basis, taxation of seller, 123
Buyer basis
    Generally, 129 et seq.
    Allocating Section 743(b) adjustments, 133
    Inside basis, 129
    Section 754 elections, 138
    Section 732(d) adjustments, 139
    Transferee's share of inside basis, 131
Capital gains and losses treatment, taxation of seller, 124
Collateral effects, 140
Contributions to partnerships distinguished, 123
Death of a partner, sale of partnership interest to survivors, 204
Form vs substance of the transaction, 186
Gains, taxation of seller on look-through gains, 128
Liquidation of partner interests distinguished, 123
Look-through gains, taxation of seller, 128
Partnership liabilities calculations, taxation of seller, 124
Retiring partner payments distinguished, 183
S corporation stock sales compared, 141
Section 754 elections, buyer basis, 138
Section 751 property, taxation of seller, 123
Section 732(d) adjustments, buyer basis, 139
Seller basis, 123
Substance doctrine, 183
Taxation of seller
    Generally, 123 et seq.
    Amount realized, 123
    Basis, 123
    Capital gains and losses treatment, 124
    Look-through gains, 128
    Partnership liabilities calculations, 124
    Section 751 property, 123

SALES OF PARTNERSHIP INTERESTS
—Cont'd
Taxation of seller—Cont'd
Unrecaptured Section 1250 gain, 123
Transferee's share of inside basis, 131

SERVICE PARTNERS
Generally, 28 et seq.
Basis, 29
Compensation of profits interest, 32
Distributions and payments for services distinguished, 171
Fixed payments, 117
Fringe benefits, 11
Guaranteed payments for services
Generally, 113, 117
Timing, 113
Income taxation of service contributions, 29
Pass-through principle, 10
Payments for services and distributions distinguished, 171
Profit sharing employee partners, 31
Profits interests, 32, 34
Safe harbor partnership interests, 37
Section 707(a) payments, 117
Self-employed taxpayer status, 10
Timing of guaranteed payments for services, 113

SERVICE PARTNERSHIPS
Capital investment partnerships distinguished, 88
Cost-sharing arrangements by sole proprietors distinguished, 208
Definition, 174
Donee partners' distributive shares, 88
Partnership property, 174
Retiring partner payments to general partners, 173
Retroactive allocations, 59

SHELTERS
Allocations of nonrecourse financing tax items, 60, 63
At-risk rules of Section 465, 20
Last-minute partners, 90
Nonrecourse Debt, this index
Nonrecourse financing, allocations of tax items, 60, 63
Outside basis limitations on loss deductions, 19
Passive activity loss rules, 22
S Corporation rules compared, 23
Section 465 at-risk rules, 20

SHIFTING TAX CONSEQUENCES RULE
Allocations of tax items, 59

SOCIAL SECURITY TAXES
Limited liability company members, 12
Pass-through principle, 12
S corporations compared, 12

SUBSTANCE DOCTRINE
Generally, 183

SUBSTANTIAL ECONOMIC EFFECT TEST
Generally, 44
See also Allocations of Tax Items, this index

SUBSTANTIALITY RULES
Allocations of tax items, 56, 58

TAX SHELTERS
See Shelters, this index

TAXABLE YEARS
Closing on death of partner, 203

TIMING OF INCOME
Generally, 9
Guaranteed payments to service partners, 113

TRANSACTIONS WITH PARTNERS
Generally, 113 et seq.
See also Contributions to Partnerships, this index
Deduction of losses on sales or exchanges, 122
Distributive shares
Fixed payments, 117
Income-related payments, 115
Minimum payments, guaranteed, 118
Partner capacity, payments in, 118
Fixed payments, 117
Gross income, payments measured by, 121
Guaranteed payments
Minimums, 118
Partner capacity, payments in, 118
Services
Generally, 117
Timing, 113
Use of capital, 113
Income, payments measured by, 121
Income-related payments, 115
Loans to partners, distributions distinguished, 171
Losses on sales or exchanges, 122
Minimum payments, guaranteed, 118
Partner capacity payments, 118
Payments measured by partnership gross income, 121
S corporation taxation rules compared, 122
Section 707(a) payments, income-related, 115, 117
Timing of guaranteed payments for services, 113
Unrelated party treatment, 113

UNREALIZED RECEIVABLES
Basis, 182
Definition, 126, 174
Retiring partner payments, 174, 182

INDEX

References are to Pages

WHAT IS A PARTNERSHIP
Generally, 206 et seq.
See also Check-the-Box Regulations, this index
Aggregate and entity approaches, 1, 6
Business expense sharing arrangements, 209
Continuity of life test, 211
Co-ownership of property, 206, 207
Corporations distinguished, 210
Cost-sharing arrangements, 208
Electing large partnerships, 215
Election out of Subchapter K, 212
Employees, profit sharing with, 209
Employment arrangements, 208
Expense sharing agreements, 209
Limited liability companies distinguished, 210
Master limited partnerships, 214

WHAT IS A PARTNERSHIP—Cont'd
Per se corporations, 211
Professional corporation statutes, 211
Profit sharing arrangements, 209
Property co-ownership, 206, 207
Publicly traded partnerships, 213
Small partnerships, Subchapter K applicability, 213
Statutory definitions, 206

WITHDRAWAL OF A PARTNER
Generally, 171, 183
See also Retiring Partner Payments, this index
Liquidation of partnership distinguished, 183

YEARS, TAXABLE
Closing on death of partner, 203

†